The Collected Courses of the Academy of European Law
Series Editors: Professor Philip Alston and
Professor Gráinne de Búrca,
European University Institute,
Florence

VOLUME IX/1

The EU, the WTO, and the NAFTA

The Collected Courses of the Academy of European Law
Edited by Professor Philip Alston and Professor Gráinne de Búrca

This series brings together the Collected Courses of the
Academy of European Law in Florence. The Academy's mission is to
produce scholarly analyses which are at the cutting edge of the two
fields in which it works: European Union law and human rights law.
A 'general course' is given each year in each field, by a
distinguished scholar and/or practitioner, who either examines the
field as a whole through a particular thematic, conceptual or
philosophical lens, or who looks at a particular theme in the context
of the overall body of law in the field. The Academy also publishes
each year a volume of collected essays with a specific theme in each
of the two fields.

The EU, the WTO, and the NAFTA
Towards a Common Law of
International Trade?

Edited by

J. H. H. WEILER

Academy of European Law
European University Institute

OXFORD
UNIVERSITY PRESS

OXFORD
UNIVERSITY PRESS

Great Clarendon Street, Oxford OX2 6DP

Oxford University Press is a department of the University of Oxford.
It furthers the University's objective of excellence in research, scholarship,
and education by publishing worldwide in

Oxford New York

Athens Auckland Bangkok Bogotá Buenos Aires
Cape Town Chennai Dar es Salaam Delhi Florence Hong Kong Istanbul
Karachi Kolkata Kuala Lumpur Madrid Melbourne Mexico City Mumbai
Nairobi Paris Sao Paulo Singapore Taipei Tokyo Toronto Warsaw

and associated companies in Berlin Ibadan

Published in the United States
by Oxford University Press Inc., New York

First published 2000
First published new in paperback 2001

British Library Cataloguing in Publication Data

Data available

Library of Congress Cataloging in Publication Data

Data available

ISBN 0–19–829874–9
ISBN 0–19–924812–5 (Pbk)

Typeset by Hope Services (Abingdon) Ltd.
Printed in Great Britain
on acid-free paper by
Biddles Ltd, *www.biddles.co.uk*

Contents

Table of Cases

Table of Treaties and Legislation

B. International

C. United Kingdom
Acts
Copyright Act 1956

Statutory Instruments

D. United States

Endangered Species Act 133

Abbreviations

AB	Appellate Body
AD	Anti-dumping
AG	Advocate General
BSE	Bovine Spongiform Encephalopathy
CAP	Common Agricultural Policy
CCP	Common Commercial Policy
CEC	(North American) Commission for Environmental Co-operation
CEN	*Comité Européen de Normalisation*
CENELEC	*Comité Européen de Normalisation Electrotechnique*
CFSP	Common Foreign and Steel Community
CJ	Creutzfeldt-Jakob (Disease)
CLC	(North American) Commission for Labor Co-operation
CU	Customs Union
CUSFTA	Canada–United States Free Trade Agreement
CVD	Countervailing Duty
DSB	Dispute Settlement Body
DSU	Dispute Settlement Understanding
ECHR	European Court of Human Rights
ECJ	European Court of Justice
ECSC	European Coal and Steel Community
EEA	European Economic Area
EMU	European Monetary Union
ERTA	European Road Transport Agreement
EU	European Union
FAO	Food and Agriculture Organization (of the United Nations)
FTA	Free Trade Agreement
GATS	General Agreement on Trade in Services
GATT	General Agreement on Tariffs and Trade
ICSID	International Centre for the Settlement on Investment Disputes
IDA	International Dairy Agreement
IGC	Intergovernmental Conference
ILO	International Labour Organisation
IP	Intellectual Property
MAI	Multilateral Agreement on Investment
MFN	Most Favoured Nation
NAAEC	North American Agreement on Environmental Co-operation
NAALC	North American Agreement on Labor Co-operation
NAFTA	North American Free Trade Agreement
NAH	New Approach to Harmonization

NAO	National Administrative Office
OECD	Organization for Economic Co-operation and Development
OIE	*Office International des Epizooties*
RSA	Regional Services Arrangements
SEAC	Spongiform Encephalopathy Advisory Committee
SPS	Sanitary and Phytosanitary Measures
TBT	(Agreement on) Technical Barriers to Trade
TED	Turtle Exclusion Devices
TEU	Treaty on European Union
TRIMS	(Agreement on) Trade Related Investment Measures
TRIPS	(Agreement on) Trade Related Aspects of Intellectual Property Rights
UNCITRAL	United Nations Commission on International Trade Law
VCLT	Vienna Convention on the Law of Treaties
WTO	World Trade Organization

1

Cain and Abel—Convergence and Divergence in International Trade Law

J. H. H. WEILER

Though born roughly in the same period, committed to similar beliefs in the virtues of liberalized trade and open markets, sharing in many instances a common legal vocabulary, the GATT and the European Communities developed over the years as the Cain and Abel of international economic law—except that in this case, Cain was cast out into the wilderness by a complacent and self-satisfied Abel. It is time to bring him back to the fold.

The social reality of the legal profession and of legal academe tells the story. With notable exceptions (as lawyers we know that a rule has not been invented to which there are not some 'notable' exceptions) specialists in European law would typically profess to a great ignorance of the law of the GATT (almost as great as that of classical public international lawyers). The converse is also largely true. The historical evolution of the two systems was perceived as deepening a gap which existed already at their inception and it also became rapidly clear who was the Abel and who was the Cain of the two evolving systems. The offerings of the GATT were considered clearly inferior to those of its regional brother. Whereas the EU could boast a commitment to a radical elimination (or harmonization) of all obstacles to trade across its internal frontiers, the GATT seemed, superficially at least, to be wedded to the more primitive notion of National Treatment—the mere elimination of discrimination. It was not only the substantive content of the material obligation which made the EU the favoured sibling. The EU could offer, too, a judicial system and a set of effective remedies which ingeniously employed national individual plaintiffs as 'Private Attorney Generals' and national legal systems as effective enforcement mechanisms. This compared favourably to the GATT's intergovernmental, semi-voluntaristic and consensual Panel system, much of which was shrouded in secrecy for many years.

This systemic growing apart was accompanied by an attitude—an attitude of dismissal or even contempt towards the law of the GATT (which like most dismissal was informed in large measure by ignorance)—and a corresponding attitude of envy, notably manifest in an influential (though in my view wholly

misguided) school of thought that would like to see the principal achievement
of the EU system—its constitutionalization—grafted on to the GATT.

With such rich legal offerings it is no surprise that in our institutions of
higher learning EU law rapidly gained a foothold. Within one generation we
have reached the stage where there are few graduates of European law faculties who have not, in one way or another, studied the law of the European
Union. By contrast, very few have had any contact with the law of the GATT;
and in a great many of our law faculties they could not have such a contact
since so few courses are offered. Of course, since there is little private practice
in the law of the GATT/WTO, the Bar has not provided for incentives to
change the blissful ignorance.[1]

And yet, for all the disciplinary distance, the EU itself is a major player in
the GATT both before and after the advent of the WTO. It plays a major role
in the shaping of the GATT/WTO and also is a classic repeat player in dispute resolution—as complainant, as a subject of complaints and as a third
party. It is one of the Gang of Four—alongside the USA, Japan, and
Canada—of international trade law.

In this context the distance between the disciplines and the general ignorance of the law of the GATT among Community lawyers and the law of the
Union among GATT lawyers has produced some troubling pathologies.

In many of the most distinguished books of instructions on the general law
of the European Community—indeed in the most distinguished of all—that
part of the law dealing with the international trade law of the EU, its conventional and non-conventional Commercial Policy, is often truncated or
missing altogether. Likewise in several of the books dealing with the Common
Commercial Policy which is often in place to implement international trade
law and, in any event, is meant to be in compliance with it, there is but a per-
functory treatment of the source of most Community obligations—the
GATT/WTO. Likewise, the practice of the Union before the instances of the
GATT is largely unknown. I have often noticed the surprise of well-seasoned
Community lawyers when they learn, for example, of the frequency with
which the Community has been held to violate its GATT and WTO obligations. Even more interestingly, you find from time to time the Community's
own international trade lawyers arguing before the instances of the
GATT/WTO positions which seem to be at odds with the European Court's
own jurisprudence on similar provisions in situations where there is no principled justification for a divergence in the jurisprudence.[2] It is even more sur-

---

[1] The Appellate Body of the WTO ruled in the Banana case that henceforth governments
may be represented before Panels and the Appellate Body itself by private lawyers. Given the
rapid growth of disputes brought to Geneva, we may expect a change in this respect too.

[2] Compare, e.g. the position of the EU in Japan—Alcoholic Beverages and the position of
the Court in its Article 95 line of jurisprudence commencing with Case 168/78 *Commission v
Italy* and Case 46/80 *Vinal v Orbat*.

prising that in many international trade law books, the EU is mentioned but its trade law is excluded.

Everything that I have said about the GATT/WTO could be said with even greater conviction about other regional systems. The NAFTA, to give but one example, is an esoteric topic to all but a handful of Community lawyers. And yet, Canada and the United States are among the largest trade partners of the European Union and its Member States. For a Community lawyer interested in trade not to know about the NAFTA is as alarming as it would be for a North American lawyer engaged in Commercial transactions with Europe to know nothing of the EU.

The WTO has made this situation increasingly untenable. The new mechanisms introduced by the WTO Dispute Settlement Understanding are not perhaps comparable to the full judicial system within the EU, but they have radically changed both the rules and legal culture concerning the adjudication and enforcement of obligations. Less transparently but no less important for this, is the hardening of certain extant GATT obligations and new WTO agreements. The *Hormones* case, let it be recalled, did not essentially turn on denial of national treatment, but on a *Dassonville*-like complaint that a non-discriminatory obstacle to trade was not justified. Even more startling perhaps, the doctrine in *Keck* can be interpreted as a more profound understanding of and respect for national regulatory autonomy. Cain and Abel seem to be making increasingly similar offerings to the God of Free Trade.

The recent banana saga unfolding simultaneously before the European Court of Justice, a WTO panel, and the Appellate Body as well as the German Constitutional Court has served as a striking and welcome example of the complexity of this situation. For the first time it came to the attention of many that the interlocking systems of trade law can have a profound effect on the most cherished foundations of European constitutionalism: that what happens in Geneva can have more than a ripple effect on Luxembourg and that if Brussels elects to disregard it, national courts might not. But even more should be said. I would first argue that you simply cannot read *critically* any of the cases in this saga—not even those before the ECJ—without a firm grasp of the law of the GATT/WTO. More generally, the material convergence which cases like *Hormones, Japan Alcoholic Beverages,* and *Canada Periodicals*[3] display, means that one can no longer disregard the doctrinal developments of the WTO even if one's primary interest rests in the internal market of the EU.

We are witnessing, thus, the emergence of a nascent Common Law of International Trade rooted in three phenomena. First in the fact that the very same regulatory measure may come simultaneously within the jurisdictional

---

[3] All decisions of the Appellate Body of the WTO are annotated on the Web Site of the European Journal of International Law www.ejil.org.

reach of more than one trade regime and may even be adjudicated simultaneously. Some regimes offer alternatives. The NAFTA offers GATT dispute resolution as an option for many categories of dispute.

Second is the fact that in the material law of disparate international trade
regimes we can see considerable convergence. In some cases the convergence
is egregious—the NAFTA simply incorporates, some times with no change,
whole chunks of the GATT—in other cases the convergence is jurisprudential, as in the law governing discriminatory tax or discriminatory internal regulation. This, of course, is the heart of the emergent Common Law.

Third is the strengthening of private parties in all regimes—once a preserve
of the EU. The NAFTA already allows private party dispute resolution of different types in relation to Anti-dumping, Countervailing Duties, Investment
(using, for instance, ICSID arbitration!), Labour, and Environmental matters. The WTO is still an intergovernmental preserve, but private actors, at
least powerful private actors, have already learnt to manipulate the system to
reach legal adjudication under the guise of intergovernmental disputes.

I am neither predicting nor advocating a full convergence—either substantive or procedural. There is much more to, say, the EU than its trade regime.
Indeed, as indicated above I find fanciful and even mischievous the advocacy
of a constitutionalized GATT. But I am claiming that there is enough convergence to justify a redefinition of the field—international economic law as
a single field comprising its various siblings and families and sharing a common doctrinal core—as close, perhaps, as the Common Law doctrines in the
Old British Commonwealth.

This volume, built on a recent series of courses at the Academy of European
Law, is a reflection of this conviction. The various contributions deal with discrete areas—in the double sense—of the international trading system but
each placing considerable emphasis on the interlocking nature of the various
components of that system. It is our conviction that this is the appropriate
way to understand and to teach this branch of the law.

2

EC External Commercial Policy after Amsterdam: Authority and Interpretation within Interconnected Legal Orders

MARISE CREMONA[1]

INTRODUCTION[2]

> The Community legal system is characterised by the simultaneous application of provisions of various origins, international, Community and national; but it nevertheless seeks to function and to represent itself to the outside world as a unified system.[3]

The 'multi-dimensional configuration of authority' within the European Union is not only a result of what Neil Walker refers to as the trend towards differentiated integration.[4] It is also a feature of a system that depends on an interaction between Community and national legal orders and international sources of rights and obligations. Indeed some of the most pointed challenges to the authority and legitimacy of the Community legal order have arisen out of the still problematic relationship between the Community institutions, the Member States and international legal obligations. Who, in this multi-layered authority structure, has the primary responsibility for determining the scope

[1] Senior Fellow, Centre for Commercial Law Studies, Queen Mary and Westfield College, University of London.

[2] This paper is a revised and slightly expanded version of the chapter 'External Economic Relations' in D. O'Keeffe and P. Twomey (eds.) *Legal Issues of the Amsterdam Treaty* (Hart Publishing, 1999). I am, as usual, much indebted to colleagues for helpful comments on earlier drafts, and especially to Gráinne de Búrca, Eileen Denza, and Kenneth Armstrong; all remaining errors and omissions are mine alone.

[3] Tesauro AG in case C-53/96 *Hermes International v FHT Marketing Choice BV*, [1998] ECR I-3603, para. 21.

[4] Walker, 'Sovereignty and Differentiated Integration in the European Union' (1998) 4 ELJ 355. Differentiated integration encompasses the opt-outs and 'pillar' structure introduced by the Treaty on European Union, and the flexibility and 'closer co-operation' provisions introduced by the Treaty of Amsterdam.

and the content of the external policy of the European Community and defining the scope and content of its international obligations? This paper is an attempt to address, in the context of the Treaty of Amsterdam, and in the limited sphere of external commercial policy, some of the issues raised by this question. The perennial questions of the balance of powers and the location of authority are sharpened by the demands of external negotiations, the need 'to represent itself to the outside world as a unified system' and to demonstrate substantive consistency in external policy to the Community's interlocutors.[5] It is not merely that the conclusion of the WTO Agreements faced the European Community with awkward competence and legal base questions. The creation of the WTO is one aspect of a dynamic in the broadening and deepening of international trade and economic relations, involving the EU in debates and initiatives which go far beyond traditional tariff negotiations.[6] Broader principles are at stake than simply the question of the extent to which the commercial policy should encompass trade in services or the protection of intellectual property rights: in the opinion of one commentator: 'The lack of clarity as to the extent of the foreign trade authority could pose the currently most important constitutional problem of the Union.'[7]

A characteristic of the Treaty's approach to commercial policy serves to emphasize this point. Article 133 [ex 113] EC gives an unusual amount of discretion to the Community legislative institutions (apart from the Parliament) as to both the form and the content of this particular common policy.[8] It is not only that any type of legal instrument can be used, both autonomous and contractual. Little guidance is given in the Treaty, apart from the generalizations of Article 131 [ex 110] and the requirement of uniformity, as to what the objectives of the common commercial policy (CCP) are to be. Nor has this gap been filled either by legislation or by systematic analysis in the case law of the Court. From this silence flows not only the debate as to the proper scope (including its use for harmonization purposes) of the CCP but

[5] Cf. Article 3 [ex C] TEU, 'The Union shall . . . ensure the consistency of its external activities as a whole in the context of its external relations, security, economic and development policies. The Council and Commission shall be responsible for ensuring such consistency and cooperate to this end.' The requirement of consistency dates from the TEU itself, the requirement to co-operate has been added by the Treaty of Amsterdam. The addition reminds us that we are not only dealing with the EC/Member State balance of power, but also with the institutional balance.

[6] Neil Walker refers to 'a thickening web of interconnections between the EU and the WTO legal orders': Walker, 'Sovereignty and Differentiated Integration in the European Union' (1998) 4 ELJ 355 at 373. The fact that the WTO can be seen as a distinct legal order is itself significant.

[7] Hilf, 'Unwritten EC Authority in Foreign Trade Law' (1997) 2 EFARev. 437.

[8] Dashwood, 'States in the European Union' (1998) 23 ELRev. 201 at 209. For a recent recognition by the Court of this wide discretion, see case C-150/94 *UK v Council (import quotas for toys from China)*, [1998] ECR I-7235, at para. 49; and case C-284/94 *Spain v Council (import quotas for toys from China)*, [1998] ECR I-7309, at para. 33.

also the significance for the Community of the obligation to adhere to WTO rules and principles.[9]

We should start with the amendment to Article 133 [ex 113] made by the Treaty of Amsterdam. The Treaty adds a fifth paragraph to this provision on the common commercial policy so that it now reads:

1. The common commercial policy shall be based on uniform principles, particularly in regard to changes in tariff rates, the conclusion of tariff and trade agreements, the achievement of uniformity in measures of liberalization, export policy and measures to protect trade such as those to be taken in the event of dumping or subsidies.

2. The Commission shall submit proposals to the Council for implementing the common commercial policy.

3. Where agreements with one or more States or international organisations need to be negotiated, the Commission shall make recommendations to the Council, which shall authorize the Commission to open the necessary negotiations.

The Commission shall conduct these negotiations in consultation with a special committee appointed by the Council to assist the Commission in this task and within the framework of such directives as the Council may issue to it.

The relevant provisions of Article 300 [ex 228] shall apply.

4. In exercising the powers conferred upon it by this Article, the Council shall act by a qualified majority.

5. The Council, acting unanimously on a proposal from the Commission and after consulting the European Parliament, may extend the application of paragraphs 1 to 4 to international negotiations and agreements on services and intellectual property insofar as they are not covered by these paragraphs.

---

[9] This obligation—the extent of which is much contested—flows essentially from Art. 131 [ex 110] EC which requires an adherence to principles of progressive trade liberalization: cases 22–24/72 *International Fruit Company NV v Produktschap voor Groenten en Fruit* [1972] ECR 1219. Among the many contributions to this debate, in which there is no space to engage here, see for example Kuilwilk, *The European Court of Justice and the GATT Dilemma: Public Interest versus Individual Rights?* (Nexed, Critical European Studies, 1996); Woolcock, 'The European Acquis and Multilateral Trade Rules: Are they compatible?' (1993) 31 JCMS 539; Everling, 'Will Europe Slip on Bananas? The Bananas judgements of the ECJ and national courts' (1996) 33 CMLRev 401; Reich, 'Judge-made "Europe a la carte": some remarks on recent conflicts between European and German constitutional law provoked by the bananas litigation' (1996) EJIL 103; Cottier, 'The Challenge of Regionalisation and Preferential Relations in World Trade Law and Policy' (1996) 2 EFA Rev. 149; Eeckhout, 'The Domestic Legal Status of the WTO Agreements: Interconnecting Legal Systems' (1997) 34 CMLRev. 11; Cottier and Schefer, 'The Relationship Between World Trade Organisation Law, National and Regional Law' (1998) 1 JIEL 83.

THE LEGISLATIVE HISTORY OF ARTICLE 133
PRIOR TO AMSTERDAM

An appreciation of the significance of this amendment requires us briefly to examine its history, which predates not only the Treaty of Amsterdam but also the Maastricht Treaty. The Dublin European Council of April 1990, which launched the pre-Maastricht intergovernmental conferences, affirmed the aim of strengthening the democratic legitimacy of the union, 'assuring unity and coherence in the Community's international action'. The Commission's proposals, in its Opinion of October 1990 and subsequently,[10] were based on the concept of a unified set of Treaty articles on external policy generally, encompassing *inter alia* a new foreign and security policy and a revised common commercial policy (CCP), renamed 'external economic policy' and expressly including the external dimension of services, intellectual property, capital, investment, establishment, and competition policy.[11] The Commission argued that this was not an extension of the existing CCP provisions, but merely a codification of the current position established by the case law of the Court of Justice. A newly defined CCP would be part of the Community's exclusive sphere of competence, at least where the Community's powers had been exercised internally.[12] This debate was taking place against the background of the Uruguay Round negotiations which were ultimately to lead to the Marrakesh Agreement establishing the WTO and the GATS and TRIPS Agreements,[13] and for the Commission the right to represent the Community over this whole field of policy was clearly of crucial importance.[14]

[10] See Intergovernmental Conferences: Contributions by the Commission, Supplement 2/91, Bull.EC., p. 65.

[11] For a full discussion, see Maresceau, 'The Concept "Common Commercial Policy" and the Difficult Road to Maastricht' in Maresceau (ed.), *The European Community's Commercial Policy after 1992: The Legal Dimension* (Martinus Nijhoff, 1993).

[12] See for example case 22/70 *Commission v Council* [1971] ECR 263; cases 3, 4, 6/76 *Kramer* [1976] ECR 1279.

[13] The General Agreement on Trade in Services (GATS) and the Agreement on Trade Related Aspects of Intellectual Property Rights (TRIPS) are Annexes 1B and 1C respectively of the Agreement establishing the World Trade Organization (WTO). The Agreements on Trade in Goods, including GATT 1994, form Annex 1A.

[14] The debate was (and is still being) conducted among commentators as well as between the Commission and the Member States; see for example Timmermans, 'Common Commercial Policy (Article 113 EEC) and International Trade in Services' in Capotorti *et al.* (eds.), *Du droit international au droit de l'integration, Liber Amicorum Pierre Pescatore* (Baden-Baden: Nomos, 1987); Eeckhout, *The European Internal Market and International Trade: A Legal Analysis* (OUP, 1994) at 20–46; Hyett, 'The Uruguay Round of the GATT: The United Kingdom Standpoint' in Emiliou and O'Keeffe, *The European Union and World Trade Law after the GATT Uruguay Round* (Wiley, 1996) at 99–101.

The Commission did not get its way. In spite of some proposals to alter the old Article 113 EC in the drafts put forward by the Luxembourg and Dutch Presidencies, Article 113 was left substantively unchanged by the Maastricht Treaty, and of course the foreign and security policy provisions were not put into the EC Treaty at all but into the new Treaty on European Union.

OPINION 1/94 ON THE WTO AGREEMENT AND THE SCOPE OF ARTICLE 133

Not only was there no codification of the Court of Justice case law on the CCP in the Maastricht Treaty, but the result demonstrated the lack of agreement as to the scope and effect of that case law. This disagreement resurfaced in 1994, as the issue of the formal conclusion of the Uruguay Round Agreements became both pressing and, increasingly, embarrassingly controversial. In its request for an opinion under Article 300(6) EC [ex 228(6)], the Commission attempted to achieve judicially what it had failed to achieve politically: a recognition of the Community's exclusive competence in the areas of external policy covered by the WTO. As the Court said in its Opinion, 'the fundamental issue is whether or not the Community has exclusive competence to conclude the WTO Agreement and its Annexes'.[15]

In a characteristically pragmatic and—some have argued—cautious opinion, the Court defused the political debate and rejected the Commission arguments in favour of exclusive competence to conclude either the GATS or the TRIPS Agreements. This is not the place for a comprehensive analysis of *Opinion 1/94* and here we will concentrate on the argument as to the scope of Article 133 [ex 113] EC.[16] First, the Court confirmed that the Multilateral Agreements on Trade in Goods (including GATT 1994) fall within the scope of Article 133 [ex 113] EC. The areas of disagreement here included ECSC products, agricultural products and the Agreement on Technical Barriers to Trade. The Court refused to accept that the specific rules in the ECSC Treaty, or those found in Article 37 [ex 43] of the EC Treaty affected the power to conclude a general trade agreement under Article 133:

[15] *Opinion 1/94* (re WTO Agreement) [1994] ECR I-5267 at para. 14.

[16] The Commission argued alternatively that exclusive competence could be based on implied powers, or on Article 95 [ex 100a] or 308 [ex 235] EC. For detailed comment see for example Arnull, 'The Scope of the Common Commercial Policy: A Coda on Opinion 1/94' in Emiliou and O'Keeffe (eds.) *The European Union and World Trade Law after the GATT Uruguay Round* (Wiley, 1996); Bourgeois, 'The EC in the WTO and Opinion 1/94: An Echternach procession' (1995) 32 CMLRev. 763; Hilf, 'The ECJ's Opinion 1/94 on the WTO: No surprise but not wise?' (1995) 6 EJIL 245; Tridimas and Eeckhout, 'The External Competence of the Community and the Case Law of the Court of Justice—Principle versus Pragmatism' (1994) 14 YEL 143.

the Community has sole competence pursuant to Article 113 [new 133] of the EC Treaty to conclude an external agreement of a general nature, that is to say, encompassing all types of goods, even where those goods include ECSC products . . .

The fact that the commitments entered into under that Agreement [on Agriculture] require internal measures to be adopted on the basis of Article 43 [new 37] of the Treaty does not prevent the international commitments themselves from being entered pursuant to Article 113 alone.[17]

This last point is significant. The conclusion of an international agreement under Article 133 [ex 113] does not necessarily prejudge the question of which Treaty provision might be the most appropriate for internal implementing measures.[18] This has implications for the decision-making process which we will consider below.

The brief conclusion in respect of the Agreement on Technical Barriers to Trade also has a wider significance. The Dutch government had argued that here competence should be shared on the ground that complete harmonization has not been achieved (and is not envisaged) in the field of technical barriers to trade, reasoning which reflects that of the Court itself in *Opinion 2/91*.[19] However, the Court stressed that the Agreement on Technical Barriers is not about harmonization of standards: the provisions of the Agreement 'are designed *merely* to ensure that technical regulations and standards . . . do not create unnecessary obstacles to international trade' and the Agreement therefore falls within the ambit of the common commercial policy.[20] Harmonization of standards is of course also a way of removing obstacles to trade, but unlike ILO Convention No. 170 (which was at issue in *Opinion 2/91*) this Agreement does not establish minimum standards. It uses the principle of national treatment, encourages the adoption of international standards and provides for specific bilateral mutual recognition agreements. It is therefore premature to regard Article 133 as representing alone, even for goods, the external aspect of Article 95 [ex 100a] EC and able to provide a complete legal base for 'positive integration' measures to harmonize substantive standards.[21]

---

[17] *Opinion 1/94* (re WTO Agreement) [1994] ECR I-5267 at paras 27 and 29.

[18] A similar point is made in relation to an agreement concluded under the development co-operation provision Art. 181 [ex 130y] together with Art. 133, where the legal base for conclusion of the agreement was held not to predetermine the legal basis for Community acts implementing co-operation: case C-268/94 *Portuguese Republic v Council* [1996] ECR I-6177 at para. 47.

[19] *Opinion 2/91* (re ILO Convention No. 170) [1993] ECR I-1061.

[20] *Opinion 1/94* (re WTO Agreement) [1994] ECR I-5267 at para. 33 (my emphasis).

[21] See Chalmers, 'Legal Base and the External Relations of the EC' in Emiliou and O'Keeffe (eds.) *The European Union and World Trade Law after the GATT Uruguay Round* (Wiley, 1996) at 58–61; and Eeckhout, *The European Internal Market and International Trade: A Legal Analysis* (OUP, 1994) at 256–8.

Turning to services, the Court rejected two extreme positions. First, that of certain Member States who had argued for a complete exclusion in principle of services from the common commercial policy:

It follows from the open nature of the common commercial policy, within the meaning of the Treaty, that trade in services cannot immediately, and as a matter of principle, be excluded from the scope of Article 113.[22]

Second, that of the Commission which had argued for the inclusion of all trade in services without any distinction (the Court pointed out) as to mode of supply. Its middle way is based upon precisely that distinction, rather than adopting a sectoral approach.[23] The key distinction made by the Court is between (1) the direct, cross-frontier supply of services where neither the supplier nor the consumer moves to the other's country, and (2) a supply of services involving either a commercial presence in the consumer's country or a movement of natural persons (whether supplier or consumer) across the external frontiers of the Member States. The Court argued that the CCP was never intended to cover the movement of persons (natural or legal), basing itself on the existence of separate chapters in the Treaty on the movement of persons, and the distinction in Article 3 EC between the common commercial policy (paragraph (b)) and the entry and movement of persons (paragraph (d)).

In textual terms this is not very convincing: there is a separate chapter of the Treaty on the free movement of goods as well as persons; and a chapter on services (although some services are said to fall within the CCP). In addition trade in goods, which the Court says 'is unquestionably covered by the common commercial policy', is of course subject to different modes of supply in the same way as services are. The Court is however recognizing a political reality which had been clearly demonstrated during the Maastricht negotiations: the sensitivity of the Member States with respect to rights of entry for third country nationals.[24]

---

[22] *Opinion 1/94* (re WTO Agreement) [1994] ECR I-5267 at para. 41.

[23] Although special account is taken of transport services in recognition of their special place in the Treaty itself. Basing itself on case 22/70 *Commission v Council* (re AETR) [1971] ECR 263, and *Opinion 1/76* (re inland waterways agreement) [1977] ECR 741, the Court finds that international agreements in the field of transport fall within the specific Treaty Title on Transport on the basis of implied powers, and not within Article 133: *Opinion 1/94* (re WTO Agreement) [1994] ECR I-5267 at paras 48–52.

[24] This recognition is displayed in other cases where the Court argues that trade in services is based in a distinctive way on a *person*—the service provider and the provider's employees. In case C-43/93 *Van der Elst v OMI* [1994] ECR I-3803, for example, the freedom to provide services across frontiers was held to imply the right of the service provider to use its own employees even where they are nationals of a non-Member State; see also case C-113/89 *Rush Portuguesa* [1990] ECR I-1417. However, the Court expressly does not extend this principle to include a right of initial immigration into the Community for the third country workers, or even a right of free circulation from one Member State to another. In *Van der Elst v OMI* the employees were legally resident within both the home and host Member States and had work permits within the home Member State of the service provider.

In relation to the TRIPS Agreement the Court also adopts a 'middle way', although on different grounds. Certain aspects of the Agreement, concerning measures to be taken at external frontiers in order to prevent the importation of counterfeit goods, reflected a pre-existing Community Regulation adopted on the basis of Article 133 EC.[25] As a measure concerning the powers and duties of customs officers at the external frontiers of the Community, Article 133 provides an appropriate legal basis for both autonomous action (the Regulation) and international commitments (the TRIPS).[26] Other parts of TRIPS, however, go far beyond the actions of customs officials; they are concerned with establishing minimum standards, a baseline of protected rights. In areas where there are no Community harmonization measures, conclusion of the TRIPS will at the same time achieve a degree of harmonization *within* the Community.[27] In the same way as with services, the Court argues that there are other Treaty articles providing a legal base for internal harmonization of intellectual property rights (Articles 94 and 95 [ex 100 and 100a] as well as Article 308 [ex 235] where the creation of a new right is envisaged) and this excludes the possibility of using Article 133 to engage in 'external harmonization' of this type. The Court argues that to grant exclusive competence to the Community to enter into international agreements to harmonize IP rights on the basis of Article 133 would lead to an evasion of the 'internal constraints' imposed on the institutions when adopting harmonization measures at the internal level.[28] The Court is not concerned solely with the 'exclusivity' of Article 133, but also with the decision-making implications: with the interinstitutional balance of power as well as that between Member States and Community. Were such a conclusion accepted, it says, 'the Community institutions would be able to escape the internal constraints to which they are subject in relation to procedures and to rules as to voting'.[29]

To have extended the scope of Article 133 to cover all trade in services and all those aspects of intellectual property rights contained in the TRIPS Agreement would have in fact got very close to the re-definition of the CCP

---

[25] Council Regulation 3842/86 laying down measures to prevent the release for free circulation of counterfeit goods OJ 1986 L 357/1. This Regulation has now been altered to reflect the TRIPS obligations: Council Regulation 3295/94 OJ 1994 L 341/8.

[26] *Opinion 1/94* (re WTO Agreement) [1994] ECR I-5267 at para. 55.

[27] *Opinion 1/94* (re WTO Agreement) [1994] ECR I-5267 at para. 58.

[28] *Opinion 1/94* (re WTO Agreement) [1994] ECR I-5267 at para. 60; although the logic of the Court's opinion in relation to agriculture (see above at n. 17) would suggest that a different legal base might be appropriate for internal harmonization measures which implement TRIPS requirements.

[29] Ibid. Arnull argues that the Court's reliance on different decision-making procedures is 'not entirely convincing' as these differences 'merely reflect the lack of coherence in the voting rules and procedural requirements' in the Treaty: Arnull, 'The Scope of the Common Commercial Policy: A Coda on Opinion 1/94' in Emiliou and O'Keeffe, *The European Union and World Trade Law after the GATT Uruguay Round* (Wiley, 1996).

in terms of a general external economic policy proposed by the Commission and rejected by the Member States at Maastricht. The Court was thus not only recognizing the sensitivity of Member States in relation to the specific subject matter under discussion, but confirming the locus of the political power to alter Treaty obligations.

THE PRE-AMSTERDAM DEBATE OVER EXTERNAL ECONOMIC POLICY

In its Opinion of 28 February 1996, requested by the Council Presidency before the formal convening of the intergovernmental conference, the Commission, under the heading 'More effective Community action', made three proposals relating to external policy which each evidence concern as to the international identity of the Community, its relationship with the Member States and the need to 'speak with one voice' in order to engage more effectively with third countries and within international organizations.[30] As applied to external economic policy, they represent a response to the compromise Opinion of the Court, a reiteration of the concern expressed in the Commission's submissions to the Court as to the difficulty of administering the WTO Agreements on a basis of shared competence.[31] Then, the Court had responded that issues of competence are logically and legally prior to the question of implementation. The impression given is that this (actually highly pragmatic and politically sensitized) Opinion is following a 'pure' theoretical path to its only logical conclusion. Matters of practical application are of 'legitimate concern' but cannot be allowed to influence the allocation of competence.[32]

In its own Opinion, the Commission argued the need to address these same concerns, if necessary by Treaty amendment, and for a 'clarification' of the common commercial policy to take account of 'the radical changes in the structure of the world economy, in which services, intellectual property and direct foreign investment play an increasingly important role'. The lack of clarity over the Community's powers in these areas leads, the Commission said, to 'needless procedural wrangles' compromising its ability to defend the interests of the Member States and their businesses.[33]

---

[30] Commission Opinion of 28 February 1996 'Reinforcing Political Union and Preparing for Enlargement'. These concerns were of course also at the heart of the proposals for the development of the common foreign and security policy.

[31] Summarized in *Opinion 1/94* (re WTO Agreement) [1994] ECR I-5267 at para. 106.

[32] Ibid. at para. 107. One is reminded of the Court's insistence that issues of legal base must be determined according to 'objective factors which are amenable to judicial review' (see for example case 45/86 *Commission v Council* (re GSP Regulation) [1987] ECR 1493).

[33] Commission Opinion of 28 February 1996, at para. 25. Without being too cynical, we can note the reference to 'businesses', part of the rhetoric of a Union/Community which is

The Treaty on European Union had repealed the old Article 116 EC, which required the Member States to proceed by common action within international organizations of an economic character. This had been replaced by the more general provision in Article 19(1) [ex J.9] TEU:

Member States shall co-ordinate their action in international organisations and at international conferences. They shall uphold the common positions in such fora . . .

Given the wider responsibilities of the World Trade Organization (WTO), the Commission argued that the Union's negotiating position in such bodies was weakened where competence was shared between the Community and the Member States as a result of difficulties both in formulating a common position and in communicating it effectively. It therefore called, rather vaguely, for the Treaty to include 'provisions explicitly designed to enable the Union to speak with one voice and thus defend all the relevant interests more effectively'.[34] More generally, in cases of shared competence, there was a need for greater integration between policies of Member States and those of the Community.[35]

In March 1997, the IGC Task Force of the European Commission in its Report on 'The IGC—state of play at the end of 1996' mentions three aspects of external policy: the CFSP reforms, defence, and external economic relations. Alongside fairly full summaries of progress (and difficulties) in respect of negotiations within the IGC on the first two, the Commission simply says of the third, 'The Commission has proposed that Article 113 [new 133] be amended to reflect the realities of modern trade relations.' The scope of the Community's external economic powers, and the problems (or otherwise) of shared competence were not the major focus of either the Reflection Group Report of December 1995 or of the European Parliament.[36] Their concern was rather the coherence of the Union's external action more generally, and specifically the relations between first and second pillar action, together with the generally recognized need to reform aspects of the CFSP.[37] Nevertheless,

more responsive to its citizens, as well as appealing to Member State concern over international competitiveness.

[34] Commission Opinion of 28 February 1996, at para. 26.

[35] Commission Opinion of 28 February 1996, at para. 27. See also the requirements of consultation and co-ordination imposed on the Community and Member States explicitly by Art. 180 [ex 130x] EC on development policy, and the duty of co-operation in cases of shared competence reinforced by the Court of Justice in *Opinion 1/94* at paras 108–9.

[36] See for example, European Parliament Intergovernmental Conference Briefing No. 24 (First update: 30 January 1996) 'Coherence of the External Action of the European Union Under the First (Community) and Second (CFSP) Pillars'.

[37] For an assessment of the changes made by the Treaty of Amsterdam to the CFSP provisions, see Monar, 'The EU's Foreign Affairs System after the Treaty of Amsterdam: A "Strengthened Capacity for External Action"?' (1997) 2 EFA Rev. 413; Schmalz, 'The Amsterdam Provisions on External Coherence: Bridging the Union's Foreign Policy Dualism?' (1998) 3 EFA Rev. 421; F. Dehousse, 'After Amsterdam: A Report on the Common Foreign and Security Policy of the European Union' (1998) 9 EJIL 525.

the draft Treaty and commentary prepared for the Dublin summit in December 1996 contains a substantive proposal for the addition of a new article alongside Article 133 which would have extended explicit treaty-making competence to the Community in the fields of services, intellectual property and direct foreign investment.

The introduction and commentary attached to the draft text of the new article in 'Dublin II' is notable for the extent to which it follows the logic and even the language of the Commission's February 1996 Opinion. The Presidency argues: 'In its external economic relations, the Community would be able to act more effectively in multilateral international organizations, notably in the World Trade Organization, to defend the interests of its Member States, its industry and workers in today's highly competitive international trading environment.'[38] The Presidency recognizes the complexity of the issue and the wide range of views among the Member States, but indicates a wide measure of support for amending the Treaty to ensure procedures that would enable the Community to act decisively and effectively. The proposed draft article would have supplemented, not replaced, the existing Article 113:

1. In the framework of multilateral international organizations, negotiations in the areas of services, intellectual property and direct foreign investment not covered by Article 113(1) [new 133] shall be conducted by the Commission in consultation with the special committee provided for in Article 113.

2. To this end, the Commission shall make recommendations to the Council which shall authorize the Commission to open and conduct the negotiations within the framework of such directives as the Council may issue to it.

3. Agreements resulting from those negotiations shall be concluded by the Council, acting on a proposal by the Commission and after consulting the European Parliament. They shall not have direct effect.

4. In exercising the powers conferred upon it by this article, the Council shall act [by a qualified majority].

5. The provisions of Article 228(4), (5), (6) and (7) [new 300] shall apply.

6. Member States and the Community shall retain their respective internal powers in the fields covered by this Article, subject to the provisions of Article 228(7).

A declaration should be included in the Final Act of the Conference to provide that the Commission would conduct negotiations with maximum transparency vis-à-vis Member States.

The draft article is striking in the ways it seeks to circumscribe the new explicit Community competence. First, the Community's powers would be limited to the negotiation and conclusion of agreements in the framework of multilateral international organizations. The WTO and OECD would

---

[38] Conference of the Representatives of the Governments of the Member States, December 1996, CONF 2500/96; Introduction to Section III, An Effective and Coherent Foreign Policy.

certainly be included; the commentary suggests that it 'would certainly not apply in organisations such as the World Bank and IMF' although there is no specific exclusion or limitation. However, bilateral or multilateral agreements with third states outside the framework of an international organization (for example within an association or free trade agreement) would not be included. Nor would autonomous measures which did not involve negotiations and agreements. Second, the new provision would of itself give rise to no transfer of internal competence from the Member States to the Community: 'Member States and the Community shall retain their respective internal powers in the fields covered by this Article.' This provision was clearly intended to address the issue discussed by the Court in its WTO Opinion: the internal decision-making implications of extending the scope of Article 133.[39]

Third, agreements concluded under the draft article 'shall not have direct effect'. This is of course an attempt to generalize (in more direct language) recital 11 in the Preamble to the Council Decision concluding the WTO Agreements: 'Whereas, by its nature, the Agreement establishing the World Trade Organization, including the Annexes thereto, is not susceptible to being directly invoked in Community or Member State courts.'[40] The legal effect of the preambular statement is doubtful: the nature and scope of treaty obligations are a matter of interpretation and therefore for the Court of Justice if not explicitly determined by the parties; a unilateral statement by the Council when concluding a treaty cannot therefore be conclusive although it may provide an indication of the parties' intentions.[41] Although the Court itself has so far not expressed a view on the effect of recital 11, both Cosmas AG and Elmer AG have cited it to support an argument that the Court's earlier case law on the (non-) direct effect of the GATT 1947 should be applied to the GATT 1994 and the WTO Agreements.[42] Tesauro AG, on the other hand, has argued that the characteristics of the new WTO system are such as

---

[39] See above at n. 29.

[40] Council Decision 94/800/EC of 22 December 1994 concerning the conclusion on behalf of the European Community, as regards matters within its competence, of the agreements reached in the Uruguay Round multilateral negotiations (1986–1994) OJ 1994 L 336/1.

[41] See for example Case 104/81 *Hauptzollampt Mainz v Kupferberg* [1982] ECR 3641, paras 13–14. The Court accepts that contracting parties are free to agree what effect the provisions of the agreement will have in their internal legal order (ibid. at para 17). It can be argued that this was done with respect to the GATS in the Introductory Note to the Schedule of Commitments of the Community and its Member States. For a discussion of this issue, see Eeckhout, 'The Domestic Legal Status of the WTO Agreements: Interconnecting Legal Systems' (1997) 34 CMLRev. 11. The effect of GATS within the Community legal order and the implications for the domestic legal order of the Member States is discussed further below.

[42] Cosmas AG in case C-183/95 *Affish BV v Rijksdienst voor de keuring van Vee en Vlees* [1997] ECR I-4315, at paras 127–8 in relation to the Agreement on Sanitary and Phytosanitary measures; Elmer AG in cases T-364/95 and T-365/95 *T. Port GmbH & Co. v Hauptzollamt Hamburg-Jonas* [1998] ECR 1023 at paras 28–9 in relation to GATT 1994.

to render the Court's objections to the direct effect of GATT 1947 'obsolete'. He stresses the unilateral nature of the preambular statement as well as the fact that it is not in the operative part of the Decision and argues from this that the recital could not 'prevent the Court from coming to a different conclusion'.[43] The provision in the Dublin draft would have purported not only to pre-empt the Court of Justice in relation to an agreement which was silent on the issue, but also to write a compulsory clause into the negotiating mandate for future agreements. The effect would have been to shift the balance of power in two senses: away from the judicial and towards the political institutions, but also away from the Council of Ministers exercising its discretion in drawing up a negotiating mandate for a specific agreement (or in adopting a concluding Decision), in favour of the Member States as authors of the Treaty.

Finally, although the Dublin draft proposes the transfer of sole negotiating competence to the Commission, this is within the framework of a mandate adopted by the Council, 'in consultation with' the Article 133 Committee and with 'maximum transparency vis-à-vis Member States'. The mandate and the Committee are both of course in the existing Article 133. The suggested Declaration on transparency reflects Member State nervousness as to the possibility of the Commission exceeding its mandate[44] and the concern of national parliaments at their exclusion under current Article 133 procedures from the process of negotiation and approval of commercial policy agreements. Whether the draft as it stood would have conferred an exclusive competence is not entirely clear. The Presidency comments that 'the resulting agreements would be concluded by the Council, with no need for national ratification procedures' and there is no doubt that the delay consequent upon the national ratifications required by mixed agreements has been, alongside the need for a 'single negotiating voice', an argument used in support of extending exclusive CCP competence over external economic relations generally. Nevertheless, unlike Article 133 as amended by the Treaty of Amsterdam, the Dublin draft would have created a new legal base for Community action, not necessarily identical in its effects to Article 133, and with an explicit retention of internal Member State competence.

---

[43] Tesauro AG in case 53/96 *Hermes International v FHT Marketing Choice BV*, judgment 16 June 1998, [1998] ECR I-3603 at paras 23–5 and 30, in the context of the TRIPS Agreement.

[44] See comment by Monar, 'The European Union's Foreign Affairs System after the Treaty of Amsterdam: A Strengthened Capacity for External Action?' (1997) 2 EFARev. 413 at 431–2.

THE AMSTERDAM AMENDMENT AND
INTER-INSTITUTIONAL BALANCE

As we have seen, the final version of the Treaty of Amsterdam contains no direct grant of treaty-making power in relation to services, intellectual property and direct foreign investment. Instead, the Council, acting on a proposal from the Commission and after consulting the European Parliament, is given the power to extend the application of Article 133 to international negotiations and agreements on services and intellectual property in so far as they are not already covered by that provision. Foreign direct investment is omitted altogether.[45] The limitations placed on Community competence by the Dublin II draft (the references to multilateral international organizations, the retention of national internal powers, the denial of direct effect) have all disappeared, except the exclusion of autonomous measures from paragraph 5. It is quite clear that, should the paragraph 5 option be exercised, the areas covered would fall within the common commercial policy and would as such be subject to the decision-making procedures of the existing CCP. These decision-making procedures have been slightly modified by the amendments to Article 300 [ex 228] EC, to give an extra degree of control to the Council: under Article 300(2) the decision to sign as well as formally to conclude agreements will be taken by the Council. As the Council will now decide to sign the agreement, it may also decide at that stage to apply the agreement provisionally before its entry into force (Article 300(2)). When acting under Article 133, the Council will take these decisions by qualified majority vote and (except exceptionally) without any formal involvement of the European Parliament.

The Treaty of Amsterdam therefore leaves the decision as to the scope of Article 133, and specifically its extension to cover services and intellectual property, to the political institutions. Arnull has argued that this is essentially a 'vindication' of the judicial caution displayed by the Court of Justice in its opinion in the WTO case.[46] However, as we have seen, the Court in *Opinion 1/94* implies that intellectual property and some services are by their nature outside the scope of the CCP; that the Treaty structure and internal institutional balance require specific alternate legal bases for external action in these

[45] FDI, as included in the Dublin II draft, was presumably intended to cover not only the 'trade related investment measures' (TRIMS) within the WTO Annex IA but also the Multilateral Agreement on Investment (MAI) then being negotiated within the OECD. TRIMS were not discussed in *Opinion 1/94* but as things stand the MAI (or other multilateral investment agreement) would most likely be concluded as a mixed agreement: see also *Opinion 2/92* (re OECD National Treatment Instrument) [1995] ECR I-521.

[46] Arnull, 'The Court of Justice After Amsterdam: A Glass Half Empty or a Glass Half Full?', paper given to the UKAEL/UACES conference on Legal Issues of the Amsterdam Treaty, 19 June 1998.

areas. The Court also reaffirms that institutional practice cannot be conclusive of the correct choice of legal base. The Article 133 amendment could thus be seen rather as a shifting of the crucial decision from the Court to the Council—or from legal to political agency. If it vindicates the Court it does so by vindicating the Court's unstated recognition that altering Article 133 in this way would have major political and constitutional implications. In this, both *Opinion 1/94* and *Opinion 2/94* on the ECHR[47] can be seen as expressions of the major constitutional shift represented by Article 5 [ex 3b] EC.[48]

The effect of the Amsterdam amendment is to treat Article 133 as a box in which to put (or not) certain aspects of external activity where it is desired that their exercise should follow certain procedures and have certain legal effects. Although this could have been achieved by way of completely new provision(s) on external competence in the fields of services and intellectual property, it would have been very difficult in this case to have excluded the European Parliament from the decision-making processes, as the Dublin II draft demonstrates. The 'common commercial policy' is used as a convenient shorthand: far from having certain inherent characteristics its content is dynamic and subject to change in a way perhaps not foreseen by the Court even in its *Opinion 1/78*.[49] The wide discretion given to the institutions as far as the contents and objectives of the CCP is concerned are of relevance here too.[50]

The institution most directly affected by the option in Article 133(5) is of course the European Parliament, which must be consulted before the option is exercised. Article 133 is the only legal base (express or implied) for concluding an international agreement that does not require at least consultation of the Parliament. Although the new provision in the Dublin II draft would have given a role, albeit only consultative, to the Parliament, the Amsterdam amendment to Article 133 leaves this aspect of the decision-making process unchanged. In practice, the Parliament is normally consulted in the case of agreements based on Article 133 under the Luns-Westerterp procedure,[51] and Parliamentary assent was actually obtained in the case of the WTO Agreement and is referred to in the recitals of the concluding decision.[52]

---

[47] *Opinion 2/94* (re ECHR) [1996] ECR I-1759; [1996] 2 CMLR 265.

[48] Dashwood argues that in *Opinion 2/94* '[the first paragraph of Article 3b] is treated by the Court . . . as expressing one of the general organising principles of the post-Maastricht constitution'; Dashwood, Commentary in 'The Human Rights Opinion of the ECJ and its Constitutional Implications' CELS Occasional Paper No. 1 (University of Cambridge, 1996) at 21; see also Hilf, 'Unwritten EC Authority in Foreign Trade Law' (1997) 2 EFARev. 437 at 449.

[49] *Opinion 1/78* (re Natural Rubber Agreement) [1979] ECR 2871; cf. the Court's reference in *Opinion 1/94* to the 'open nature' of the CCP: see text above at n. 22.

[50] See text above at n. 8.   [51] OJ 1982 C 66/68.

[52] Council Decision 94/800/EC of 22 December 1994 concerning the conclusion on behalf of the European Community, as regards matters within its competence, of the agreements reached in the Uruguay Round multilateral negotiations (1986–1994) OJ 1994 L 336/1.

However, the formal position is significant and the Parliament is sensitive to the distinction, hence its intervention in the WTO Opinion, arguing against an extension of Article 133 to cover services and intellectual property.[53]

The TRIPS agreement provides an illustration of this. The TRIPS is more than merely an agreement to work towards the harmonization of standards. If it were so limited, then it would be possible to argue that the legal base for internal (implementation) measures would not be pre-empted by using Article 133 as a legal base for the conclusion of the external agreement.[54] However, as the Commission and Court agree, 'since TRIPS lays down rules in fields in which there are no Community harmonisation measures, its conclusion would make it possible at the same time to achieve harmonisation within the Community'.[55] The 'internal constraints' in relation to voting and involvement of the Parliament in adopting autonomous internal measures under Articles 94, 95, or 308 would have been evaded in the areas harmonized by the TRIPS. This is not to say that all further internal Community harmonization of IP rights would be pre-empted: for example, the TRIPS contains a so-called 'minimum clause' allowing parties to adopt legislation granting more extensive protection to right-holders. However, certain (internal) policy-choices have been constrained by TRIPS obligations, and were Article 133 to have been used, those obligations would have been created without following the internal decision-making procedures. As the Court points out, IP rights are at least as much about internal trade as international trade.[56] We are therefore not only concerned with the appropriate legal base for concluding an international agreement, but also with the implications of the agreement for internal harmonization measures.

There is a further dimension to this question. Under Article 133 (both as it stands and after the Amsterdam amendment) no consultation of Parliament is necessary. If on the other hand a legal base utilizing the Community's implied powers is used then the Parliament must be involved.[57] However under Article 300(3) its involvement is limited to consultation, even in cases where the adoption of the internal act requires the co-decision or co-operation procedures under Articles 251 or 252 EC. Exceptionally, the assent of Parliament is required where the agreement establishes an association under

---

[53] See also the Parliament's successful challenge to the Council decision concluding the EC–US agreement on procurement: Case C-360/93 *European Parliament v Council* [1996] ECR I-1195. The decision concluding the agreement had been based solely on Art. 133 (then Art. 113). Following its *Opinion 1/94*, the Court held that as the agreement covered aspects of services going beyond mere transfrontier supply involving no movement of persons, Art. 133 could not form the sole legal base (at para. 27).

[54] See text above at n. 18.

[55] *Opinion 1/94* (re WTO Agreement) [1994] ECR I-5267 at para. 58.

[56] Ibid. at para. 57.

[57] For intellectual property, this would be Arts. 94, 95, and/or 308 [ex 100, 100a, 235]. For services this would be Arts. 47(2), 55, and 95 [ex 57(2), 66, 100a].

Article 310, where it establishes a 'special institutional framework', where it has 'important budgetary implications' and (more significantly in this context) where it entails amendment of an act already adopted under the co-decision procedure. This means that where implied powers are used to conclude an agreement which aims to harmonize national legislation, the role of Parliament will vary according to whether this is an area already subject to internal EC harmonizing measures which may need amendment. If it is an area where no harmonization has as yet taken place within the Community (as in the case of TRIPS), not only is the Parliament limited to a consultative role, but future internal action (which may be based on provisions requiring co-decision) may be pre-empted or at least circumscribed.

THE AMSTERDAM AMENDMENT AND EXCLUSIVITY

The second major aspect of Article 133 is the exclusivity of the powers it grants to the Community. The effect of the amended Article is to leave the Council to decide (unanimously) when and whether to move external competence in the fields of services and intellectual property into exclusivity.

A number of questions immediately arise. First is the extent to which exclusivity is an inseparable part of the application of Article 133. Exclusivity as it applies to paragraphs 1–4 of Article 133 is (unlike the decision-making procedure) a characteristic of the common commercial policy identified by the Court of Justice and not explicit in the Treaty itself. Could the Council then decide to 'extend the application of paragraphs 1 to 4 to international negotiations and agreements on services and intellectual property' *without* extending exclusivity into these areas, effectively limiting the extension to the decision-making aspects of Article 133? On one view[58] the full competence granted by Article 133(5) includes the theoretical possibility of making a more limited transfer. The answer turns on whether exclusivity, although not explicit, could be said to be implicit in the concept of 'uniform principles' on which the common commercial policy is to be based and thus an inseparable part of the nature of a 'common commercial policy'. There is no doubt that the Court of Justice, in *Opinion 1/94*, regards exclusivity as an attribute of the common commercial policy; it refers to 'the exclusive competence conferred on the Community in matters concerning the common commercial policy by Article 113 [new 133] of the EC Treaty' and uses similar language in discussing the possible application of Article 133 to services and intellectual property.[59] Were the Council to deny exclusivity in the context of exercising

[58] Thanks to Eileen Denza for her comments on this section.
[59] *Opinion 1/94* (re WTO Agreements) [1994] ECR I-5267 at para. 22. The Court also refers to the exclusive nature of Art. 133 in the context of its application to services at para. 51 and at paras 60 and 65 in relation to intellectual property.

the option granted by Article 133(5), it would thus be redefining the nature of the common commercial policy as hitherto generally accepted,[60] and would reinforce a view of the CCP which does not depend on any inherent characteristics.[61]

A second question is closely connected. Does exclusive external competence necessarily imply exclusive internal competence (a form of parallelism)? Or, putting it another way, could Community powers really be exclusive externally over a whole field (such as intellectual property) where they clearly are not yet exclusive internally? This echoes the discussion in *Opinion 1/94* of whether Article 133 could cover the harmonization of standards and it is possible to read passages in the Opinion as taking this view of the effect of using Article 133 as a legal base.[62] However it is also clear that in the opinion of the Court this would be an undesirable outcome. Hyett argues for a parallel approach, but with the exercise of internal powers taking the lead: 'the external competence of the Community should move in step with what happens internally within the Community'.[63] As he points out, this approach has a practical as well as a constitutional justification: if the Commission (as the key policy-maker) is not yet acting in a particular field at the internal level, it will not yet have developed the expertise to act effectively in external negotiations.[64] It will also of course be much harder to agree a common negotiating mandate within the Council in an area where common rules have not yet been agreed at the internal level, and the proper level (Community or Member State) at which implementing measures should be adopted may be contentious. The question posed brings out the difference between the 'exclusivity' of the common commercial policy, and exclusivity in the context of implied external powers. In so far as services and intellectual property are within the scope of *implied* external powers, the Court said in *Opinion 1/94* that: 'Only in so far as common rules have been established at internal level

---

[60] Some authors have argued that the CCP, especially a CCP extended to cover services, should not be fully exclusive; for a summary of the arguments see Eeckhout, *The European Internal Market and International Trade: A Legal Analysis* (OUP, 1994) at 32–4. Eeckhout argues in favour of an exclusive CCP but suggests that the adoption of uniform principles by the Community leaves room for implementation at least in part by the Member States.

[61] See text above at n. 49.

[62] See above at n. 20. The Court rejected the Netherlands government argument that Art. 133 should not be used as a legal base for international harmonization in the field of technical barriers to trade, not on the ground that Art. 133 *could* be used for this purpose but on the ground that the Agreement on Technical Barriers to Trade was not a harmonization measure.

[63] Hyett, 'The Uruguay Round of the GATT: The United Kingdom Standpoint' in Emiliou and O'Keeffe, *The European Union and World Trade Law after the GATT Uruguay Round* (Wiley, 1996) at 98–100.

[64] However, even in cases of shared competence, the Commission will tend to act as negotiator and spokesperson for the Community and Member States: see below at n. 70.

does the external competence of the Community become exclusive.'[65] However, the Community's CCP powers have been held to be exclusive even where they have not (yet) been fully exercised, any Member State action in the meantime requiring specific authorization.[66] This classic approach to exclusivity under Article 133 would not extend easily to a broadened CCP including intellectual property and services, areas (unlike the customs union) in which strict exclusivity does not apply internally.

The option offered by the Amsterdam amendment could thus be used in two ways; either to move these sectors of external policy into exclusivity *before* they acquire that status as implied external powers via the exercise of internal powers, or as a way of allowing the political institutions to adapt the Treaty's external commercial-policy mechanisms to reflect the progressive development of internal policy. In the latter case, the effect of exercising the option as far as exclusivity is concerned may be in part declaratory, as existing implied competence may already have become exclusive.

This last point raises a third question. To what extent would the exercise of the option be a once-and-for-all decision, applying to the whole of 'services' or 'intellectual property' in so far as they are not already covered by Article 133? On the one hand it would be difficult to interpret Article 133(5) as permitting 'transfer' on a case-by-case basis for individual agreements: it is hard to see the point of the Council deciding—unanimously and after consulting Parliament—to sign and conclude a specific agreement by qualified majority vote and without Parliamentary consultation. On the other hand, it seems entirely possible that the Council would wish to transfer specific service sectors ('air transport', 'procurement of services', 'financial services') into Article 133. If a transfer does take place in this graduated way, some of the difficulties raised above concerning exclusivity will be less acute. The Member States (through the Council) will be happier to accept exclusive external competence over a delimited aspect of services (or IP), and this approach would also allow for a gradual evolution of Community competence to reflect the development of internal policies. It may even be envisaged that a decision might be taken

---

[65] *Opinion 1/94* (re WTO Agreements) [1994] ECR I-5267 at para. 77. A little later (para. 85) the Court accepts that very exceptionally external powers may become exclusive without a prior exercise of internal powers, as was the case in respect of the Rhine/Moselle Inland Waterways Agreement at issue in *Opinion 1/76* [1977] ECR 741, but refuses to apply this to the WTO Agreements.

[66] Case 41-76, *Suzanne Criel, née Donckerwolcke and Henri Schou v Procureur de la République au tribunal de grande instance de Lille and Director General of Customs* [1976] ECR 1921 at para. 32. See also *Opinion 1/75* (re OECD Understanding) [1975] ECR 1355. For examples of authorization see Art. 134 [ex Art. 115] EC as interpreted in *Donckerwolcke*, and Council Decisions 69/494 OJ 1969 L326/39 and 97/351 OJ 1997 L 151/24 authorizing automatic renewal and continuing in force of provisions governing matters within the CCP contained in friendship, commerce, and navigation treaties between Member States and third states.

to apply Article 133 to certain types of agreement within a particular service sector (to market access agreements, for example, but not to harmonization agreements).

Lastly, what would be the implications of *not* exercising the Article 133 option, and retaining the *status quo* of shared competence? The Commission has, as we have seen, argued before the Court and in the IGC negotiations, in favour of bringing all external commercial relations (or at least everything within the scope of the WTO) within Article 133 on grounds of more efficient external representation. The Court's response has been to stress the duty of co-operation between the Member States and the Community institutions, not only in the negotiation phase, but also in the implementation of mixed agreements.[67] This is especially important where, as in the case of the WTO Agreements, the areas of respective competence are 'inextricably linked'[68] and in fact not expressly allocated in the concluding instrument or elsewhere. The *FAO fisheries agreement* case illustrates the kinds of problem that arise where there is disagreement over the scope of a proposed action in the context of a mixed agreement.[69]

As far as the WTO is concerned, a practice appears to be emerging at least within the context of dispute settlement procedures that the Community will act jointly with the Member States, whether as the subject of a complaint or as a complainant.[70] The alternative might lead to great difficulty if not all Member States supported a Community-led complaint. As in the negotiation of mixed agreements, where the Commission may present a single negotiating position adopted as a common position by the Member States and Community in co-operation, consensus is in effect required. It is also clearly undesirable to require third countries to take difficult and contentious decisions as to the proper party to a dispute settlement procedure. Some of the WTO agreements, notably Annex 1A containing GATT 1994 and the other multilateral Agreements on Trade in Goods, fall within the common commercial policy and thus within the Community's exclusive competence.[71]

---

[67] *Opinion 1/94* (re WTO Agreements) [1994] ECR I-5267 at paras 108–9. See also *Opinion 2/91* (re ILO Convention No. 170) [1993] ECR I-1061 at para. 36, Art. 10 [ex 5] EC and Art. 3 [ex C] TEU.

[68] *Opinion 1/94* at para. 109.

[69] Case C-25/94 *Commission v Council* (FAO fisheries agreement) [1996] ECR I-1469. For detailed discussion of these issues, see MacLeod, Hendry, and Hyett, *European Community External Relations: Law and Practice* (Oxford University Press, 1996) at 155–62, 171–89.

[70] A. Rosas, 'The EC and WTO Dispute Settlement: Some reflections on practice and doctrine', paper given to 37th London-Leiden Meeting, 'The WTO and the European Union', between the Europa Institute, University of Leiden and the British Institute of International and Comparative Law, 27 June 1998.

[71] *Opinion 1/94* (re WTO Agreement) [1994] ECR I-5267 at paras 27–33. Elmer AG argues that exclusive competence is not just a matter of internal allocation of powers, but has

Others, notably Annex 1B containing the GATS and Annex 1C containing the TRIPS Agreements, are a matter of shared competence. As both the Community and its Member States are members of the WTO and parties to the WTO Agreement and all its Annexes, with no express provision on respective competence written into the Agreement, they must both be considered responsible for any breach as far as third parties are concerned.[72] In the case of a mixed agreement such as this, both the Member States and the Community are under a Community obligation to respect the agreement in its entirety[73] and the allocation of competencies is essentially an internal matter.[74]

As we shall see in the next section, the need for a common position in matters of interpretation of treaty obligations is also becoming apparent. The difference between exclusive and mixed competence appears less important in practice than in theory.

MIXED AGREEMENTS AND JUDICIAL EXCLUSIVITY

The question of exclusivity is increasingly clearly linked to the relationship between international and national and/or EC rules, and more specifically to the question of the direct effect of international agreements. Within Community law, direct effect has been seen in part as an issue of effective enforcement of rules and in part as an example of the constitutionalization of EC law.[75] The direct effect of GATT 1947, denied by the Court of Justice,

implications for third states as requiring exclusive international responsibility: in cases T-364/95 and T-365/95 *T. Port GmbH & Co. v Hauptzollamt Hamburg-Jonas* [1998] ECR 1023 at para. 16: 'In the relations between Member States of the WTO, and hence parties to GATT 1994, I consider that it follows from Article 59(1)(a) of the Vienna Convention on the Law of Treaties of 23 May 1969 that GATT 1994 has replaced GATT 1947 with effect from 1 January 1995, when GATT 1994 entered into force. The WTO Agreement, and hence GATT 1994, was concluded, as regards commercial policy, by the Community, which, under Article 113 of the Treaty, has exclusive competence for commercial policy. Accordingly, claims arising from GATT 1994 can only be addressed to the Community and not to the various Member States.'

[72] See Tesauro AG in case 53/96 *Hermes International v FHT Marketing Choice BV*, [1998] ECR I-3603 at para. 14: 'In these circumstances it should be recognised that the Member States and the Community constitute, vis-à-vis contracting non-Member States, a single contracting party or at least contracting parties bearing equal responsibility in the event of failure to implement the agreement.'

[73] See Art. 300(7) EC [ex 228(7)] and case 12/86 *Demirel v Stadt Schwäbisch Gmund* [1987] ECR 3719 at para. 11.

[74] See *Ruling 1/78/Euratom* (Nuclear Materials) [1978] ECR 2151, at para. 35.

[75] Case 26/62 *Van Gend en Loos* [1963] ECR 1. See Mancini, 'The Making of a Constitution for Europe' (1989) 26 CMLRev. 595; Weiler, 'The Transformation of Europe' (1991) 100 Yale LJ 2403.

has been argued for on both these grounds.[76] Giving direct effect to an international agreement deprives the Member States (and national courts) of discretion as to *how* to implement the obligation articulated in Article 300(7). The Court of Justice has insisted that, in the context of an agreement concluded under Article 133, the issue of the effect of a Community agreement within the legal order of Community Member States is a matter for EC law alone. A Community agreement is 'an integral part of Community Law' and its interpretation is therefore (as far as the Community legal order is concerned) a matter ultimately for the Court of Justice.[77] As the Court held in *Kupferberg*:

> It follows from the Community nature of such provisions that their effect in the Community may not be allowed to vary according to whether their application is in practice the responsibility of the Community institutions or of the Member States and, in the latter case, according to the effects in the internal legal order of each Member State which the law of that State assigns to international agreements concluded by it. Therefore it is for the Court, within the framework of its jurisdiction in interpreting the provisions of agreements, to ensure their uniform application throughout the Community.[78]

To what extent does this principle of (what may be termed) judicial exclusivity apply to agreements—such as the GATS and the TRIPS—where competence is shared between Community and Member States? Does the whole agreement become 'an integral part of Community law' or only those parts that are within Community competence? And if the latter is the case, does it then follow that the Court does not have jurisdiction to interpret (including the determination of direct effect) those parts of the agreement that do not form a part of Community law? For the WTO agreements, these questions are sharpened by the fact that the Council Decision concluding them specifies that the multilateral agreements 'are hereby approved on behalf of the European Community *with regard to that portion of them which falls within the competence of the European Community*'.[79] As Eeckhout has argued, although there is no certain answer as yet to these questions, there is a strong case for

---

[76] Cases 22–24/72 *International Fruit Company NV v Produktschap voor Groenten en Fruit* [1972] ECR 1219; case 267–269/81 *Amministrazione delle Finanze dello Stato v SPI SpA* [1983] ECR 801; case C-69/89 *Nakajima* [1991] ECR I-2069; case C-280/93 *Germany v Council* (bananas) [1994] ECR I-4737. See also Petersmann, *The GATT/WTO Dispute Settlement System. International Law, International Organizations and Dispute Settlement* (Kluwer Law International, 1997) and works cited at n. 9 above.

[77] See case 181/73 *Haegeman* [1974] ECR 449.

[78] Case 104/81 *Hauptzollampt Mainz v Kupferberg* [1982] ECR 3641 at para. 14. The Court refers here only to the effect *in the Community* of provisions of Community agreements: the determination of direct effect by the Court of Justice only affects the Community legal order, not that of the other Contracting Party/ies.

[79] Council Decision 94/800/EC of 22 December 1994, OJ 1994 L 336/1, Art. 1 (emphasis added).

giving one answer rather than sixteen to the question of the domestic legal status of all the WTO Agreements, and not only the GATT (which already falls within exclusive competence).[80] This case would become even stronger were the option in the Amsterdam amendment to be exercised and the fields covered by the GATS and TRIPS to move into exclusive Community competence.

However, as far as the WTO rules are concerned, the Court is again in a number of ways allowing the political institutions and the Member States to set the trend. First, by denying that the GATT is capable by its nature of creating directly enforceable rights, and that in the internal legal order of the Community its effects are dependent on the existence of internal Community legislation, the Court is effectively shifting the burden of ensuring enforcement of GATT from the courts to the legislator.[81] As Cosmas AG has pointed out:

It can be inferred from the Court's case-law that, until the Community has adopted the necessary implementing measures for the purpose of fulfilling its obligations under GATT, it cannot be compelled to do so by judicial means by the operators concerned.[82]

The case law on the GATT, and especially *Germany v Council*[83] and *Commission v Germany*,[84] thus have the effect of leaving the implementation and enforcement of WTO/GATT obligations to the political institutions.[85]

Second, in its most recent judgment on this issue, in the *Hermes* case, the Court comments neither on the assumption made by the referring Dutch judge that the relevant provision of the TRIPS agreement is directly effective,[86] nor on the preambular statement in the decision concluding the WTO

[80] Eeckhout, 'The Domestic Legal Status of the WTO Agreements: Interconnecting Legal Systems' (1997) 34 CMLRev. 11 at 14–24.

[81] Case 70/87 *Fediol v Commission* [1989] ECR 1781; case C-69/89 *Nakajima v Council* [1991] ECR I-2069; case C-280/93 *Germany v Council* (bananas) [1994] ECR I-4737.

[82] Cosmas AG in case C-183/95 *Affish BV v Rijksdienst voor de keuring van Vee en Vlees* [1997] ECR I-4315, at para. 120, n. 97.

[83] Case C-280/93 *Germany v Council* [1994] ECR I-4973, in which the Court held that the provisions of GATT cannot—in the absence of implementing legislation—be taken into account in assessing the lawfulness of a Community regulation in an action brought by a Member State.

[84] Case C-61/94 *Commission v Germany* [1996] ECR I-3989, in which the Commission challenged national measures as incompatible with GATT-based Community commitments in an action based on Art. 226 [ex 169] EC.

[85] A point made by Tesauro AG in Case C-53/96 *Hermes International v FHT Marketing Choice BV*, [1998] ECR I-3603, at para. 35 of his Opinion.

[86] Case C-53/96 *Hermes International v FHT Marketing Choice BV*, [1998] ECR I-3603. See Opinion of Tesauro AG at para. 8 for a reference to the Dutch court's order for the reference. Tesauro also points out (at para. 20, n. 28) that the French government, in its submissions at the oral hearing had (while denying the Court's jurisdiction to interpret Art. 50) urged the Court to rule on the issue of direct effect so as to avoid the risk of divergent national interpretations.

agreements to the effect that none of the agreements are susceptible of being directly invoked in Community or Member State courts.[87]

These examples of judicial restraint are in the first place concerned with the respective roles of courts and legislator in determining the relationship between interconnecting legal systems. However, alongside *Opinion 1/94* they may also reflect the Court's views on the need for a political consensus within and among the Member States (as well as within and among the 'political' institutions) in working out the constitutional implications of submission to an external legal order. As such they can be regarded as an example of subsidiarity as a guiding principle of the Court's interpretative power.[88] As Hilf points out, 'with regard to foreign affairs powers, the ECJ is proving to be on the whole not so much a dynamic and driving factor of integration, but rather an institution which *safeguards the federal balance* between the Community and its Member States'.[89] The fact that the TRIPS is a mixed agreement may also be a factor here; as in *Demirel*,[90] the Court in *Hermes* clearly wished to avoid any discussion of the putative allocation of obligations between Community and Member States.[91] It did not take up the Advocate General's invitation to reconsider the issue of direct effect, but neither did it take the opportunity to reassert its current position on the GATT in the context of TRIPS. Instead, it relies on the fact that although the point had been argued before the Court, the national court had not actually asked it to rule on the question.[92]

---

[87] Council Decision 94/800/EC of 22 December 1994 concerning the conclusion on behalf of the European Community, as regards matters within its competence, of the agreements reached in the Uruguay Round multilateral negotiations (1986–1994) OJ 1994 L 336/1, recital 11. See text above at n. 40ff. for differing views as to the effect of this recital.

[88] De Búrca suggests that the subsidiarity principle may be reflected in the Court's reasoning in *Opinion 2/94* (re ECHR), 28 March 1996, [1996] ECR I-1759; [1996] 2 CMLR 265; in this case the Court insisted on the need for formal treaty amendment (thus engaging national constitutional procedures) as a pre-condition for accession to the ECHR. See de Búrca, 'The Principle of Subsidiarity and the Court of Justice as an Institutional Actor' 36 JCMS 217 at 225.

[89] Hilf, 'Unwritten EC Authority in Foreign Trade Law' (1997) 2 EFARev. 437 at 454, emphasis in the original.

[90] Case 12/86 *Demirel v Stadt Schwäbisch Gmund* [1987] ECR 3719.

[91] See Case C-53/96 *Hermes International v FHT Marketing Choice BV*, at paras 24–5.

[92] This was also the reason given by the Court in case C-183/95 *Affish BV v Rijksdienst voor de keuring van Vee en Vlees* [1997] ECR I-4315, at para. 28, in which one party had raised the issue of direct effect of one of the WTO Agreements, but the referring national court had not included it among the questions asked. See also joined cases T-364/95 and T-365/95 *T. Port GmbH & Co. v Hauptzollamt Hamburg-Jonas*, judgment of the Court of 10 March 1998 [1998] ECR I-1023 at paras 58–67 where a different strategy was used to avoid (re)considering the issue of direct effect of GATT 1994. In both cases, the Advocates General had concluded that the reasoning behind the earlier case law on GATT 1947 still applied and that the WTO agreements were not directly effective. In case C-149/96 *Portugal v Council*, judgement of 23 November 1999, the Court finally discussed the issue and confirmed its earlier pre-WTO case law.

The national court had, however, asked for an interpretation of Article 50 of the TRIPS agreement, and while not denying the implications of the fact that TRIPS is a mixed agreement, the Court does not display such reticence in relation to its substantive interpretative jurisdiction. A number of governments[93] had argued that the Court had no jurisdiction to interpret Article 50 of TRIPS (which deals with provisional measures ordered by judicial authorities to prevent infringement of intellectual property rights) since the provision in question falls within Member State competence and thus does not fall within the scope of application of Community law.[94] The Court asserted its authority to interpret Article 50 by relying on the fact that the Regulation on the Community trademark contains a provision on provisional measures.[95] Since the Community is a party to, and bound by, the TRIPS, the TRIPS will apply to the Community trademark; and national courts, when interpreting national law on provisional measures in connection with the Community trademark, must do so as far as possible in the light of the wording and purpose of TRIPS. That being so, the Court of Justice has jurisdiction to interpret Article 50 of TRIPS. This jurisdiction also applies, the Court held, even in cases such as the present where it was national trademark rights rather than the Community trademark that were at issue. Not only do national courts have a discretion to assess their need for a preliminary ruling;[96] in addition, where a provision may apply to situations falling within the scope of both national and Community law, it is in the Community interest that the provision should be interpreted uniformly.[97]

Article 99 of the Community Trademark Regulation even envisages that the provisional measures will be applied by national courts in accordance with their own domestic laws as applied to national trademarks (there is no harmonization of national law on provisional measures by the Regulation). Nevertheless, in so far as Article 50 of TRIPS is relevant to these domestic laws, the Court of Justice holds that it has jurisdiction to interpret the provision. In a neat sideways move the Court side-steps the issue of direct effect and asserts the relevance of TRIPS to the proceedings in the national court by using—in language redolent of *Marleasing*[98]—the interpretative principle sometimes referred to as 'indirect effect':

---

[93] The French, Netherlands and UK governments.

[94] Case C-53/96 *Hermes International v FHT Marketing Choice BV*, [1998] ECR I-3603 at para. 23.

[95] Regulation 40/94/EC OJ 1994 L 11/1, Art. 99.

[96] Case C-53/96 *Hermes* at para. 31, citing *inter alia* cases C-297/88 and C-197/89 *Dzodzi* [1990] ECR I-3763 at paras 34–5.

[97] Case C-53/96 *Hermes* at para. 32, citing *inter alia* case C-130/95 *Giloy v Hauptzollamt Frankfurt am Main-Ost* [1997] ECR I-4291 at para. 28.

[98] *Marleasing SA v La Comercial Internacionale de Alimentacion SA* C-106/89 [1990] ECR I-4135.

The courts referred to in Article 99 of Regulation 40/94, when called upon to apply national rules with a view to ordering provisional measures for the protection of rights arising under a Community trademark, are required to do so, as far as possible, in the light of the wording and purpose of Article 50 of the TRIPS Agreement.[99]

The Court cites, 'by analogy', a passage in *Commission v Germany*.

The primacy of international agreements concluded by the Community over provisions of secondary Community legislation means that such provisions, must, so far as is possible, be interpreted in a manner that is consistent with those agreements.[100]

In this latter passage the Court was referring to the interpretation of Community legislation; in *Hermes* the national courts referred to would be interpreting national law. The Court has already claimed jurisdiction to interpret the GATT in a case where the national court was considering the compatibility of a national law with the GATT, on the explicitly policy-based foundation of the need for uniform interpretation of GATT rules throughout the Community:

It is important that the provisions of GATT should, like the provisions of all other agreements binding the Community, receive uniform application throughout the Community. Any difference in the interpretation and application of provisions binding the community as regards non-Member countries would not only jeopardize the unity of the commercial policy . . . but also create distortions in trade within the Community . . . It follows that the jurisdiction conferred upon the Court in order to ensure the uniform interpretation of Community law must include a determination of the scope and effect of the rules of GATT within the Community . . . In that regard it does not matter whether the national court is required to assess the validity of Community measures or the compatibility of national legislative provisions with the commitments binding the Community.[101]

The GATT, however, unlike the GATS or TRIPS, is within the Community's exclusive competence; *Hermes* extends this principle to cases of shared competence.

Does the emphasis on the Trademark Regulation imply that in its absence the Court would have denied jurisdiction? *Hermes* still leaves open the question whether, in the absence of a 'Community dimension' such as the Community Trademark Regulation, the Court would claim jurisdiction to interpret a mixed agreement such as the TRIPS. The gradual evolution of Community law into areas covered by the TRIPS, foreseen by the Court as a possibility in *Opinion 1/94*[102] would suggest that it should do so 'in order to

---

[99] Case C-53/96 *Hermes* at para. 28.

[100] Case C-61/94 *Commission v Germany* (International Dairy Arrangement) [1996] ECR I-3989 at para. 52.

[101] Cases 267–269/81 *SPI and SAMI* [1983] ECR 801, at paras 14–15.

[102] *Opinion 1/94* (re WTO Agreements) [1994] ECR I-5267 at para. 104.

forestall future differences of interpretation'.[103] Were the option under Article 133(5) to be exercised, and intellectual property and services generally to fall within exclusive external competence, then the logic of *SPI and SAMI*[104] would require an interpretative jurisdiction for the Court of Justice over the whole of the GATS and TRIPS. In the current situation of shared competence, action at Community level requires a justification not only in terms of formal jurisdiction but also in terms of effectiveness.[105] Thus, the need for a uniform (and more effective) enforcement of TRIPS throughout the Community may justify a 'judicial exclusivity' here too, even in the absence of an exercise of the Article 133(5) option. If the Community is, with respect to third states, responsible for the effective performance of obligations under the agreement as a whole it is clearly important that a uniform view is adopted throughout the Community as to the scope of those obligations.[106] The need for Member States (and their courts) to accept the interpretative jurisdiction of the Court of Justice in these cases can be seen as an expression of the duty of 'close co-operation' in the management of mixed agreements, which is founded on Article 10 [ex 5] of the EC Treaty.[107] The adoption of a common position on the implementation of mixed agreements implies a common position on their interpretation.

It should also be borne in mind that one of the practical attractions of the mixed agreement has always been the absence of the need to delineate the respective spheres of Community and Member State competence (unless the other Contracting Parties insist). This attraction would be substantially reduced, not least for the Court, if its interpretative jurisdiction were to be excluded from aspects of a mixed agreement falling within Member State competence. Apart from being highly sensitive, the inter-connectedness of the provisions of an agreement (or even of several agreements, as in the case of the WTO agreements) would render any attempt to separate the two an extremely difficult exercise. So far the Court has always avoided this problem.[108] From this perspective, the 'judicial exclusivity', evidenced in *Hermes*

---

[103] Case C-53/96 *Hermes* at para. 32.   [104] See n. 101 above.

[105] Art. 5 [ex 3b] EC; see also the discussion of subsidiarity and the interpretative role of the Court in de Búrca, 'The Principle of Subsidiarity and the Court of Justice as an Institutional Actor' 36 JCMS 217.

[106] This is a general point applicable in principle to all mixed agreements and not only TRIPS. See text at n. 72 above, and Tesauro AG in *Hermes* at para. 20.

[107] See Tesauro AG in *Hermes* at para. 21. For the duty of close co-operation, see, *inter alia*, *Opinion 1/94* [1994] ECR I-5267, paras 108–9; for the duty on Member States, based on Art. 10 [ex 5] EC, to respect their Community obligations even where exercising their own external competence, see joined cases 3, 4, and 6/76 *Cornelis Kramer and others* [1976] ECR 1279, paras 40–6. See also J. H. J. Bourgeois, 'The European Court of Justice and the WTO: Problems and Challenges', in this volume at section II.2.2, final paragraph.

[108] See for example Case 12/86 *Demirel v Stadt Schwäbisch Gmund* [1987] ECR 3719, and Case C-53/96 *Hermes* at para. 25.

as a claim to interpretative jurisdiction, can be seen as reluctance to delimit definitively the scope of Community competence and thus pre-empt the choices of the political institutions and the Member States as far as the implementation of TRIPS is concerned. The Court may be seeking to 'safeguard the federal balance' between Community and Member States,[109] but in this task unity and coherence between the constituent parts may be more important than a clear separation of powers.

Would there then be no limits to the Court's interpretative jurisdiction in respect of mixed agreements? The shared competence at issue in the case of the WTO Agreements is not one which involves areas reserved to the *exclusive* competence of Member States.[110] Community competence in areas covered by the GATS and TRIPS may be only potential (in the sense that it has as yet been effectively exercised only over limited aspects of the fields covered by these agreements), but the Court is clear that it could develop further. In fact the Court suggests, in *Opinion 1/94*, that a Community-wide initiative would be a solution to distortions in the cohesion of the internal market that the Commission claimed would be caused by differential national approaches to third country services and intellectual property rights.[111] If on the other hand a provision in a mixed agreement related to a field within exclusive Member State competence, or a field of activity where the Court's jurisdiction has been expressly excluded by Article 46 [ex L] TEU, it is probable that the Court would have no interpretative jurisdiction.[112] Even here, the provision may need to be interpreted in order for the Court to 'police the borderline', and perhaps to ensure consistency with other provisions of the agreement which form part of Community law.[113]

CONCLUSION

The most striking aspect of the Amsterdam amendment to Article 133 is the way in which the Treaty now leaves the extension of the scope of the common commercial policy open for future decision without specifying on what basis that decision should be made, or indeed whether a newly extended commercial policy should possess all the characteristics (such as exclusivity) of the existing policy. Treaty amendment requires full constitutional procedures within each Member State and these should not be short-circuited even if all the Member State representatives in Council agree (for example by using

---

[109] See n. 89 above.
[110] *Opinion 1/94* (re WTO Agreement) [1994] ECR I-5267, paras 41 and 104.
[111] *Opinion 1/94* (re WTO Agreement) [1994] ECR I-5267, paras 79 and 90.
[112] See Tesauro AG in *Hermes* at para. 18, basing himself on *Demirel* (see n. 90 above).
[113] See case C-170/96 *Commission v Council* (transit visas), [1998] ECR I-2763.

Article 308 [ex 235] EC.[114] Of course the full formal amendment procedure has been used in the case of Article 133 but this technique of delegation of the decision to a future Council of Ministers is becoming a recognized practice, if not quite a trend. It can also be seen in the *passerelle* in Article 42 TEU (formerly Article K.9), and in Article 2 of the 'Protocol integrating the Schengen acquis into the framework of the European Union', under which the Council is to determine the proper legal base for each element of the Schengen *acquis* (whether under Title VI TEU or under Title IV EC). It is also in evidence in the provisions for 'closer cooperation' in Articles 40, 43, and 44 TEU and Article 11 EC; these contain special decision-making procedures but no provision for national constitutional requirements.[115]

All these cases, in different ways, involve decisions as to appropriate legal base, with the implications they carry as to the respective powers of the different institutions (including the Court of Justice) and the balance between Community and Member State powers. We have become accustomed to what appeared to be a clear distinction between the initial determination of available legal bases by the Member States as authors of the Treaties, and the determination of the appropriate legal base for a specific measure, which is a function (ultimately) of the Court acting under Article 220 [ex 164] EC.[116] This distinction is becoming blurred. In the case of Article 133(5), the allocation of legal base will be for the political institutions, with no substantive principles laid down as to when or whether the option should be exercised or reference to the theoretical allocation of competence discussed at such length in *Opinion 1/94*. It is an open question, for example, whether external competence in relation to the supply of services involving the movement of persons should be exclusive before the Community has a fully worked-out common policy towards third country nationals.

The pragmatic solution in Article 133(5) is of course at least in part an agreement to disagree—or rather an agreement to postpone agreement to a future unspecified date—in the sense that it reflects the lack of consensus

---

[114] Dashwood, Commentary in 'The Human Rights Opinion of the ECJ and its Constitutional Implications' CELS Occasional Paper No. 1 (University of Cambridge, 1996) at 24. See also Dashwood, 'States in the European Union' (1998) 23 ELRev. 201 at 211. *Opinion 2/94* (ECHR) 28 March 1996, [1996] ECR I-1759; [1996] 2 CMLR 265 at para. 30.

[115] As participation in 'closer cooperation' will be voluntary on the part of each Member State, however, it will always be possible for a Member State to insist on following specific internal procedures before participating. In comparison, the possible extension of citizenship rights under Art. 22 [ex 8e] EC explicitly requires adoption in accordance with national constitutional requirements (as well as involving the Council, Commission, and European Parliament).

[116] The Court will only become seized of a legal base issue where there is an unresolved dispute between the institutions and/or the Member States, but it has always insisted on the legal character of the question: see above at n. 32.

between the Member States at the time of Amsterdam as to the proper (potential) scope of the Community's common commercial policy and its effect on internal decision-making powers. It is also (as are the other examples mentioned) an attempt to avoid the decisional paralysis caused by such disagreements, an aspect of especial importance in the context of external commercial policy.

Both the caution of the Court of Justice in *Opinion 1/94*, its reticence over the issue of direct effect in *Hermes*, and its use of the principle of indirect effect in the same case indicate a sensitivity to these factors. The assertion of interpretative jurisdiction in *Hermes* was very carefully done, but carries with it a powerful presumption in favour of uniformity of interpretation of international agreements, mixed or not, within the Community legal order (including the courts of the Member States) even where there has been as yet little or no internal harmonization. The Court has an interest in maintaining the unity of the international representation of the Community, as well as a unity in the delimitation of its international obligations; however unity is not the same thing as exclusivity. The Member States have practical as well as legal reasons for developing and keeping to common positions in the external commercial field. Where real differences remain as to the allocation of competence, unity may be best served by not insisting on exclusivity.

3

Adjudicative Legitimacy and Treaty Interpretation in International Trade Law: The Early Years of WTO Jurisprudence

ROBERT HOWSE*

INTRODUCTION

The creation of the World Trade Organization (WTO) in 1995 has often been identified with the establishment of a system for adjudicative resolution of disputes which, in its effectiveness and sophistication surpasses what has been achieved by other international tribunals, such as the International Court of Justice.[1] Under the WTO, Members, i.e. states parties to the various treaties under the WTO umbrella (known as 'covered agreements') including the successor treaty to the original 1947 GATT, have access to dispute settlement as of right; unlike with the original GATT, where a consensus of the Member States was required in order for dispute settlement rulings to become binding, under the WTO a ruling will be adopted as binding unless all the Members, including the winning party, vote *against* its adoption (negative consensus); determinations of when and how the losing party must act to implement a ruling are subject to arbitration; and should the losing party not

* Various students and other participants at the European Academy, July 1998, who heard the course on which this chapter was based have been very helpful to me in their reactions to my initial efforts to state the thesis in this chapter, especially Liz Tuerk, Christoph Feddersen, Arne Varndaele, and Sung-joon Cho, as well as students at the University of Michigan Law School, where I taught as a visiting professor in the Fall of 1998. In addition to my enormous debt to Petros Mavroidis—from whom I have learned more than I can express about these matters—I am grateful for challenging conversations with Bill Davey, Joseph Weiler, Arthur Appleton, Kerry Rittich, Julie Soloway, David Kennedy, Craig Scott, and Karen Knop. I alone am of course responsible for the argument, and all its shortcomings.

[1] See for example, E.-U. Petersmann, 'How to Reform the United Nations: lessons from the International Economic Law Revolution', 2 *UCLA J.Intl.L. and Foreign Affairs* 185 (1997–8); E.-U. Petersmann, 'How to Reform the United Nations: Constitutionalism, International Law and International Organizations', *Leiden J.Intl.L.* 421 (1997).

implement a ruling in accord with the findings of the arbitrator, retaliation (a withdrawal of trade concessions to the losing party by the winning party) is automatically authorized. Moreover, legal determinations of the tribunal of first instance (known as a panel) may be appealed to the Appellate Body, a standing tribunal of seven jurists, three of whom sit on each case.[2]

There are a number of perspectives from which one could examine the early results of the operation of this system. One obvious perspective would be that of practical success, the ability to effectively settle disputes in a timely and cost-efficient fashion. Another perspective would be that of trade liberalization as a value: to what extent has the jurisprudence generated by the new system produced rulings that unleash the liberalizing and integrating potential of WTO legal strictures? This chapter will adopt yet another perspective in its assessment of the first four years of dispute settlement—that of legitimacy. What are the characteristics of international adjudication that tend to allow for the rulings of these tribunals to be considered as legitimate by those whose values or interests are implicated or affected? To what extent has the jurisprudence of the WTO to date displayed or exemplified these characteristics?

The context of this focus on legitimacy is what I perceive as a significant, and perhaps growing, cleavage between the enthusiasts of globalization through law—for whom the WTO system represents a major advance towards legally rigorous economic integration—and its critics, who greet the increasing constraint on the scope for domestic democratic regulation by the international economic order with suspicion and anger.[3] Two related but distinct concerns are, first, that the legal and institutional arrangements of globalization have themselves privileged certain interests and values over others—in particular the interests and values of liberal trade over distributive justice, environmental concerns, the protection of human health and safety—and, secondly, that (at the same time) these legal and institutional arrangements have made it much more difficult for these kinds of values and interests to be effectively protected through democratic governance, which can only occur in a meaningful way at the national level and below. These concerns played a large role in the mobilization of international civil society against the proposed Multilateral Agreement on Investment, negotiated within the OECD.[4]

---

[2] These procedures are codified in the WTO *Understanding on Rules and Procedures Governing the Settlement of Disputes* [hereinafter, in the text, DSU or Dispute Settlement Understanding]. This, along with all the other 'covered agreements' under the WTO umbrella, as well as related legal instruments, such as various ministerial decisions and declarations associated with the various treaties, may be found in World Trade Organization, *The Results of the Uruguay Round of Multilateral Trade Negotiations: The Legal Texts* (Geneva: WTO, 1995).

[3] These responses are discussed in a respectfully critical spirit in D. Rodrik, *Has Globalization Gone Too Far?* (Washington DC: Institute for International Economics, 1997).

[4] See the main 'manifesto' of these groups, T. Clark and M. Barlow, *MAI: The Multilateral Agreement on Investment and the Threat to Canadian Sovereignty* (Toronto: Stoddart, 1997).

From a formal or positivistic perspective on legitimacy, of course, the law of the WTO poses no problem inasmuch as that law has been ratified according to the internal constitutional arrangements of the Member countries—to the extent that these are democratic, the WTO law itself can be understood as the result of democratic choice *within* national polities. Obviously, questions might arise as to the extent to which such choices were made based upon informed democratic debate and deliberation about their implications; but advocates of the WTO system usually present such questions as really matters that are solely relevant to internal legal and constitutional arrangements of Members, and therefore not a problem for the system itself. Yet, even with respect to outcomes within democratic polities, formal legitimacy of this kind rarely provides closure on the issue of whether those affected by a decision can fully accept it as a legitimate outcome—as Joseph Weiler argues, in the context of the European Union, 'social legitimacy' is distinct from, and certainly not exhausted by, formal legitimacy.[5]

With respect to dispute settlement under the GATT, the trade liberalization elites were not unaware of the limits of formal legitimacy, if only because, prior to the new WTO rules, the effectiveness of the system explicitly depended on the willingness of the states parties to adopt rulings as binding and to implement them, which could obviously be influenced by 'social legitimacy'. The main approach at the GATT to the gap between formal and social legitimacy relied heavily on the potential of validating dispute settlement outcomes as the product of technical, institutional expertise about the trading system. This in turn would depend on a broad consensus among 'experts' as to what this competence consisted in, ultimately underpinned by a shared understanding about the goal or telos of the system—enhancement of economic welfare through trade liberalization. This approach is well articulated by Robert Hudec, describing in particular an early era of GATT dispute settlement: 'Legal rulings were drafted with an elusive diplomatic vagueness. They often expressed an intuitive sort of law based on shared experiences and unspoken assumptions. Because of policy cohesion within this community, the rate of compliance with these rather vague rulings was rather high.'[6]

This kind of general strategy for legitimating international adjudication is well-described by Richard Falk: 'the authoritativeness of an interpretation

---

[5] J. H. H. Weiler, 'The Transformation of Europe', (1991) 100 *Yale L.J.* 2403 at 2466–77. As Weiler pointedly notes: 'Most popular revolutions since the French revolution occured in polities whose governments retained formal legtimacy but lost social legitimacy.' (at 2469). One important exception to the indifference among trade law experts to the democratic deficit in trade law formation is Bronckers, 'Better Rules for a New Millenium: A Warning against Undemocratic Developments in the WTO', *Journal of International Economic Law* (forthcoming).

[6] R. Hudec, *Enforcing International Trade Law: The Evolution of the Modern GATT System* (Salem, New Hampshire: Butterworths, 1993), 12.

derives, in part, from the cohesiveness of the elite creating an aura of objectivity for its interpretative claims and, thereby, soliciting voluntary acquiescence from the general public.'[7] Many features of GATT dispute settlement practice can be explained by the following of this strategy.[8] Dispute settlement panel members under GATT were mostly junior to middle-level trade diplomats, or retired trade diplomats, expected to take advice from the technocrats/experts in the GATT Secretariat in crafting their legal rulings; in fact the Secretariat, not the panels, typically drafted the rulings. The Secretariat decided on who was proposed to serve on panels, another means of insuring that outcomes reflected the technocratic consensus. Academics and independent jurists were unwilling to engage in very much open and critical scrutiny of panel rulings. Proceedings were secret, and the difficulty of obtaining relevant documents—and indeed the panel decisions themselves, until derestricted and published much later—made such informed outsiders who existed dependent on good relations with members of the Secretariat, who held control over crucial information. Normatively, the GATT elite embraced economic liberalism—the notion that everyone could be better off, or more prosperous as a consequence of freer trade—as the substantive telos of the system. As David Kennedy has shrewdly observed, this was not from actual *laissez-faire* dogmatism, but from a pragmatic sense that, *in fact*, this goal could command the consensus needed to hold together the coherence of the system, strengthening its legitimacy against the dark, nationalist, protectionist forces of domestic politics that always threaten to bring it down.[9]

This entire strategy of legitimation became problematic once GATT dispute settlement panels were faced with the adjudication of issues where the need to address competing values was explicit and unavoidable. This occurred with the notorious *Tuna/Dolphin* rulings in the early 1990s. At issue were US trade sanctions to enforce a regime to protect dolphins for biodiversity reasons (a regime that applied domestically within the United States as well, and could thus be argued to be non-discriminatory at least in its basic structure). Article XX of the GATT explicitly allowed otherwise GATT-inconsistent measures where 'necessary' to protect animal life or health (XX(b)), or 'in relation to' the conservation of exhaustible natural resources. These provisions on their face called for adjudication of potentially competing trade liberaliza-

---

[7] R. Falk, 'On Treaty Interpretation and the New Haven Approach: Achievements and Prospects', 8 *Va. J.Int.L.* 323, 326.

[8] The following characterization is derived from the more extensive discussion in M. J. Trebilcock and R. Howse, *The Regulation of International Trade*, (2nd edn., forthcoming, London and New York: Routledge, 1999), ch. 3: 'Dispute Settlement'.

[9] D. Kennedy, 'The International Style in Postwar Law and Policy: John Jackson and the Field of International Economic Law', (1995) 10 *Am. U. J.Int.L. & Policy* 671, especially at 677–9. While he is writing of John Jackson specifically, he seems to be invoking Jackson as an exemplar of a certain 'style' in international economic law and policy.

tion and environmental values. However, faced with such a challenge, the panels resorted to the traditional strategy, manipulating the text of the GATT so as to produce a result that simply excluded the possibility of justification of such measures, thereby largely disenabling entire provisions of the GATT treaty.[10] Once the text of the GATT itself presented the challenge of adjudication of competing values, the very strategy by which the system had ensured legitimacy in the past came back to haunt it. Secrecy, the centralized management of interpretation by bureaucrats, the exclusion of controversial material that could not easily be appreciated from the perspective of trade liberalization as the single goal or value driving the system, the rejection of participation by interested stakeholders (represented for instance by environmental NGOs) all now served to rob the outcome of social legitimacy.[11] Ultimately, the system, as Nichols notes, was saved from a full-blown legitimacy crisis by what its guardians had usually regarded as a weakness, the possibility of the losing party blocking adoption of dispute rulings.[12]

Under the WTO, as already noted, this safety valve is no longer available. At the same time, many more treaty provisons under the new WTO system involve, in an obvious and explicit way, the adjudication of competing values. Whether in determining if required risk assessment procedures for health and safety regulations have been followed in interpreting the WTO agreements on Technical Barriers to Trade and on Sanitary and Phytosanitary Measures, or deciding if a Member has respected the criteria for compulsory licensing of patents in the Agreement on Trade-Related Intellectual Property, including 'adequate remuneration' to the patent holder, the WTO dispute settlement panels cannot avoid making complex trade-offs between public values. Further, while some features of the WTO dispute settlement system preserve elements of the GATT 'elite cohesion' strategy, such as secrecy of deliberations and pleadings, others actually serve to undermine that strategy, in particular the existence of an Appellate Body. With an adjudicative institution separate, to some extent, from the technocratic culture of the Secretariat, and empowered to openly review and scrutinize panel decisions, the myth—maintained even by many academic commentators in the past—that those

---

[10] *United States—Restrictions on Imports of Tuna*, (1991) 30 I.L.M. 1594; *United States—Restrictions on Imports of Tuna*, (1994) 33 I.L.M. 936. For a systematic critique of the legal argumentation employed in the ruling, see R. Howse and M. J. Trebilcock, *The Regulation of International Trade* (London and New York: Routledge, 1996), ch. 15: 'Trade and the Environment', and 2nd edn., forthcoming, 1999.

[11] For an insightful discussion of some of the deeper implications of the controversy surrounding the *Tuna/Dolphin* rulings, see B. Kingsbury, 'The Tuna-Dolphin Controversy, the World Trade Organization, and the Liberal Project to Reconceptualize International Law', *Yearbook of International Environmental Law 1995* (Oxford: Oxford University Press, 1995).

[12] P. Nichols, 'Comments on Ch. 5' in J. S. Bhandari and A. O. Sykes (eds.), *Economic Dimensions in International Law: Comparative and Empirical Perspectives* (Cambridge: Cambridge University Press, 1997).

decisions represent technical expertise underpinned by a consensus about competence rather than contestable legal interpretations, is no longer sustainable.

These considerations suggest that, even from an internal perspective of effective 'regime management', there is an urgency to seek a new basis for the 'social legitimacy' of dispute settlement outcomes, a basis sensitive to the concern of critics or sceptics concerning the project of global economic liberalism that the whole undertaking of international trade law is tilted towards the privileging of free trade against other competing, relevant values of equal or greater legitimacy in themselves.

Perhaps the most ambitious attempt at mapping such an alternative is to be found in the 'stakeholder model' of WTO dispute settlement propounded by Richard Shell.[13] This model entails opening up the WTO dispute settlement process to all stakeholders, through extension of standing rules to include private parties, as well as incorporation of various social and environmental norms *within* WTO law, such that stakeholders could actually use the WTO system to enforce such norms against Member States. As Shell himself acknowledges, this proposal would entail very significant reforms in the law of the WTO, including the dispute settlement procedures themselves.[14] It has been the object of important criticisms, even from those who are sympathetic to the overall project of making the WTO system responsive to diverse stakeholders.[15]

A more moderate or institutionally conservative perspective on legitimacy—nevertheless incorporating the core normative idea of Shell's stakeholder model that 'trade policy must come to reflect trade-offs that citizens make among their needs as members of national communities and as consumers, workers, and investors participating in the emerging global business civilization'[16]—might begin with the observation that, in domestic public law litigation, contemporary regulatory theory and practice widely understands courts as engaged in the adjudication of competing values, and may yield use-

---

[13] R. Shell, 'Trade Legalism and International Relations Theory: An Analysis of the World Trade Organization', (1995) 44 *Duke L.J.* 829, reprinted in R. Howse (ed.), *The World Trading System: Critical Perspectives on the World Economy, vol. II Dispute Settlement* (London and New York: Routledge, 1998), 333–416.

[14] Ibid., 370 ff.

[15] See for example the extended critique of Phillip Nichols, 'Participation of Non-Governmental Parties in the World Trade Organization: Extension of Standing in World Trade Organization Disputes to Non-Government Parties', (1996) 17 *U. Pa. J.Int.Econ.L.* 295. One not insignificant criticism of Shell's reliance upon standing is that: 'Only those interest groups whose resources were not exhausted at the domestic level could take advantage of standing before the World Trade Organization. In other words, rather than resulting in a democratization of trade policymaking, expansion of standing might instead be a boon to a select group of well-monied interest groups.' (318–19.)

[16] R. Shell, n. 13 above, at 381.

ful lessons as to how this may be done legitimately, especially where the tribunal understands itself as accountable to a far wider range of stakeholders than would normally exercise, or be able to exercise, a right to standing as a party to the proceedings.[17] It has often been assumed by international lawyers that the manner in which diversity of values and perspectives is managed in domestic litigation is not possible at the international level. Thus, Ian Johnstone suggests: 'Because an international tribunal cannot fully reflect the value diversities of all States subject to it, it can never receive the degree of acceptance and confidence bestowed on domestic courts.'[18] However, this may assume wrongly that *within* domestic polities there is a relatively high degree of homogeneity of values, which is certainly not the case for pluralistic liberal democracies. Thus, in the *domestic* context, Cass Sunstein defines the central question of law in terms of the reality that judges 'must operate in the face of a particular kind of social heterogeneity: sharp and often intractable disagreements on matters of basic principle'.[19] The possibility that the legitimacy of adjudication at the international or supranational level is not sharply distinguishable, or completely different, from legitimacy at the national level animates the recent work of Helfer and Slaughter on surpanational adjudication, which has been strongly influenced by the study of the European Court of Justice and the European Court of Human Rights.[20]

In light of this possibility, the present chapter seeks to examine the extent to which the jurisprudence of the Appellate Body of the WTO to date exemplifies the ingredients of legitimacy in adjudication of conflicting values that are evident from the theory and practice of domestic public law litigation, as well as present in Helfer and Slaughter's own analysis of the legitimacy of adjudication, which moves back and forth, as I shall do, between the international, supranational, and domestic levels. Such an assessment should shed light on whether in fact the kind of radical reforms suggested by Shell, for example, are actually a *sine qua non* for legitimacy. It may have implications, as well, for more fundamental critiques that suggest that the whole project of globalization is structurally and essentially wedded to the supremacy of economic liberalism over other, more or less competing, public values.

I have gleaned from the literature on the legitimacy of adjudication what I believe are three necessary elements in legitimacy in the adjudication of

---

[17] See, for instance, A. Chayes, 'The Role of the Judge in Public Law Litigation', (1976) 89 *Harv.L.Rev.* 1281.

[18] I. Johnstone, 'Treaty Interpretation: The Authority of Interpretive Communities', (1991) 12 *Mich. J.Int.L.* 371. But see, for a contrary view, C. Scott, 'Bodies of Knowledge: A Diversity Promotion Role for the UN High Commissioner for Human Rights' in P. Alston and J. Crawford (eds.), *The Future of UN Human Rights Monitoring* (Cambridge: Cambridge University Press, 1998).

[19] C. Sunstein, *Legal Reasoning and Political Conflict* (New York: Oxford University Press, 1996), 3.

[20] 'Toward a Theory of Effective Supranational Adjudication', (1997) 107 *Yale L.J.* 273.

competing values: fair procedures; coherence and integrity in legal interpretation; and institutional sensitivity. These three elements in some respects can be understood as a grouping of the detailed 'checklist' of Helfer and Slaughter. But, as they themselves say of their own checklist, this kind of categorization is a 'first step' towards understanding the challenge of supranational adjudication rigorously.[21] With respect to the three elements I have identified, they should not be understood as categories for which I claim some kind of abstract or formal validity—their usefulness, at least to me, is simply in understanding and unpacking the phenomena at issue.

FAIR PROCEDURES

Fair procedures can play an important role in the legitimation of adjudicative decisions, especially where conflicting public values are at issue. In the first place, it should be recognized that democratic theory, at least in its main contemporary liberal formulations, is to a significant extent proceduralist.[22] Democratic legitimacy for decisions, including those of the more directly representative organs, derives not simply, or even largely, from an authorization by a crude majoritarian, or mass will (the elected dictatorship of, for example, Carl Schmitt) but from the fact that complex procedures and institutional disciplines have been followed.[23] Generally, the procedures include: requirements that deliberation occur before decision; opportunities for opposing sides or parties to be heard and to attempt to persuade one another; and some means of participation for those affected by the decision (at a minimum, publicity, so that they can be aware of how they are affected, and understand the manner in which the decision itself was arrived at). And legislators and elected executives, as well as adjudicators, are constrained, in most liberal democracies, by rules on conflict of interest, and at a minimum, prohibitions on bribery or the taking of public decisions for purely personal advantage.

[21] 'Toward a Theory of Effective Supranational Adjudication', (1997) 107 *Yale L.J.* 273, at 298.

[22] The most sophisticated exploration of the relationship of legal procedure to democratic legitimacy in the contemporary literature is J. Habermas, *Between Facts and Norms: Contributions to a Discourse Theory of Law and Democracy*, trans. W. Rehg (Cambridge, MA: MIT Press, 1996). A different account of liberal democratic justice, more liberal (in the traditional sense) and less democratic than that of Habermas, J. Rawls, *A Theory of Justice* (Cambridge, MA: Harvard Belknap, 1970), also emphasizes the relationship of fair procedures to legitimacy. This illustrates that the manner in which fair procedures can contribute to legitimacy is itself subject to philosophical dispute. My own discussion will emphasize elements in fair procedure that tend to be common, at least in a broad sense, to these different, divergent accounts.

[23] T. Franck, 'The Emerging Right to Democratic Governance', (1992) 86 *A.J.I.L.* 46, at 50.

These, rather obvious, reflections suggest that there may actually be considerable common ground between the manner in which fair procedures function to legitimate *adjudicative* decisions where conflicting values are at issue and the manner in which they contribute to the legitimacy of legislative and executive decisions in such cases. Thus, while the former are clearly taken, especially at the international level, at a far greater remove from direct assertion of majoritarian will, the extent of this 'democratic deficit', and its impact on the legitimacy of these decisions, may well depend upon how far the procedures for adjudication stray from the norms of procedural fairness that are also, in somewhat different form, essential ingredients in the validation of the latter, 'democratic' decisions.[24] Indeed one might even suggest that the farther removed the decision-maker is from responsibility to a particular electorate, the greater the extent to which legitimacy depends on procedural fairness itself. Thus, the following observation of Cappelletti might apply *a fortiori* to international adjudicative bodies: 'The legitimacy or credential of the judiciary, unlike that of the other strictly political organs, does not derive from the fact that it represents an electorate, to which it is directly or indirectly responsible. Rather, democratic legitimacy accrues to the judiciary through the fundamental right to respect for the guarantees of "natural justice".'[25]

The legitimating impact of fair procedures can, rather evidently, be seen in the willingness of those affected by a decision adversely, or who would have argued for a different kind of balance between conflicting values, to accept the decision as a fair outcome.[26] Such acceptance does not preclude, of course, the tendency to argue that the substance of the dispute was badly adjudicated by the tribunal, or that the law itself needs to be changed. But, in the international trade context, it does preclude a convincing claim that the deciding institutions themselves deserve to be rejected as having the authority to decide the question—a kind of claim often made in the past, and one that has threatened considerable damage to the world trading system.

Under the GATT, in the wake of the *Tuna/Dolphin* rulings, the 'democratic deficit' claim about dispute settlement was frequently expressed in terms of the illegitimacy of 'three faceless bureaucrats in Geneva' deciding, for

---

[24] In the European Union, one observes that concerns about the 'democratic deficit' are much more frequently, or at least vehemently, directed at the activity of the European Commission and Council, rather than the European Court of Justice or European Court of Human Rights. I believe this 'puzzle' can be explained at least in part by the fact that the former institutions embody or are seen to embody elements of non-transparent bureaucratic diktat and secretive élite bargaining, while the latter follow procedures that embody norms of publicity, transparency, deliberation, justification, and participation, which are closely linked to the legitimacy of 'democratic' outcomes.

[25] M. Cappelletti, *Giudici legislatori?* (Milan, 1984) (translation by the author).

[26] L. Helfer and A.-M. Slaughter, 'Toward a Theory of Effective Supranational Adjudication', n. 20 above, at 284.

instance, the limits to which a democratic government can further goals of global environmental protection. It should be noted that the objection is not simply that this be decided in Geneva (away from national democratic institutions), but that it be decided in a certain manner by certain kinds of persons. The decisions emanated from panels that deliberated in secret, largely unconstrained by procedural norms, and which systematically rejected participation from those affected, other than GATT member states, even when in the non-intrusive form of *amicus curiae* briefs. The results of this process, the panel decisions, were usually not de-restricted or made public until actual adoption by the membership, thereby precluding any broader public deliberation about their merits prior to adoption. At the same time, no mechanism for appeal of these panel rulings existed.

Within the GATT 'insider' community, the lack of procedural constraint on decision-making has often been viewed with a great deal of pride, and frequently contrasted with the cumbersome legalism of domestic adjudicative processes.[27] Read narrowly, the WTO Dispute Settlement Understanding (DSU) represents only a modest departure from this anti-proceduralist bias.[28] Proceedings of panels remain secret (Art. 14), including the pleadings of the parties to the dispute and third parties (Art. 18.2), and there is no mechanism for participation of affected non-governmental actors in the proceedings, for instance formal intervenor status. Selection of panelists themselves remains controlled by the bureaucracy, now the WTO Secretariat.

On the other hand, the DSU places on panels certain general duties which could be taken to imply elements of fair procedure. The most important of these is the duty 'to make an objective assessment of the matter before [the panel], including an objective assessment of the facts of the case' (Art. 11). Also, the DSU continues the trend under GATT to codification of certain customary working procedures, at least for efficacy or 'housekeeping' purposes. For example, the practice of defining the panel's mandate in its terms of reference is entrenched in Article 7.2 of the DSU. Perhaps most importantly, the DSU provides for appeal of panel decisions to the new Appellate Body, on grounds of error of law (Art. 17.6). While the appellate decision is to take place rapidly following on the release of the panel ruling (90 days), this nevertheless allows a space for deliberation and critique with respect to the panel ruling, both by affected stakeholders, as well as by governments, experts and academics. This space is guaranteed by the recent practice of releasing decisions of panels publicly on the Internet immediately following the release of the final panel report to the parties themselves; further, while deliberations and pleadings of panels remain secret, the arguments of parties and third par-

---

[27] Hudec, n. 6 above.
[28] For a detailed guide to the Dispute Settlement Understanding, see the excellent new work of D. Palmeter and P. Mavroidis, *Dispute Settlement in the World Trade Organization: Practice and Procedure* (The Hague: Kluwer, 1999).

ties are summarized *in extenso* in the introductory parts of panel reports, and the practice has been followed of reproducing in the published panel report expert testimony or advice, where it has formed part of the panel's evidentiary record. The practice of summarizing the pleadings did exist under the old GATT system, but of course coming too late to play a role in the public scrutiny of the panel's work (since this material was normally publicly available only after the adoption by the membership of the panel report as a binding settlement of the dispute), it was of little value in terms of procedural fairness. Obviously, the existence of appellate review changes this considerably.

The early decisions of the Appellate Body are in several respects encouraging from the perspective of the evolution of a conception of procedural fairness which can contribute to the legitimacy of WTO adjudication of conflicting values. First of all, the Appellate Body has rapidly seized on the codification of GATT working procedures in the DSU and interpreted these provisions in terms of an ideal of 'due process', rather than technical efficiency or efficacy in the settlement of disputes. Thus, in *Desiccated Coconut*, the AB held that Article 7.2 of the DSU, which on its face does little more than set out the practice of establishing the terms of reference of the panel and instruct the panel to address legal provisions cited by parties in the terms of reference, imposes a requirement that all claims that a party is intending to make in the dispute be contained in the Terms of Reference, and that claims the complainant is making be in the first instance contained in its request for a panel. Here, the AB referred to 'an important due process objective', which is to 'give the parties and third parties sufficient information concerning the claims at issue in the dispute in order to allow them an opportunity to respond to the complainant's case'.[29] In *Indian Patents*, on similar due process grounds, the AB held that a party must specify the exact legal provision in a WTO agreement that it is relying on, in order for a claim related to that provision to be adjudicated, even if the claim itself has appeared in the Terms of Reference.[30]

Of course, implicit in these various rulings by the AB is the notion that conformity of panel with WTO procedural rules is *subject* to appellate review. A narrow reading of the DSU provisions on appellate review could suggest that only a panel's substantive legal findings with reference to the claims made by the parties are reviewable. Article 17.6 of the DSU states that 'an appeal shall be limited to issues of law covered in the panel report and legal interpretations developed by the panel'. 'Issues of law' and 'legal interpretations' might have been read to include only the 'issues' and 'interpretations' concerning whether a WTO *Member or Members* has violated a WTO

---

[29] *Brazil—Measures Affecting Desiccated Cocunut*, Report of the Appellate Body, WT/DS22/AB/R, 21 February 1997.

[30] *India—Patent Protection for Pharmaceutical and Agricultural Chemical Products*, Report of the Appellate Body, WT/DS50/AB/R, 19 December 1997, para. 92.

Agreement, since it is these issues and interpretations that relate directly to the panel's jurisdiction as embodied in its Terms of Reference. In embracing a broader interpretation, the AB has clearly underscored the view of the DSU as embodying *justiciable due process rights*.

Perhaps the most dramatic example of this has been the manner in which the AB has breathed life into the duty of the panel 'to make an objective assessment of the matter', and in particular an 'objective assessment of the facts'. As noted above, the scope of appellate review is limited to matters of law, but through understanding the duty of the panel to make an 'objective assessment' as a *legal* duty, the AB has interpreted the DSU as establishing procedural disciplines on how the panel deals with the evidence before it. Thus, in the *Hormones* case, the AB stated: 'The duty to make an objective assessment of the facts is, among other things, an obligation to consider the evidence presented to a panel and make factual findings on the basis of that evidence. The deliberate disregard of, or failure to consider, the evidence submitted to a panel is incompatible with an objective assessment of the facts'.[31] While the threshold for a finding of breach of this duty was set relatively high by the AB, namely evidence of bad faith or egregious error, the AB also held in *Hormones* that where a panel decides to disregard evidence as irrelevant, this finding of non-relevancy is itself a finding of law, subject to appellate review (para. 143). Finally, in the *Periodicals* case, the AB found that a lack of proper legal reasoning could 'be based on' inadequate factual analysis, especially where the legal test being applied by a panel is highly contextual, requiring a case-by-case appreciation of specifics (in this instance, the determination of whether products are 'like' for purposes of examining whether tax or regulatory treatment treats 'like' foreign products as well as domestic products). Thus, in *Periodicals*, the AB invalidated a legal finding of the panel because, first of all, it had not made its finding based upon the evidence available to it on the record, and secondly, had instead, as it were, invented evidence, referring to a hypothetical comparison of two products not based upon the facts on the record.[32] In sum, even where its behaviour is not so egregious as to constitute a violation of the duty to make an 'objective assessment' under DSU Article 11, a panel's mishandling or disregard of the evidence on the record may well affect the sustainability of its legal conclusions upon appeal.

The significance of these developments for the legitimacy of dispute settlement outcomes where conflicting values are at stake must be appreciated in light of the pattern of behaviour of pre-WTO/GATT panels in cases overtly or obviously implicating competing values, such as *Tuna/Dolphin*. In such cases the legitimacy of the panels was further undermined by their explicit

---

[31] *EC Measures Concerning Meat and Meat Products (Hormones)*, Report of the Appellate Body, WT/DS26/AB/R, WT/DS48/AB/R, 16 January 1998, para. 133.

[32] *Canada—Certain Measures Concerning Periodicals*, Report of the Appellate Body, WT/DS31/AB/R, 30 June 1997, 22–3.

choice simply to disregard evidence that related to the impact of the measures in dispute on non-trade values and interests (in fact protected under the text of Article XX of the GATT through a series of exceptions to trade disciplines), thereby arbitrarily giving primacy to free trade over all the other values at issue in the dispute.[33] More generally, as Helfer and Slaughter suggest: 'A guaranteed capacity to generate facts that have been independently evaluated, either through a third-party fact-finding process or through the public contestation inherent in the adversary system, helps counter the perception of self-serving or "political" judgments.'[34]

A rather different, and more indirect, way in which the AB has strengthened the role of fair procedures in the legitimacy of WTO dispute settlement outcomes is through its decision that private legal counsel may attend at and plead in WTO proceedings at the appellate level,[35] a right recently extended by a panel to include representation by such lawyers at the panel level.[36] Private attorneys, often trained in the context of domestic litigation processes, are more likely to discern and care about due process than governmental lawyer/diplomats, much of whose 'legal' experience may consist in treaty negotiations or informal resolution of disputes through arbitration and conciliation. Thus, the complainants, in opposing the notion that private counsel may plead before the WTO dispute settlement organs, argued that this would amount to a 'fundamental change in the premises' underlying the WTO dispute settlement system, presumably the premises that dispute settlement is fundamentally about a practical way for governments to manage their trade disagreements, as opposed to an adversarial litigation process with the corresponding procedural norms. Moreover, while the Member seeking to be represented by private counsel (and others supporting its claim) argued the case for private lawyers in significant measure in the language of traditional diplomatic law—the sovereign prerogative to choose the delegates representing one's country in any international conference or meeting—the Appellate Body, in the presence of textual silence about this matter in the DSU itself, chose to emphasize the right as a due process right in litigation, not simply a diplomatic prerogative or privilege.

Of great long-term significance, however, is another finding of the Appellate Body related to dispute settlement procedure, contained in the

---

[33] See P. Nichols, 'Corruption in the World Trade Organization: Discerning the Limits of the World Trade Organization's Authority', (1996) 28 *N.Y.U. J.Intl.L. & Pol.* 711.

[34] L. Helfer and A.-M. Slaughter, 'Toward a Theory of Supranational Adjudication', n. 20 above, at 303.

[35] *European Communities—Regime for the Importation, Sale and Distribution of Bananas,* Report of the Appellate Body, AB-1997–3, WT/DS27/AB/R, 9 September 1997.

[36] *Indonesia—Certain Measures Affecting the Automobile Industry,* Report of the Panel, WT/DS54,55,59 64/R, 2 July 1998.

recent *Turtles*[37] ruling. The AB reversed the panel's decision that a panel is prohibited under the DSU from receiving information in the form of *amicus curiae* briefs from non-governmental organizations. Since these organizations may often speak for stakeholders concerned with the non-trade interests and values at issue in a dispute, the legitimacy of a decision that adjudicates competing values may well be enhanced by the fact of their input, and to the extent their voices can be seen to be taken seriously and weighed in the balance. As Trocker suggests, in a study of the impact of *amicus* submissions at the European Court of Human Rights, in principle, the consideration of such submissions offers the possibility of a 'formidable antidote to the risk that the judicial power become an élite, destined to leave behind the too vulgar democratic process, blinded by the prejudice that it can divine the consensus of the community without seeking confirmation in reality . . .', or a hedge against the 'danger of judicial over-reaching or bias, expressed in the admonition of Justice Oliver Wendell Holmes, that "it is a misfortune if a judge reads his conscious or unconscious sympathy with one side or the other prematurely into the law, and forgets that what seems to him to be the first principles are believed by half his fellow men to be wrong".'[38] The relationship between *amicus* participation and democratic legitimacy in the international law context has been directly addressed by Dinah Shelton, who has argued for a more expansive view of such participation at the International Court of Justice: 'The long-term institutional interests of the Court may be best served by ensuring that its opinions are based upon the fullest available information and reflect consideration of the public interest, as well as the desires and concerns of the litigating parties.'[39]

The panel's legal interpretation of the DSU was based on the simple, and simplistic notion that, because the DSU explicitly *authorizes* panels to 'seek' information from practically any source that it deems appropriate, the DSU must, by implication, *prohibit* a panel from accepting non-requested information (other than submissions of the parties or third parties, which are entitled to consideration by virtue of other provisions of the DSU). But of course

[37] *United States—Import Prohibition of Certain Shrimp and Shrimp Products,* Report of the Appellate Body, WT/DS58/AB/R, 12 October 1998 [hereinafter in text, *Turtles*].

[38] N. Trocker, 'L'"Amicus Curiae" nel giudizio davanti alla Corte Europea dei Diritti Dell'Uomo', (1989) 35 *Rivista di Diritto Civile* 119, at 124 (translation by author).

[39] D. Shelton, 'The Participation of Nongovernmental Organizations in International Judicial Proceedings' 88 *A.J.I.L.* 611, at 625. In this sense, the possibility of *amicus* intervention addresses the relationship between stakeholder participation and legitimacy that is crucial to Shell's 'Stakeholder Model' of dispute settlement, but without some of the risks of moving to a system where non-governmental actors have full standing as parties before the WTO dispute settlement organs; excellent *amicus* may well be within the financial reach of NGOs that would likely be bankrupted by the need to participate in proceedings as parties in order to counter the arguments of 'deep pocket' non-governmental actors, such as multinational corporations.

there is nothing inconsistent logically between an *explicit authorization* to seek information and an *implicit permission* to consider non-solicited information that is provided or brought to the panel's attention. Since, as Palmeter and Mavroidis note, 'few formal procedural rules govern the operation of panels',[40] if the DSU were really to limit a panel's powers to those specifically authorized, its ability to function would be largely hobbled. That the right to seek information would be among the few prerogatives explicitly set out in the DSU is understandable; one of the fundamental differences between the two main kinds of domestic legal system (civil and common law) concerning the powers inherent in an adjudicator's fact-findng role is whether these extend to the 'inquisitorial' function of seeking information not brought to the attention of the adjudicator by the litigants, or through the briefs of intervenors. In civil law systems, crudely speaking, such an inquisitorial role is generally assumed as a normal judicial power, whereas in most kinds of litigation it would not be seen as appropriate in the common law world. In the presence of such divergent understandings of the appropriateness of an adjudicator 'seeking' information, an explicit authorization was clearly appropriate, given the choice of Members of the WTO to opt for the inquisitorial model.

In the case of *amicus* briefs, by contrast, there is a wide range of domestic and international practice that suggests, in contemporary circumstances, that the discretion to consider such briefs has become widely (if not entirely universally) assumed as an appropriate judicial right, implicit in the function of the tribunal to make a judgment having heard all the relevant facts and arguments.[41]

In *Turtles*, in holding that panels may consider unsolicited information in the form of *amicus* briefs, the AB found that an appropriate interpretation of the meaning of the right to 'seek' information must logically include the right to consider unsolicited information: when a panel grants leave to an intervenor to file an *amicus* brief, it is 'seeking' the information in that brief (para. 107). In effect, the intervenor is presenting 'unsolicited' or 'unrequested information' only in the attenuated sense that she is the first mover, as it were, in a process by which the panel may, through the explicit act of granting leave, 'seek' the information. This interpretation of the *amicus* brief as 'sought' information, is consistent with general practice both in domestic and

---

[40] D. Palmeter and P. Mavroidis, *Dispute Settlement in the World Trade Organization: Practice and Procedure*, n. 28 above, at 73.

[41] For practice with respect to *amicus* submissions in various domestic and international tribunals see: Y. Laurin, 'L'*amicus curiae*', 3603 *La semaine juridique: doctrine—jurisprudence— textes* (1992), 345 at 345–8; E. Angell, 'The Amicus Curiae: American Development of English Institutions' 16 *Intl. & Comp. L.Q.* 10017 (1967) (claiming that the *amicus* practice was known already to Roman law); N. Trocker, 'L' "Amicus Curiae" nel giudizio davanti alla Corte Europea dei Diritti dell'Uomo', (1989) 35 *Rivista di Diritto Civile* 119; D. Shelton, 'The Participation of Nongovernmental Organizations in International Judicial Proceedings', n. 38 above.

international tribunals, where the granting of leave by the tribunal is a necessary precondition to its consideration of any information that may be offered
by *amici*.[42]

The AB, however, went considerably beyond this (in itself quite sound)
basis for finding that panels can accept *amicus* briefs from non-governmental
organizations, and read the meaning of the right to 'seek' information in
Article 13 of the DSU in light of a panel's *duty* to make an objective assessment of the facts in Article 11. The AB noted:

> The thrust of Articles 12 and 13 taken together, is that the DSU accords to a panel
> established by the DSB, and engaged in a dispute settlement proceeding, ample and
> extensive authority to undertake and to control the process by which it informs itself
> both of the relevant facts of the dispute and of the legal norms and principles applic-
> able to such facts. That authority, and the breadth thereof, is indispensably necessary
> to enable a panel to discharge its duty imposed by Article 11 of the DSU to 'make an
> objective assessment of the matter before it, including an *objective assessment of the
> facts of the case* and the *applicability of and conformity with the relevant covered agree-
> ments*. . .' (para. 106; emphasis in original)

The notion that a panel might not be able to discharge its duty under Article
11 but for the *full* breadth of its authority to obtain information under
Articles 12 and 13, suggests that in some circumstances, the consideration of
amicus briefs may actually be necessary to a panel discharging its Article 11
duty to make an objective assessment. Thus, while the AB has clearly indicated that only submissions of the parties and third parties to panels are to be
considered by the panels as a matter of right (para. 101), the panel's *discretion*
to decide to grant leave for an *amicus* to submit, and to consider or not consider the information provided once leave has been granted, will nevertheless
be subject to the panel's *general* duty to make an objective assessment of the
matter before it. For instance, if an *amicus* submission provides crucial information about environmental effects in a dispute that concerns competing
free-trade and environmental issues, a panel's failure to give leave, or to consider the information, could well be a violation of a duty to make an 'objective assessment', which must take into account the competing values and
interests at stake in the interpretation of the treaty. Similarly, a choice in such
a dispute to give leave to a pro-export lobby group to file, but not an environmental group with equally or more crucial information or arguments,
might well be an abuse of discretion, amounting to a violation of the duty to
make an objective assessment. Further, along the lines of the *Periodicals* ruling, discussed above, once leave has been granted there is little doubt but that
the information contained in an *amicus* submission forms part of the record
of the case—in some circumstances, a panel's legal analysis may be defective

---

[42] Shelton, n. 39 above, at 618: 'As a procedural step, potential amici generally must request
leave of the court to file . . .'

because of its failure to base its factual analysis, at least in part, on the information in question. In sum, it is arguable that the Appellate Body has legal tools available to it to preserve the legitimacy of the dispute settlement system in the adjudication of competing values against the risk that panels will selectively silence or marginalize non-governmental voices that may speak most credibly or competently to some of the competing values at issue in the legal dispute.

COHERENCE AND INTEGRITY IN LEGAL INTERPRETATION

Integrity and coherence in legal interpretation contribute to the legitimacy of a tribunal adjudicating competing values, through providing assurance that the tribunal's decisions are not simply a product of its own personal choice of the values that should prevail in a given dispute. Nichols suggests:

One area in which it will be particularly difficult for the World Trade Organization to reach consensus is the interface between promoting free trade, on the one hand, and other societal values, such as protecting the environment, labor standards or human rights, on the other. As complex as the interface may be, the World Trade Organization must address it if the organization is to become a credible institution. It is almost certain that these questions will come before the Appellate Body; coherent answers by the Appellate Body will do much to legitimize the organization.[43]

There are strong and more modest versions of this claim. The strong claim is that by 'applying' the law in a rational and coherent way the tribunal rises above politics, proves its 'neutrality', and in effect largely dispenses with the need to engage in actual explicit trade-offs between conflicting values.[44] The more modest claim would be that coherence and integrity contribute to the tribunal's legitimacy not by obviating the need to adjudicate conflicting values but by disciplining such adjudication;[45] the offering of reasons for decisions based on the legal materials, and consistent with the reasons given in other cases provides a transparent, public basis for critique and contestability of the manner in which the tribunal has handled the legal materials in the presence of competing values. But for the doctrine produced by the *aspiration* of adjudicators to coherence and integrity, even the critical project of exposing to democratic contestability the policy choices that adjudicators make indirectly or more or less covertly would never get off the ground.[46]

[43] P. M. Nichols, 'GATT Doctrine', 36 *Virginia J.Intl.L.* 379, at 463–4.

[44] With some nuances and qualifications Helfer and Slaughter tend to adopt this stronger version: Helfer and Slaughter, 'Toward a Theory of Effective Supranational Litigation', n. 20 above, at 312–14.

[45] P. M. Nichols, 'GATT Doctrine', n. 43 above, at 383–4.

[46] What the critical theory, for instance, of Duncan Kennedy does not seem to fully appreciate is that by rendering possible the critique and (democratic) contestability of the policy and

Traditionally, the trade policy elite that staffed the GATT Secretariat and the panelists themselves, as well as some academics in the field, tended to view the actual legal text and doctrine of the GATT as a manipulable tool to achieve whatever result a particular case could be understood to support; the negative legitimacy effects of this practice were particularly visible in the *Tuna/Dolphin* panel decisions. In the first decision, the panel invented a territorial limitation on the ability of a state to justify otherwise GATT-inconsistent unilateral environmental trade measures under Article XX of the GATT—such measures could only be justified where necessary to protect the domestic environment of the country taking the measures. After much criticism by environmentalists of the legal *bona fides* of the first ruling, in the second *Tuna/Dolphin* case the panel stated that such a territorial limitation was without a basis in the text or the negotiating history of the GATT, but then invented a new limitation to get the same result: measures could only be justified under Article XX if their environmental impact did not depend on other countries changing their own policies. Then, finally, a panel dealing with a more recent unilateral measure, a US embargo to prevent the import of shrimp fished in a manner that threatens endangered species of sea turtles, invented yet another different limitation on Article XX justification in order to exclude such environmental measures—they *per se* constituted an 'abuse' of GATT rights that fell afoul of the chapeau of Article XX, which requires that, to be justified under any part of that Article, measures should not be applied in a manner that causes unjustified or arbitrary discrimination between countries where the same conditions prevail. The panels, in effect, turned GATT doctrine into a moving target, eluding a sustained critique of any given manipulation.

The Appellate Body, in the first few years of its jurisprudence, has done much to address the problem of lack of coherence and integrity in panel legal interpretation. First of all, it has insisted that panels must take seriously the wording of the treaty text, and especially that they must neither impose limitations on Members' rights that are not based in the text, nor interpret the text in such as way as to render actual wording irrelevant or inutile.[47] The tendency of panels to assume they understood the general purpose of a provision,

---

value choices that judges make through, in the first instance, a critique of doctrine against its own aspiration of rationality and coherence, the critical project may render adjudication *more*, not less, democratically legitimate, through providing insurance against the risk that judges will be able to make, under the guise of rationality, policy choices that are non-transparent and non-(democratically) contestable. Cf. D. Kennedy, *A Critique of Adjudication (fin de siecle)* (Cambridge, MA: Harvard University Press, 1997). Doctrinalists and Crits may be comrades in arms.

[47] *United States—Standards for Reformulated and Conventional Gasoline*, Report of the Appellate Body, adopted 20 May 1996, WT/DS2/AB/R, at 22; *Japan—Taxes on Alcoholic Beverages*, Report of the Appellate Body, WT/DS8, 10–11/AB/R, 4 October 1996, at 12.

and to give sense to it in light of that purpose, without regard to the individual words and phrases, almost always resulted in rulings tilted towards one particular value among the competing values at stake, namely that of liberal trade—since the purpose invariably understood by the panel was the greatest possible discipline on barriers to trade. Thus, in the *Hormones* case, the panel interpreted a requirement that Members not take trade restrictive sanitary and phytosanitary measures unless they are 'based on' international standards to mean that such measures must conform with such standards, assuming that the stricter meaning was intended, given the purported purpose of the treaty to eliminate trade-restrictive effects of regulatory diversity through harmonization. True to the fast and loose approach described above, in light of its assumption about 'purpose', the panel picked out the stricter language of conformity with international standards from a quite different legal provision in the same treaty, and then read that meaning into the less strict requirement that measures be based on international standards, in light of its view of 'purpose'. In reversing this finding, the Appellate Body noted one of the main reasons why attention to the details of the text is important to legitimacy when competing values are being adjudicated: the detail of the text itself may reflect a 'delicate and carefully negotiated balance . . . between these shared, but sometimes competing, interests of promoting international trade and of protecting the life and health of human beings'.[48]

The emphasis of the AB on the exact wording of the WTO treaty texts could at first glance, and especially in light of the debate about 'textualism' in statutory interpretation in domestic law,[49] be understood as a sweeping rejection of teleological reading of treaty language in favour of rigid literalism. However, it is important to read the textualism of the Appellate Body in light of its more fundamental jurisprudential choice to understand the WTO Dispute Settlement Understanding as incorporating the canons of treaty interpretation in Articles 31 and 32 of the *Vienna Convention on the Law of Treaties*. Article 3 of the DSU states that the purpose of the WTO dispute settlement system 'is to clarify the existing provisions of [the covered] agreements in accordance with customary rules of interpretation of public international law' (3.2). According to the Appellate Body, this language mandates the application of Articles 31 and 32 of the *Vienna Convention* to the interpretation of the WTO treaties.[50] Article 31 of the *Vienna Convention* states that provisions of a treaty

---

[48] *EC—Measures Concerning Meat and Meat Products (Hormones)*, Report of the Appellate Body, n. 31 above, para. 177.

[49] See, generally, W. Eskridge, 'The New Textualism', (1990) 37 *UCLA L.Rev.* 621. For a recent illustration of how a textualist theory of interpretation can be permeated by a concern with purpose and principle, see Akhil Reed Amar, "Intratextualism', 112 *Harvard Law Review* (1999) 747.

[50] *Japan—Taxes on Alcoholic Beverages*, Report of the Appellate Body; *United States—Standards for Reformulated and Conventional Gasoline*, Report of the Appellate Body, 17.

be given their ordinary meaning in context and in light of the treaty's object and purpose; thus, in emphasizing the importance of the exact words, the AB is not endorsing narrow literalism and eschewing teleological interpretation; rather it is taking the words as the necessary beginning point for an interpretive exercise that includes teleological dimensions. Most importantly, it is rejecting the tendency of the panels to *assume* a certain purpose prior to careful textual interpretation, thereby taking a shortcut to the establishment of treaty meaning that bypasses the exact text. This prevents the interpeter from having to 'test' their view of purpose against the exact words used in the treaty, a necessary safeguard against the importation or prioritization of a single purpose into a legal text crafted to balance diverse, and possibly competing, values.[51]

In some senses, the very decision to follow these general public international law interpretative norms enhances the legitimacy of the dispute settlement organs in adjudicating competing values—because these norms are common to international law generally, including regimes that give priority to very different values, and are not specific to a regime that has traditionally privileged a single value, that of free trade.[52] This significance is highlighted by another interpretive issue in the *Hormones* case. A traditional GATT-specific canon of interpretation[53] was that where a provision of the treaty allows an 'exception' to a trade-liberalizing obligation, the burden of proof falls on the party invoking the 'exception'—an approach that clearly privileges free trade over other, competing values, assuming that the latter, embodied in the exception, cannot easily dislodge the former, regardless of the nature of

[51] As Cass Sunstein notes in the context of domestic public law adjudication: 'Statutory terms—not legislative history, nor legislative purpose, nor legislative "intent"—have gone through the constitutionally specified procedures for the enactment of law. Largely for this reason, the words of a statute provide the foundation for interpretation, and those words, together with widely shared conventions about how they should be understood, often lead to uniquely right answers, or at least sharply constrain the territory of legitimate disagreement. Resort to the text also promotes goals associated with the rule of law: the statutory words are available to affected citizens, and it is in response to those words that they can most readily order their affairs. An emphasis on the primacy of the text also serves as a salutary warning about the risks of judicial use of statutory purpose and of legislative history, both of which are, as we will see, subject to interpretive abuse.' C. Sunstein, *After the Rights Revolution: Reconceiving the Regulatory State* (Cambridge, MA: Harvard University Press, 1990), 114.

[52] Nichols discusses some of the GATT-specific interpretive canons that evolved before the WTO adoption of customary interpretive rules in public international law: for instance an exception to trade-liberalizing obligations is to be interpreted narrowly and whenever an exception is at issue the party that seeks to invoke it bears the burden of proof that it meets the specific criteria for the exception. Clearly, in both these cases, these canons assume the primacy of trade liberalization as a value in treaty interpretation. 'GATT Doctrine', (1996) 36 *Va. J.Int.L.* 379, at 434–5.

[53] For an early critique of the tendency to seal off GATT law from public international law more generally, see P. Mavroidis, 'Das Gatt als self contained Regime', (1991) 6 *Recht der internationalen Wirtschaft*.

the matter in dispute. In *Hormones*, the panel applied this traditional GATT-specific approach to a provision of the Sanitary and Phytosanitary Agreement, but the Appellate Body reversed its finding on burden of proof, instead emphasizing that 'merely characterizing a treaty provision as an "exception" does not by itself justify a "stricter" or "narrower" interpretation of the provisions than would be warranted by examination of the ordinary meaning of the actual treaty words, viewed in context and in light of the treaty's object and purpose . . .' (para. 104). Because, as Palmeter and Mavroidis note, the *Vienna Convention* rules 'do not give grounds for preferring one portion of the text over another, construing the former broadly and the latter narrowly', they are likely to result in interpretations that do not unduly or unjustifiably privilege one of the competing values at issue over the others.[54]

A further respect in which the adoption of the *Vienna Convention* rules for the interpretation of the WTO treaties is likely to enhance the legitimacy of adjudication of competing values is suggested, in particular, by Article 31(3)(c) of the *Vienna Convention*, which provides that 'any relevant rules of international law applicable in the relations between parties' shall be brought to bear on the interpretation of a treaty. This mandates the consideration of *non*-WTO international legal rules in the interpretation of WTO treaties—rules that may reflect or prioritize other values and interests than those of trade liberalization, thus countering the undue privileging of the latter in WTO interpretation. In the *Turtles* case, the AB referred in a number of important respects, to international environmental law in interpreting the provisions of Article XX of the GATT as it related to the possibility of justifying otherwise GATT-inconsistent trade measures aimed at protection of endangered species (in this case, sea turtles). Faced with the interpretive question of whether living species of animals (in this case, endangered species of sea turtles) could be considered 'exhaustible natural resources' within the meaning of Article XX(g) of the GATT, the AB referred to a range of international environmental agreements, including the 1982 *United Nations Convention on the Law of the Sea, The Convention on Biological Diversity*, and the *Convention on the Conservation of Migratory Species of Wild Animals*. Perhaps more importantly, in assessing the implications of the unilateral nature of the US measures for the consistency of their application with the 'chapeau' of Article XX—which requires that application not result in 'unjust' or 'arbitrary' discrimination or a 'disguised restriction on international trade'—the AB, unlike the *Tuna/Dolphin* panels, did not simply invent its own limitation on unilateralism as a means of protecting the environmental commons; instead, it referred to a baseline in actual international environmental law, that contained in the *Rio Declaration*. Thus, since, among other

---

[54] D. Palmeter and P. Mavroidis, *Dispute Settlement in the World Trade Organization: Practice and Procedure*, n. 28 above, at 84–5.

international legal instruments, Principle 12 of the *Rio Declaration* called for the avoidance of unilateral measures—with a solution based on consensus being preferred whenever possible—the AB could find that, against this baseline, the failure of the United States to negotiate seriously with the complainants towards a consensus-based solution, while having already negotiated successfully with other members, constituted 'unjustified' discrimination (paras. 168–72).

Yet another important aspect of the deployment of international environmental law in this case is the AB's decision to provide interpretation of the treaty (in this case, the term 'exhaustible natural resources') based on *evolving* international law much more than on the purported original understanding of the negotiators of the 1947 GATT, as reflected in the negotiating history (*travaux préparatoires*). This preference for dynamic or evolutionary over originalist interpretation is reflected in the structure of the *Vienna Convention* itself; subsequent agreements and understandings between the parties, as well as any relevant rules of international law (obviously including custom, which is necessarily evolutionary[55]) are primary, *obligatory* sources of treaty interpretation according to Article 31, whereas *travaux*, according to Article 32 are optional, and secondary sources, which may only be resorted to when the application of Article 31 results in a remaining ambiguity, or a 'manifestly absurd or unreasonable' interpretation of the treaty text, or to 'confirm' an interpretation based on other sources.

In justifying evolutionary or dynamic interpretation in *Turtles* the AB did not, however, explicitly refer to the structure of the *Vienna Convention*; instead, citing an Advisory Opinion of the ICJ on Namibia, the AB suggested that some provisions of treaties are 'by definition, evolutionary' (para. 130). The AB thought that 'natural resources' fell into this category, because the preamble to the *WTO Agreement* envisaged future action, 'in accordance with the objective of sustainable development, seeking both to protect and preserve the environment and to enhance the means for doing so . . .' It thus seemed logical that, from the perspective of WTO law, the interpretation of a generic expression like 'natural resources' should track the evolving effort to define the meaning and scope of sustainable development to which the Members com-

---

[55] Thus, a dispute settlement panel under the North American Free Trade Agreement, when faced with the issue of whether a reference to GATT rights and obligations in NAFTA meant only those rights and obligations that existed at the time the NAFTA was negotiated, rejected such a 'frozen' interpretation, insisting that it would be contrary to the evolutionary nature of the GATT system; the panel noted a reference to customary international law as well in NAFTA, suggesting that given that custom is inherently and inevitably evolutionist, a 'frozen rights' approach to the incorporation of international law into NAFTA was simply not viable. *In the matter of Tariffs Applied by Canada to Certain US-Origin Agricultural Products*, Final Report of the Arbitral Panel Established Pursuant to Article 2008 of the North American Free Trade Agreement, 2 December 1996, see especially para. 134.

mitted themselves in the preamble.[56] The text-specific grounds for the choice of an evolutionary or dynamic interpretation of the text in this case arguably obscured the more general rationale for applying dynamic as opposed to 'static' originalist interpretation.

Retrospective, originalist interpretation almost inevitably privileges the supposed intentions and expectations of a fairly narrow 'interpretive community', that of the treaty negotiators, over the broader community affected by interpretive decisions, the community implicated in the notion of democratic or social legitimacy.[57] Traditionally, under GATT, resort to the *travaux* constituted a pervasive and largely uncontroversial interpretive practice.[58] Despite the pronouncements of the Appellate Body about following the *Vienna Convention* approach rigorously, so ingrained is the originalist instinct that John Jackson pronounces scepticism about whether in actual practice recourse to the negotiating history will be any less pervasive or unconstrained in the future.[59]

Extensive reliance on *travaux* is entirely rational in light of the understanding of legitimacy that underpinned traditional GATT practice, an understanding argued earlier in this chapter to be untenable in light of the increasingly explicit and persuasive conflict of values implicated in dispute settlement: on this older understanding, legitimacy emerges through a ruling's consistency with the general consensus among the trade policy élite—negotiators, academic specialists, practising diplomats—concerning what the text

---

[56] A similar argument for dynamic interpretation from the generality of the actual treaty language can be found in M. P. Van Alstyne, 'Dynamic Treaty Interpretation', 146 *U. Pennsylvania L.R.* (1997) 687, discussing the *Convention on the International Sale of Goods*: 'Notions such as "reasonableness", "cooperation" and "good faith" mean little in isolation. They take on substantive meaning only through a consensus in the relevant interpretive community on the appropriate context for their application' (at 776). However, as is suggested in this passage, the underlying issue is the scope and nature of the appropriate 'interpretive community', as discussed below.

[57] The distinction between the 'narrow' interpretive community constituted by the treaty's drafters and the broader interpretive community concerned with subsequent effects and practice is drawn by I. Johnstone, 'Treaty Interpretation: The Authority of Interpretive Communities', 12 *Mich. J.Int.L.*(1991) 371 , n. 18 above, at 385–93. Johnstone, however, remains within the technocratic understanding of interpretive legitimacy challenged in this chapter, so he draws even the broader interpretive community in terms of claims to expert knowledge, rather than to a stake in the values and interests affected by the interpretation of the treaty.

[58] Nichols, 'GATT Doctrine', n. 52 above, at 430.

[59] J. H. Jackson, *The World Trade Organization: Constitution and Jurisprudence* (London: Pinder/RIIA, 1998), 94–5. It should be noted however that Jackson's approach to the role of *travaux* is complicated, for instance, in an article in the early 1990s on trade and environment, he tended to discount the significance of the negotiating history; J. H. Jackson, 'World Trade Rules and Environmental Policies: Congruence or Conflict?', 49 *Washington and Lee L.R.* (1992) 1227.

is really about.[60] It is really the expectations of this group that count, even in terms of broader social legitimacy.[61] If, however, as I have argued, a decision's legitimacy depends upon the manner in which it handles a conflict of values held by diverse stakeholders, then taking into account, in an even-handed way, the actual understandings and expectations of those diverse stakeholders, as they evolve in social practice, will be crucial to legitimacy. Fortunately, these evolving understandings and expectations will often find expression in the kind of subsequent understandings and agreements, and (necessarily evolving) international legal rules, referred to in Article 31 of the *Vienna Convention.* This may include: international environmental law, international labour law,[62] and international human rights law, as it is developing in light of what Saskia Sassen refers to as an 'equity-oriented agenda . . . focused . . . on equity and distributive questions in the context of a globally integrated economic system with immense inequalities in the profit-making capacities of firms and the earning capacities of households'.[63] WTO interpretation which reflects the emerging law of the 'other' agenda of globalization, as exemplified in the already-noted invocation of various international environmental conventions by the AB in *Turtles,* also serves a 'structural' coherence function, assuring that WTO law evolves in a manner that reduces, rather than enhances, conflict and inconsistency with evolving law in other international legal regimes.[64]

In *Turtles,* the AB actually followed the sequence prescribed by the *Vienna Convention,* resorting to the drafting history of the GATT only after it interpreted the chapeau of Article XX employing the means of interpretation prescribed by Article 31 of the *Vienna Convention* (para. 157 and accompanying footnote). The AB thus examined the exact wording of the chapeau in order to come to the conclusion that its effect was to make the individual exceptions listed in paragraphs (a) to (j) of Article XX limited and conditional in nature. It then, and only then, resorted to the *travaux* to 'confirm' its textual interpretation of the chapeau of Article XX. In the earlier *Reformulated Gasoline*

---

[60] See the observations of Hudec, n. 6 above.

[61] Falk, 'On Treaty Interpretation and the New Haven Approach: Achievements and Purposes', n. 7 above, at 326.

[62] See R. Howse, 'The World Trade Organization and the Protection of Worker's Rights', 3, *Journal of Small and Emerging Business* (1999), 131.

[63] S. Sassen, *Losing Control: Sovereignty in an Age of Globalization* (New York: Columbia University Press, 1996), 26.

[64] Advocating dynamic interpretation of statutes in the domestic public law context, William Eskridge suggests that even seemingly originalist contemporary approaches, like that of Antonin Scalia, acknowledge that dynamic or evolutionary interpretation may be required for horizontal coherence, 'reconciling many laws enacted over time, and getting them to "make sense" in combination, necessarily assumes that the implications of a statute may be altered by the implications of a later statute'. W. Eskridge, *Dynamic Statutory Interpretation* (Cambridge, MA: Harvard University Press, 1994), 119, quoting Judge Scalia in *United States v Fausto,* 484 US (1988) 439, at 453.

case, the AB also resorted to the negotiating history to interpret the chapeau of Article XX as addressing itself to the avoidance of 'abuse' of the various exceptions permitted within individual paragraphs of Article XX. However, it did so only after having interpreted the 'express terms' of the chapeau to support this conclusion. Thus, the invocation of the negotiating history here, just as would subsequently be the case in *Turtles*, was for purposes of merely confirming an interpretation according to Article 31 of the *Vienna Convention*— a use of *travaux* explicitly authorized by *Vienna Convention* Article 32.

Two early cases may appear at first glance as examples of loose invocation of *travaux* by the AB. In the *Japanese Alcohol* case, the AB interpreted two textual provisions, including a main operative provision and an *Ad* article providing interpretive gloss on that main operative provision, as both being treaty language with equal legal status.[65] It did so without first examining closely the language and structure of the two provisions in their interrelationship, instead stating at the outset that the *travaux* supported such a reading, in showing that both provisions were negotiated and agreed to at essentially the same meeting. What, however, the AB might have been attempting to do here was not to use the *travaux* as a supplementary means of interpretation, but rather to classify the status of the *Ad* article, or Interpretive Note, as a source of law within the meaning of Article 31 of the *Vienna Convention*, i.e. as a *preliminary* to its application of Article 31. Thus, the issue it was addressing might have been framed as whether the *Ad* article is itself a term of the treaty or rather, within the meaning of Article 31(a) of the *Vienna Convention*, an agreement between the parties relating to the treaty, and thus part of the 'context' rather than the treaty itself.

Yet another use of the *travaux* that seems at first glance to confirm Jackson's theory occurred in the *Bananas* case.[66] In *Bananas*, the AB was interpreting the language of a Waiver that permitted a derogation from the GATT Article I obligation of Most Favoured Nation treatment, so as to allow preferential treatment of imports from developing countries who were members of the *Lome Convention*. The Waiver permitted a derogation only to the extent 'required' by the *Lome Convention*. The issue was whether 'required' included all preferential treatment forseen or aspired to in the language of the *Convention* or only those specific preferences expressed as binding obligations of the EC. Without examining the ordinary meaning of the word 'required', the AB resorted to the negotiating history of the Waiver, noting that the parties had rejected a request by the EC and the developing country members of *Lome* for a waiver to grant preferentiality as 'forseen' by the *Lome Convention*, explicitly replacing the word 'forseen' by 'required', thus emphasizing the

---

[65] *Japan—Taxes on Alcoholic Beverages*, Report of the Appellate Body, n. 47 above, at 24 and footnote.

[66] *European Communities—Regime for the Importation, Sale and Distribution of Bananas*, Report of the Appellate Body, WT/DS27/R, 22 May 1997, para. 168.

stringency implied in that term. Now the AB could have come to this conclusion simply by considering that the ordinary meaning of the expression 'required' implies obligatory force, not mere aspiration or encouragement to behaviour.

It should be remembered, however, that the *treaty* provision that the AB was interpreting here was Article I of the GATT, not the Waiver. In examining the Waiver, it was arguably considering a subsequent agreement between the parties, within the meaning of *Vienna Convention* 31(3)(a). But the *Vienna Convention* also permits consideration of subsequent practice between the parties concerning interpretation of the treaty. Here, then, the negotiating history of the *Waiver* could be viewed from the perspective of interpretation of the operative treaty provision, Article I of the GATT, as part of subsequent practice with regard to interpretation of Article I, showing the disinclination of the parties in subsequent practice to apply Article I in a too liberal or relaxed fashion, even when the goal of assisting developing countries was at issue. In sum, even though it did refer to 'negotiating history' of a subsequent agreement, the AB never really left *Vienna Convention* Article 31 in this instance.

Another way in which the AB has strengthened legitimacy of dispute settlement through coherence and integrity is through strengthening the precedential weight of panel and Appellate Body reports. As Palmeter and Mavroidis suggest: 'Continuity and consistency are valuable attributes in any legal system: application of the same rules to the same factual issues, independently of the parties involved—treating like cases alike—is an important source of legitimacy for any adjudicator.'[67] Traditional GATT practice was that previous panel reports need not be followed, although they could be considered by panels; this was based on the notion that an adopted panel ruling constituted a legally binding settlement only of the particular dispute between the particular parties. The lack of *stare decisis* allowed panels a great deal of freedom in manipulating the law to achieve a given result that they intuited to be the best one from their professional appreciation for the needs of the 'system'. I have already alluded to the 'moving target' that constituted panel jurisprudence on trade and environment, with panels shifting legally ground from one case or another for the result (exclusion of trade measures to protect the global environment from GATT justification) in order to diffuse scrutiny or criticism of how the adjudication of conflicting values was handled in the previous case. A related example, which perhaps illustrates a further dimension of the discipline that *stare decisis* can impose on an adjudicator's inappropriate privileging of one value over another in the adjudication of competing values, is that of the finding, also in the *Tuna/Dolphin* cases, that

---

[67] D. Palmeter and P. Mavroidis, *Dispute Settlement in the World Trade Organization: Practice and Procedure*, n. 28 above, at 41.

products cannot be considered 'unlike' within the meaning of Article III of the GATT—and thus treated differently without violating the non-discrimination obligation of Article III—on the basis of their production methods, but only on the basis of some characteristic of the product as such. This ruling produced the result, which the panels clearly desired, that trade measures based on environmental externalities created in the production of a product would be considered not as 'internal regulations' within the meaning of Article III but as *per se* violations of Article XI of the GATT (quantitative restrictions), regardless of whether domestic products creating similar externalities were equally banned from the market. This was because imported products creating the externalities could not be considered 'unlike' to domestic products that did not create the externalities. Had a principle of *stare decisis* been in operation, at a minimum the panels would have been forced to explain their deviance from a suggestion of a different panel just a few years before—that process and production methods might indeed be one respect in which products might be considered 'unlike' for purposes of Article III[68]—and yet another panel, which held that Article III applied to measures that were based not on any physical or other 'essential' characteristics of a product, but rather the juridical circumstances of their production (namely the violation of intellectual property rights of US nationals).[69]

While falling short of creating a strict rule of *stare decisis*, the AB has nevertheless held that panels 'should' take into account previous adopted panel reports, which create 'legitimate expectations' concerning future dispute settlement outcomes.[70] As Palmeter and Mavroidis suggest, the implication of this rule is that panels are bound to follow previous panel jurisprudence, unless they provide a reasoned explanation for a departure in approach.[71] This is arguably close to the practical significance of *stare decisis* in those domestic legal systems that recognize the principle: in such systems, courts sometimes do reverse their approach to a legal question, but when they do so, they explain the reasons for overruling themselves with care and explicitness. From the perspective of legitimacy, this attenuated justificatory meaning of *stare decisis* is in any case the most significant—the aim is to discipline results-oriented manipulation of the law, which the requirement of explaining for a deviation from previous reasonings should suffice to serve.

---

[68] *Japan—Customs Duties, Taxes and Labelling Practices on Imported Wines and Alcoholic Beverages*, BISD 34S/83, 1987, para. 5.7.

[69] *United States—Section 337 of the Tariff Act of 1930*, BISD 36S/345, 1989. See Howse and Regan, 'The Product/Process Distinction: An Illusory Basis for Disciplining Unilateralism in Trade Policy', 11 *EJIL* (2000) (forthcoming).

[70] *Japan—Taxes on Alcoholic Beverages*, Report of the Appellate Body, n. 47 above, at 11 ff.

[71] D. Palmeter and P. Mavroidis, *Dispute Settlement in the World Trade Organization: Practice and Procedure*, n. 28 above, at 40–2.

INSTITUTIONAL SENSITIVITY

A third ingredient in the legitimacy of WTO dispute settlement understood as the adjudication of conflicting values is, I believe, institutional sensitivity. In the course of interpreting provisions of the WTO Agreements, panels and the AB will be required to subject to interpretation and scrutiny a wide range of laws and policies, both domestic and international, which address a range of diverse values and interests. In approaching these laws and policies, the panels and the AB should be sensitive to their institutional strengths and weaknesses in relation to other actors who may have particular expertise or a particular stake in these laws and policies. Often this is expressed as a general exhortation to deference or 'restraint'[72] in adjudication. Jackson suggests that 'there should be *some* measure of deference, at the international dispute settlement level in the dispute settlement process, to national government decisions'.[73] These formulas are not very helpful for several reasons. First of all, they give little guidance as to how far restraint or deference should go in a given interpretive context. Secondly, the notion of deference, as is explicitly evidenced in Jackson's formula, tends to imply that what is at stake is the international level of decision-making yielding the domestic level. Yet in some very important contexts, the relevant institution with a claim to superior legitimacy may not be domestic at all, but some other international regime (international environmental legal regimes for instance in cases surrounding trade measures to protect endangered species). Thirdly, the notion of deference or restraint suggests that *when* the panel or AB's institutional analysis points to some other institution having some particular competence or credibility in dealing with a factual or legal issue, the only option in WTO dispute settlement is simply to *yield* to the determination of that body. This tends to exclude other, important options, such as the panel nevertheless still making its own determination (which may be different from that of the other institution) but giving special weight to aspects of that other institution's analysis which draw on its particular competency or legitimacy.

In order to understand the need for institutional sensitivity as an ingredient in legitimacy in WTO dispute settlement, one should be aware of the manner in which, traditionally, GATT panels failed to display such legitimacy—this is deeply connected to the assumption that they were enforcing a single value, free trade, from which perspective it would be hard to imagine than any other institution would have anything relevant to say that could

[72] Nichols, 'GATT Doctrine', n. 52 above, at 464: 'If panels within the World Trade Organization do not exhibit restraint, they could undermine public confidence in the organization.'

[73] J. H. Jackson, *The World Trade Organization: Constitution and Jurisprudence*, n. 59 above, at 90.

compete, in terms of competence and authority, with the GATT itself. A particularly good illustration of this attitude is to be found in the summary dismissal of environmental information from other organizations in the *Tuna/Dolphin* case, including information on international environmental law. But perhaps an even more egregious example was the panel's rejection of an explicit attempt of another international organization, the World Health Organization, to bring its competence to bear upon issues of health regulation as they emerged in the *Thai Cigarette* case.

In *Thai Cigarette*, Thailand sought to defend import restrictions and discriminatory tax treatment with respect to American cigarettes as justifiable under Article XX(b) of the GATT as 'necessary' for public health reasons.[74] Thailand argued that American cigarettes posed a particular health risk, because of their attractiveness to young people who might otherwise not take up the habit—an attractiveness in part due to advertising and marketing campaigns carefully targeted at youthful populations in developing countries. Thailand had sought to deal with the problem by a variety of measures, which included advertising bans, public information campaigns, and health warnings on cigarette packages, as well as the prima-facie GATT-inconsistent measures at issue.[75] In finding that these less-restrictive alternatives were adequate to Thailand's public health purpose, the panel simply ignored evidence from the World Health Organization that opening up markets to American cigarettes in a number of Latin American and Asian countries has led to increased smoking. The WHO had found that in the real world regulatory context faced by these developing countries, US multinationals had the resources to circumvent advertising bans, either finding loopholes in the laws or evading compliance efforts.[76]

This case illustrates not only one dimension of institutional *insensitivity* but two: not only insensitivity to the competence of the WHO, but also to the local knowledge of the Thai regulators, attempting to achieve regulatory goals in a real world environment known intimately to them, but not known at all to the panel. Thus, the panel felt perfectly confident that it could assess what alternatives might be available to achieve the regulatory objective in question by a purely abstract analysis, without any openness to what institutions with relevant local knowledge had found about the 'real world' in which they were attempting to regulate.

---

[74] *Thailand—Restrictions on Importation of and Internal Taxes on Cigarettes*, Report of the Panel, (1990) 37 BISD 200.

[75] *Thailand—Restrictions on Importation of and Internal Taxes on Cigarettes*, Report of the Panel, (1990) 37 BISD 200, para. 24.

[76] 'The WHO representatives stated that the experience in Latin America and Asia showed that the opening of closed cigarette markets dominated by a state tobacco monopoly resulted in an increase in smoking. Multinational tobacco companies had routinely circumvented national restrictions on advertising through indirect advertising and a variety of other techniques' (n. 75 above, at para. 55).

When we turn to the recent decision-making of the WTO Appellate Body, I think we can see a contrasting trend towards institutional sensitivity emerging, although perhaps not as consistently as would be desirable from the perspective of legitimacy. In *Hormones*, as well as in the early case of *Underwear*,[77] the Appellate Body rightly rejected any crude or rigid rule in favour of deference to findings of national authorities. In *Hormones*, the AB went on to suggest a spectrum of deference which, with respect to fact-finding, lay somewhere between *de novo* review of the facts at issue and 'total deference to national authorities' (para. 117). In itself this seems as imprecise as Jackson's formula of '*some* deference'. However, in grounding its notion of a spectrum on the duty to 'make an objective assessment of the facts', the AB seems to be pointing towards the more adequate notion that the weight to be given to factual determinations of other institutions will depend on some assessment of the relative competence and credibility of those institutions in the handling of the particular facts at issue. Similarly with respect to legal interpretation, the AB suggested that the law 'directly on point' was the Article 11 duty to make 'an objective assessment of the matter before [the panel]'. This is really the notion of institutional sensitivity *within* the discharge of the panel's duty to 'make an objective assessment'—not the delegation of a part of that duty to some other institution.

It is instructive to examine the actual deployment in *Hormones* of this incipient notion of institutional sensitivity. In *Hormones*, the AB was, in part, considering provisions that left open to some extent the degree of fit required between an assessed risk and the domestic regulatory measure in question. These provisions required that SPS measures be 'based on an assessment, as appropriate to the circumstances, of the risks to human, animal or plant life or health . . .'[78]

The general aspect of institutional sensitivity that the AB was applying here is stated somewhat earlier in the Report: '. . . a panel charged with determining, for instance, whether "sufficient scientific evidence" exists to warrant the maintenance of a particular measure may, of course, and should bear in mind that responsible, representative governments commonly act from perspectives of prudence and precaution where risks of irreversible, e.g. life-terminating, damage to human health are concerned' (para. 124). One should give weight here to these representative institutions, since in the *context* of risk regulation (as opposed to academic scientific discussion), their responsibility to protect their citizens gives a particular weight to their determinations, in contrast to the abstract scientific discourse. Similarly, this last finding is a further illustration of why deference is an inadequate notion to reflect a taking into account of relative institutional competence and credibility in dispute settle-

[77] *United States—Restrictions on Imports of Cotton and Man-Made Fibre Underwear*, Report of the Appellate Body, WT/DS24/R, 8 November 1996, 7.8–7.10.
[78] WTO, *Agreement on the Application of Sanitary and Phytosanitary Measures*, Art. 5.1.

ment. For here the choice was not simply between the panel imposing its own, more limited conception of 'risk assessment' on a WTO Member's internal institutions on the one hand, and deference to the 'domestic' on the other; it was also a choice between one of two different alternative institutional authorities outside the WTO, the one represented by science/technocracy and the other by democratic regulation that responds to the manner in which ordinary people perceive and handle risk in the everyday world.[79] The AB chose to understand science as playing a role *within* democratic justification of regulation; it was prepared to show some institutional sensitivity to internal regulatory authorities, while not simply excusing them from the need to show that their regulation can be understood as the product of public justification, in which science would have some role to play.

Of course, these various applications of institutional sensitivity in *Hormones* illustrate the important insight that the particular competence of an institution to which weight must be given in a particular interpretive context need not be (technocratic/ scientific) *expertise-based*—true to the conception of what is required for legitimacy when competing values are being adjudicated, it may just as likely be based on the institution's particular reponsibility to or claim to representivity of stakeholders or constitutents whose values and interests are at issue in the dispute (social/political/ cultural knowledge). Here, inasmuch as domestic or internal institutions are generally more capable of democratic representation, institutional sensitivity *will* cash out in terms of an appreciation of the need to allow domestic institutions to effectively respond to their constituents. This is something akin to a notion of subsidiarity[80]—the idea that presumptive normative weight should be afforded to outcomes of lower levels of authority on the assumption that those levels are closer to the people whose values and interests are at stake. In treaty interpretation this would translate into the tendency to adopt the interpretation of a given treaty provision which is least constraining of regulation that is 'closer to the people'. In *Hormones*, the AB expressed this idea through the international law notion of *in dubio mitius*: in the presence of two plausible

---

[79] On the difference between technocratic and democratic perspectives on risk and its regulation, see C. Sunstein and R. Pildes, 'Experts, Economists, and Democrats', in C. Sunstein, *Free Markets and Social Justice* (Oxford: Oxford University Press, 1997). Sunstein and Pildes argue that expert scientific judgment can play a role in 'an appropriately structured deliberative process' for *democratic* regulation, for example in correcting actual empirical error or prejudice about the facts, but that many factors that would not play a role in expert scientific judgment about risk have a legitimate place in risk determinations from a democratic perspective. The AB's approach to the meaning of 'scientific' risk assessment *within* the process of democratic regulation, and to the meaning of the requirement that regulations be 'based on' a scientific assessment of risk seems highly consistent with this insight of Sunstein and Pildes.

[80] See C. Cogianesi and K. Nicolaidis, 'Securing Legitimacy: Subsidiarity and the Allocation of Governing Authority' in S. Woolcock, *Subsidiarity in the Governance of the World Economy* (Cambridge: Cambridge University Press, 1999, forthcoming).

interpretations, the one that is less onerous, or constraining of the party accepting the obligation, should be adopted (para. 165 and accompanying footnote). In other cases, the AB has rejected interpretations of obligations under WTO treaties that were based not on the strict language of the treaty, but rather on an expansive notion of the complainant's 'reasonable expectations' from a provision of the treaty.[81] I prefer to understand these interpretive moves as the subsidiarity aspect of institutional sensitivity, since the legacy of *in dubio mitius* is that of deference to sovereignty, which is increasingly questionable as a value in itself, while democracy is arguably less contestable as a value in itself,[82] or at least as a value which is relevant to the kind of social legitimacy that informs the perspective of this chapter.

In contrast to *Hormones*, several other decisions of the Appellate Body display an inadequate appreciation of the need for institutional sensitivity; however, as I shall argue, each of these could be understandable as a reaction against the demand not for institutional sensitivity as such, but for deference, i.e. that the AB simply adopt or accept the determinations of some other institutional authority.

In *Salmon*, the AB overruled a determination by the panel that a risk analysis by the Australian government, apparently justifying an import ban on non-heat-treated salmon, was an adequate 'risk assessment' for purposes of the WTO Agreement on Sanitary and Phytosanitary Measures.[83] On this last issue, the Appellate Body relied upon the panel's own characterization of the Australian risk analysis as vague or imprecise in a number of respects. The panel itself had held that despite these defects the document qualified as a scientific assessment of risk within the meaning of the SPS Agreement. The *Salmon* panel found that the risk assessment provided by Australia was defective in various respects as against the standards of *scientific experts*, but that it would suffice from the perspective of the legal requirements of the SPS Agreement. But the panel was right not to come to an *automatic* finding that the risk assessment was inadequate for purposes of trade law, taking into account the institutional context as one of democratic regulation, not laboratory experiments. Citizens demand that their representatives respond to many different risks, in a timely fashion that prevents extensive damage being done before precautions can take effect. The time and money that real-world gov-

---

[81] See, for example, *India—Patent Protection for Pharmaceutical and Agricultural Chemical Products*, Report of the Appellate Body, n. 30 above. This interpretive approach also demonstrates how textualism may act as a constraint or discipline on the tendency of panels to interpret the WTO agreements in light of the single value of free trade, understanding the text of the treaty not as reflecting a balance of values but as a springboard for a liberalizing, integrationist trajectory.

[82] T. Franck, 'The Emerging Right to Democratic Governance', n. 23 above.

[83] *Australia—Measures Affecting Importation of Salmon*, Report of the Appellate Body, WT/DS18/ AB/R (1998).

ernments can spend to investigate all possible individual risks and alternative risk responses prior to enacting regulations are limited, as the AB itself had seemed to recognize in *Hormones*, at least in a general way. In *Salmon*, Australia had produced a document of several hundred pages with extensive scientific and regulatory analysis of the problem.[84] At the same time, the AB's rejection of the Australian Report may well have been justified in the result; the Report was less democratically transparent than an earlier document in the way in which it described risks, tending to conceal or blur the stark choice to take very restrictive measures to deal with what were in almost all cases very low probability risks. Its real defect was not a shortfall from abstract scientific standards, but a defect from the perspective of rational democratic deliberation about risk; thus, in this case democratic legitimacy could not be consistently invoked as a basis for institutional sensitivity.

In the *Bananas* case, in the course of interpreting the scope of a Waiver from Article I obligations that facilitated the EU providing trade preferences to developing countries pursuant to the *Lome Convention*, the AB found itself with the task of interpreting what was 'required' by the *Convention*, since as already noted, the Waiver relieved from the MFN obligation only to the extent that this was necessary to achieve what was 'required'. The EU argued that the panel should have deferred to the understanding of the *Lome* parties—the EU and a range of developing countries—as to what the *Convention* required. Now, because the interests of stakeholders not parties to the *Convention* in how broadly or narrowly it might be interpreted were directly at issue (banana exporters from non-*Lome* countries), simple deference to the understanding of the parties themselves would *not* have been appropriately institutionally sensitive. Yet the AB went to the opposite extreme, suggesting that the *Convention* should be read in complete abstraction from the practice of the parties, as if it had become by virtue of the reference in the Waiver, an integral part of the WTO law itself. There are many references to other international agreements in various WTO instruments, and the reading of these agreements as if they were simply *trade* law would attenuate the possibility that such agreements represent benchmarks that are relevant where panels are addressing trade-offs between free trade and other values that may be represented by these other international legal regimes. Institutional sensitivity as an ingredient in the legitimacy of adjudication of competing values would argue for taking into account the institutional competence and credibility of those preoccupied with these other legal orders in their interpretation, and thus at a minimum taking into account 'practice' surrounding these other agreements

[84] Australian Quarantine and Inspection Service, Department of Primary Industries and Energy, *Salmon Import Risk Analysis: An assessment by the Australian Government of quarantine controls on uncooked, wild, adult, ocean-caught Pacific salmonid product sourced from the United States of America and Canada*, Final Report, December, 1996, Canberra, available at www.dpie.gov.au/aqis/homepage/public/reports/salmon.html.

in the broadest sense—dispute rulings, views of the official organs responsible for the administration and development of the regime, opinions of stakeholders and experts preoccupied with the regime in question and the values and interests that it puts to the front and centre. But, again, since *outsiders* may also have a legitimate stake in interpretation, the posture of complete deference may well not be warranted.

A parallel lack of institutional sensitivity to that exemplified in *Bananas* was displayed by the AB in its treatment of domestic arrangements for the enforcement of intellectual property rights in the *Indian Patents* case.[85] The AB rejected India's claim for deference with respect to its own determination that certain administrative instructions would provide the legal security for patents required by the WTO Agreement on Trade-Related Intellectual Property Rights, even without implementing legislation (para. 66). As in *Bananas*, complete deference to another institutional authority (in this case domestic) would not have been appropriate, since outsiders (in this case, foreign patent holders) had an interest not necessarily recognizable or recognized by the domestic institutional authority. Nevertheless, again, the AB has arguably gone to the opposite extreme, in holding that WTO dispute settlement organs can interpret domestic law without even taking into account domestic institutional competence in the interpretation of this law.

CONCLUSION

In the conclusion to his classic article on GATT doctrine, Nichols—drawing on the example of the European Court of Justice—makes the bold suggestion that legitimacy in legal interpretation by the WTO dispute settlement organs may serve to legitimize the World Trade Organization as a whole.[86] If one returns to the premises beginning the investigation in this chapter, this suggestion does have some plausibility. Inasmuch as one can understand the critics of economic globalization as being motivated not by a reaction against the legal rules of international trade themselves, but the institutional and interpretative behaviour of the official guardians of those rules (the *Tuna/Dolphin* controversy), the Appellate Body may have already achieved some success in moving towards a new ground for legitimacy of the trading system as a whole. Those with a critical bent may well point out, however, that cases like *Hormones* and *Shrimp* were, in the *result*, not 'wins' from the perspective of non-free trade values. The measures were still found in violation, though on narrower, and more carefully circumscribed grounds. This raises the spectre that the Appellate Body, in discovering 'rationalizing legal analysis', to use an expression of Roberto Unger, may simply have found a more satisfactory way

---

[85] N. 30 above.   [86] 'GATT Doctrine', n. 52 above, at 465.

to achieve the kinds of results that the GATT élite had been seeking all along. Yet, as I have already suggested,[87] the analytical tools of critical legal scholarship have been honed on adjudicative rulings that have claimed to display the kind of legitimacy that is now reflected, however imperfectly or incompletely, in the emerging jurisprudence of the Appellate Body. Thus, while for economic globalization's 'liberal' friends, of which I am one, the AB jurisprudence opens up new possibilities for legitimation, for economic globalization's critics, it at the same time opens up new spaces for critique and contestation, in which critical legal scholars may especially find themelves more at home. But globalization's 'liberal' friends should welcome these latter possibilities as well, for the law of international economic integration, having survived and/or been reshaped by such critique and contestation, will possess all the more social legitimacy.

[87] See n. 46 above.

4

The European Court of Justice and the WTO: Problems and Challenges

JACQUES H. J. BOURGEOIS

INTRODUCTION

The topic chosen for this chapter prompts the question why the World Trade Organization, as an international organization, and the various Agreements that form an integral part of the Agreement establishing the World Trade Organization (hereinafter for brevity's sake: WTO law) raise problems and are challenges for the Court of Justice of the European Communities (hereinafter the ECJ) that are specific enough to merit an analysis. In other words this topic begs the question whether the issues of the status of WTO law in the EC legal system and of the judicial enforcement of WTO law in that system, have aspects that set them apart from the same issues as they raise or rather do not raise in other jurisdictions.

Generally speaking the EC-specific challenges and problems for the ECJ are related on the one hand to the status of the EC in the WTO and on the other to the ECJ's jurisdiction as it is organized by the EC Treaty. These two items are dealt with in sections I and II. Section III addresses the status of international agreements in the EC legal system and section IV deals with the status of the WTO in the EC legal system.

I THE STATUS OF THE EC IN THE WTO

The EC was not a contracting party to the General Agreements on Tariffs and Trade 1947 (hereinafter the GATT); the EC Member States were. However, the EC had over the years acquired the status to all intents and purposes of a contracting party. All trade agreements and accession protocols negotiated in the GATT framework provided in their final provisions that the agreements were open for acceptance 'by contracting parties to the GATT and by the EEC' (or 'EC'). Moreover, notwithstanding this formal distinction in such final provisions between GATT contracting parties and the EC, the substantive and procedural provisions of these Agreements treat the EC like a GATT contracting party. In addition, since 1970, most agreements negotiated in the GATT framework were accepted by the EC alone, i.e. without 'acceptance' by EC Member States as such.[1]

The EC exercised practically all rights and fulfilled practically all obligations under GATT law in its own name like a GATT contracting party. Since about 1960 all GATT contracting parties had accepted such exercise of rights and such fulfilment of obligations by the EC and had asserted their own GATT rights, even in dispute settlement proceedings relating to measures of individual EC Member States, almost always against the EC.[2] Although this cannot be described as a case of State succession, the EC had effectively replaced, with the consent of the other GATT contracting parties, its Member States as bearers of rights and obligations under the GATT.

At the outset of the Uruguay Round of Multilateral Trade negotiations, the EC was faced with the issue of the scope of its authority under the EC Treaty in the field of international economic relations, in particular with respect to trade in services and trade related aspects of intellectual property rights, which were a first in GATT history. The issue was put on the back-burner and the negotiations were conducted according to the procedures normally followed for GATT negotiations, albeit that the European Commission (hereinafter: the Commission) negotiated for both the EC and the EC Member States.[3]

The creation of the World Trade Organization (hereinafter: the WTO) offered the opportunity to draw the formal international law consequences of these developments in two respects: first, by stipulating that the EC would be a WTO Member and, second, by making clear that the EC replaced the EC Member States. When this matter arose two political constraints led the Commission not to stand up for the second consequence. First, the matter was discussed in a meeting of the Council of the European Union (hereinafter: the Council) in November 1993, that is after the Maastricht Treaty on the European Union had entered into effect with some difficulty and it was thought wise not to push this issue at that stage. Second, around this time the last hurdles facing the approval by the Council of the results of the Uruguay Round had to be cleared and Sir Leon Brittan, followed by the Commission,

---

[1] With the exception at the end of the Tokyo Round of multilateral trade negotiations of two agreements and the part of the Tariff Protocol relating to ECSC products. See for a comment J. H. J. Bourgeois, 'The Tokyo Round Agreements on Technical Barriers and on Government Procurement', 19 CML Rev. (1982) 5 at 22.

[2] See E. U. Petersmann, 'The EEC as a GATT Member—Legal Conflicts between GATT Law and European Community Law' in M. Hilf, F. G. Jacobs, E. U. Petersmann, *The European Community and GATT* (Kluwer, Deventer, 1986), 23 at 37–8.

[3] See the description by P. van den Bossche, 'The European Community and the Uruguay Round Agreements' in John H. Jackson and Alan A. Sykes (eds.) *Implementing the Uruguay Round* (Clarendon Press, Oxford, 1997), 23 at 56–7.

thought it preferable not to table yet another contentious issue and not to upset an apple cart that was already in danger of being out of balance. The end-result was Article XI of the Marrakesh Agreement establishing the World Trade Organization stating that the contracting parties to GATT 1947 (including thus all the EC Member States) and the European Communities shall become original Members of the WTO.[4]

From the perspective of the EC and its Member States this rather anomalous dual membership may in the end prove to be a bad solution. Under GATT 1947 the other contracting parties had accepted pragmatically the EC as a single entity on the grounds that one should not open the Pandora's box of a review of the GATT in order to formally substitute the EC for its Member States. The solution of Article XI of the WTO Agreement carries with it the risk that all these efforts will come to naught. There are indications that other WTO Members may not continue to show the same forbearance and are tempted to exploit the dual membership of the EC and EC Member States. What was in the GATT a patient acceptance of a passing eccentricity may turn in the WTO into a lingering handicap for both the EC and its Member States.

The very fact that EC Member States are WTO Members alongside the EC is in itself bound to raise issues in relation to the position of the ECJ on WTO law. As far as GATT 1947 was concerned, the ECJ could take the view that as a result of the substitution of the EC for the Member States in relation to commitments under GATT, it had the final word on the interpretation of GATT provisions, even in relation to the compatibility of Member States legislation with GATT.[5] This argument is no longer possible. In line with Article XI of the Agreement establishing the WTO, both the EC and the Member States signed the Final Act.

It is true that the ECJ has stated that the division of powers between the EC and the Member States is a domestic question in which third parties have no need to intervene.[6] The Commission probably relied on this when it had recorded in the minutes of Council meeting 7/8 March 1994 its view that: 'the Final Act . . . and the Agreements thereto fall exclusively within the competence of the European Community'.[7] However, that does not allow the *a-contrario* inference that the fact that the Member States and the EC are formally WTO Members is irrelevant for the division of powers within the EC legal system.

---

[4] WTO, *The Uruguay Round Results. The Legal Texts* (Geneva, 1995), 6.
[5] *Amministrazione della Finanze dello Stato v Società Petrolifera Italiana (SPI) and SpA Michelin Italiana (SAMI)* [1983] ECR 801, paras 15 and 17.
[6] Ruling 1/78 [1978] ECR 2151, para. 35.
[7] Cited in ECJ Opinion 1/94 [1994] ECR I-5267, para. 5.

At any rate the Agreement establishing the WTO and the agreements that form part of it were approved by the Council on behalf of the EC expressly 'as regards matters within its competence'.[8] The need to accord an '*effet utile*' to the joint WTO membership of the EC and the Member States is inescapable. It must mean something about the division of powers within the EC and this in turn raises issues in relation to the ECJ's jurisdiction. As will be seen such issues have arisen in relation to other agreements concluded jointly by the EC and the Member States and in relation to the TRIPS Agreement, one of the agreements annexed to the Agreement establishing the WTO.

II JURISDICTION OF THE COURT OF JUSTICE OF THE EUROPEAN COMMUNITIES

Only those aspects of the jurisdiction of the ECJ that are particularly relevant for the subject of this chapter are assessed. The analysis is necessarily selective.

An Overview

1. *The Principle of Limited Jurisdiction*

The ECJ has no inherent jurisdiction; it has jurisdiction only in so far as the EC Treaty and similar instruments have conferred jurisdiction upon it, as results from Article 4 (new Art. 7), paragraph 1 EC Treaty. Such jurisdiction may be implied. The implied jurisdiction exists where there is a prevailing need for it in order to fill a lacuna in the system of remedies expressly provided for, such as where the complete absence of any other form of legal redress creates a serious injustice and is inconsistent with the rule of law in the EC.[9]

Although the concept of 'a Community based on the rule of law' appears nowhere in the EC Treaty, the ECJ relied on this concept to develop a more general theory on which it based such implied jurisdiction. In *Les Verts* the ECJ stated that:

[T]he European Economic Community is a Community based on the rule of law, inasmuch as neither its Member States nor its institutions can avoid a review of the question whether the measures adopted by them are in conformity with the basic constitutional charter, the Treaty . . .

and that

---

[8] Council Decision of 22 December 1998 (OJ 1994 L 336/1).
[9] Cf. K. P. E. Lasok, *The European Court of Justice. Practice and Procedure*, 2nd edn. (Butterworths, London 1994), 9.

the Treaty established a complete system of legal remedies and procedures designed to permit the Court of Justice to review the legality of measures adopted by the institutions.[10]

In a subsequent case, the ECJ was of the view that in order to perform its task under Article 164 (new Art. 220) EC it had to be able to guarantee the maintenance of the institutional balance and the respect for the European Parliament's prerogatives. Although Article 173 (new Art. 230) EC did not provide for an application for annulment by the European Parliament, the ECJ concluded that it had jurisdiction in an annulment proceeding brought by the European Parliament to the extent that the purpose of the proceeding was to protect the European Parliament's prerogatives.[11] This freedom of the ECJ to intervene in the absence of express authority to do so allows the correction of defects in the system of remedies created by the Treaties.[12] In this, the implicit jurisdiction of the ECJ finds its justification and its limits.

2. Acts Susceptible to Judicial Review by the ECJ

Article 173 (new Art. 230) EC Treaty provides for an action of annulment against acts adopted jointly by the European Parliament and the Council, acts of the Council, of the Commission and the European Central Bank, other than recommendations or opinions, and of acts of the European Parliament intended to produce legal effects *vis-à-vis* third parties.[13]

In the area of external relations two developments in the case law are noteworthy in this respect.

(a) A decision of the Council to Leave it to EC Member States to Negotiate an International Agreement

In the *ERTA* case the Commission had recommended to the Council that it be authorized to re-negotiate on behalf of the EC the European Road

---

[10] CJEC, Judgment of 23 April 1986, *Les Verts v European Parliament*, [1986] ECR 1339 (consideration 23).

[11] The 'Chernobyl case' *European Parliament v Council* [1990] ECR I-2041: contrast this to the so-called 'Comitology case' *European Parliament v Council* [1988] ECR 5615. For a comment on the latter case J. Weiler, 'Pride and Prejudice—Parliament c. Council', 14 EL Rev. (1989) 334.

[12] A. Arnull, 'Does the Court of Justice have inherent jurisdiction?' 27 CML Rev. (1990), 683 at 701.

[13] Note that the *ius standi* of a private applicant is limited to:
- decisions addressed to that applicant
- decisions addressed to others which is of direct and individual concern to the applicant
- decisions taken in the form of a regulation which is of direct and individual concern to the applicant

(Art. 173, new Art. 230 para. 4, EC).

Transport Agreement to be entered into with third countries in the framework of the United Nations. The Council resolved that the (then) six EC Member States should negotiate on their own behalf and become individual parties to ERTA. The Commission challenged the Council proceedings in the ECJ, which considered that the Commission application was admissible. Referring to the wording of Article 173 (new Art. 230) EC Treaty the ECJ reasoned that:

Since the only matter excluded from the scope of the action for annulment . . . are 'recommendations or opinions'—which by the final paragraph of Article 189 [EC Treaty] are declared to have no binding force—Article 173 treats as acts open to review by the Court all measures adopted by the institutions which are intended to have legal force.[14]

The ECJ went on to analyze the content and purpose of the Council proceedings and was of the view:

It thus seems that in so far as they concerned the objective of the negotiations as defined by the Council, the proceedings of 20 March 1970 could not have been simply the expression or the recognition of a voluntary co-ordination, but were designed to lay down a course of action binding on both the institutions and the Member States, and destined ultimately to be reflected in the term of the [EC] regulation [that would have to be amended following the conclusion of ERTA].

In the part of its conclusion relating to the negotiating procedure, the Council adopted provisions which were capable of derogating in certain circumstances from the procedure laid down by the [EC] Treaty regarding negotiations with third countries and the conclusion of agreements.[15]

The ECJ concluded that:

. . . the proceedings of 20 March 1970 [i.e. the position taken by the Council] had definitive legal effects both in relations between the Community and the Member States and in the relationship between the institutions.[16]

In the same vein, in *Commission v Council (FAO)* the ECJ considered that a Council decision according to which the EC Member States rather than the EC should vote in the FAO for the adoption of an agreement on fisheries conservation measures had legal effects. The ECJ consequently held that the Commission application for annulment of that decision was admissible.[17]

(b) International Agreements

Once the text of an agreement has been initiated or authenticated in some form by the Commission, the Council 'concludes' the agreement, following

---

[14] *Commission v Council* [1971] ECR 263, para. 39.
[15] [1971] ECR 263, para. 53.   [16] [1971] ECR 263, para. 55.
[17] [1996] ECR I-1469.

either a simplified procedure or a more complicated procedure involving two or three stages. In doing so, the Council approves the agreement and decides on such steps as are required to express the Community's consent to be bound by the agreement by whatever means are applicable.

In EC practice, 'conclusion', within the meaning of the relevant EC Treaty provisions (Articles 114, 228, and 238 (Art. 114 now repealed, new Arts 300 and 310)), thus covers simultaneously two different measures: the measure whereby the *internal* procedure to conclude an agreement is completed and the measure whereby the EC binds itself *internationally*. This final act of the Council takes the form of a decision or a regulation. The decision or regulation, to which the international agreement is appended, is published in the Official Journal of the EC. A notice announcing the agreement's international entry into effect may appear subsequently in the Official Journal.

Beyond a certain analogy to legal systems providing for legislative approval of international agreements, these EC Treaty provisions do not offer much guidance on the status and effects of international agreements in the EC legal system, except that under Article 228 (new Art. 300), paragraph 7 EC agreements 'concluded' under these conditions are 'binding on the institutions of the Community and on Member States'.

The institutional provisions are silent on the question of whether and how an international agreement binding on the EC becomes part of EC law. They do not contain any indication of the Treaty framers' views on what, for convenience, are called the 'monist' and the 'dualist' approaches. The practice followed by the EC institutions does not offer much guidance either. In some cases the practice seems to reflect a 'dualist' attitude; in other cases it reflects a 'monist' one. The choice of a regulation (by definition 'directly applicable') rather than a decision for the purpose of approving an international agreement normally implies that a regulation was in that case necessary to ensure direct efficacy to an agreement which was itself considered 'self-executing'. It can thus be seen as the expression of a 'dualist' attitude. However, that choice may also be influenced by other considerations, such as the need to adopt simultaneously complementary provisions requiring the use of a regulation. For its part, the ECJ has demonstrated that it does not attach much weight to the type of legal act used for the purpose of deciding whether an agreement has become part of Community law and is directly enforceable.[18]

On the other hand, in EC practice, legislation implementing an international agreement, i.e. transforming it into EC legislation, is considered necessary only where the agreement both entails precise legal obligations and

---

[18] E.g. in *Bresciani* [1976] ECR 129, the ECJ allowed the applicant in the main case to rely on the Yaounde agreement although this international agreement had been approved by a decision and not by a regulation.

requires changes of, or additions to, rules in force internally, or where the provisions of the agreement, in order to be implemented in a clear and effective manner, call for special measures of internal law.

The question thus arises whether an international agreement concluded by the EC is an act of an EC institution within the meaning of Article 173 (new Art. 230) EC Treaty open to challenge or whether only the decision to conclude an international agreement can be the subject of a review of legality by the ECJ.

France v Commission[19] related to the 1991 Agreement entered into by the Commission and the US government regarding the application of their competition laws. France brought an action under Article 173 (new Art. 230) EC for a declaration that this agreement was void, i.e. on the ground that the Commission was not competent to conclude such an agreement.

On the admissibility of the action the ECJ took the following position:

In its defense, the Commission raises the question whether the French Government should have challenged the decision whereby it authorized its vice-president to sign the agreement with the United States on its behalf, rather than challenging the agreement itself.

Suffice it to note that, in order for an action to be admissible under the first paragraph of Article 173 of the EEC Treaty, the contested act must be an act of an institution which produces legal effects (see Case 22/70 *Commission v Council* [1971] ECR 263 (the 'ERTA' case)).

The Court finds that, as is apparent from its actual wording, the agreement is intended to produce legal effects. Consequently, the act whereby the Commission sought to conclude the agreement must be susceptible to an action for annulment.

Exercise of the powers delegated to the Community institutions in international matters cannot escape judicial review, under Article 173 of the Treaty, of the legality of the acts adopted.

The French Republic's action must be understood as being directed against the act whereby the Commission sought to conclude the Agreement. Consequently, the action is admissible.[20]

This rather short reasoning of the ECJ may be clarified by the following excerpt of the opinion of Tesauro AG (footnotes omitted).

Nevertheless, the Commission has argued that under Article 173 the Court may review only acts of the institutions, which clearly cannot encompass an agreement which, being an act that has come into being with the participation of a non-member country, is not — nor can it be considered — a unilateral act of a Community institution. The case-law in which the Court affirms that it has jurisdiction to interpret agreements as well by way of a preliminary ruling confirms, in the Commission's

---

[19] [1994] ECR I 3641.   [20] [1994] ECR I-3641, paras 13–17.

view, that only the decision to conclude an agreement and not the agreement itself can be the subject of a review of legality.

In that regard, it should be noted first of all that the relevant case-law of the Court does not by any means rule out the possibility of challenging an agreement directly. In fact, quite the opposite is true, as suggested by the weight of evidence.

Let us remember that in justifying its jurisdiction to interpret by way of a preliminary ruling agreements concluded by the Community with non-members countries, the Court has equated such agreements with acts of the institutions. Thus, in its judgment in *Haegeman*, the Court expressly stated that an agreement concluded under Article 228 of the Treaty constitutes 'so far as concerns the Community, an act of one of the institutions of the Community within the meaning of subparagraph (b) of the first paragraph of Article 177' and that 'the provisions of the Agreement, from the coming into force thereof, form an integral part of Community law'.

Since in the same judgment the Court referred to the Council decision relating to the conclusion of the Agreement in question, the aforesaid statement has been interpreted as meaning that the Court's jurisdiction to interpret provisions of international agreements can be exercised only because of the existence of an executive act. The fact remains, however, that, even in subsequent judgments, the Court reiterated, for purposes of interpretation, that agreements, so far as concerns the Community, are to be treated as acts of the institutions.

Still more important for the purposes of this case is the fact that the Court's jurisdiction to carry out an *a posteriori* review of legality in relation to international agreements concluded by the Communities has already been affirmed by the Court unequivocally, albeit in an *obiter dictum*, in Opinion 1/75. In that Opinion, the Court stated that 'the question whether the conclusion of a given agreement is within the power of the Community and whether, in a given case, such power has been exercised in conformity with the provisions of the Treaty is, in principle, a question which may be submitted to the Court of Justice, either directly, under Article 169 or Article 173 of the Treaty, or in accordance with the preliminary procedure'.

It is clear, therefore, first of all that the possibility of review under Article 173 (as well) arises from the exercise of the Community's external powers being subject to compliance with the procedural and substantive rules laid down by the Treaty, and secondly that the possibility of direct review of the agreements concluded by the Community is by no means excluded since the Court has expressly stated that it can review, in proceedings under Article 173, whether the power to conclude an agreement has been exercised in accordance with the provisions of the Treaty.

Admittedly, the Court has not so far had occasion to exercise that power of *a posteriori* review in a specific case, although it has already ruled on the legality of a Community act relating to the conclusion of an agreement. The question remains, therefore, for the purposes of this case, whether such review is permissible only indirectly, that is to say where it is carried out as a result of an action challenging the regulation or decision relating to the conclusion of the agreement, or also where the agreement is challenged directly.

It seems to me that the question is merely one of form. In my view, under the Community legal system which makes provision for judicial review, without exception, of all the acts and practices of the institutions, of individuals and of the Member States, which affect the system itself, it is not reasonably possible to exclude review of the legality of the procedure for concluding an agreement with a non-member country. The possibility of doing so on the basis of a complaint expressly directed at the agreement as such or at the act connected therewith, or else at an implied act, strikes me as a secondary and wholly irrelevant matter.[21]

The ECJ, however, adhered to the more formalistic approach. It did not annul the agreement. It declared void the act whereby the Commission sought to conclude the agreement with the US.

Some might consider that in so doing the ECJ followed a dualist approach in that it distinguished between the agreement which France sought to have declared void and the Commission decision on the conclusion of this agreement. This is doubtful. Under the monist approach the domestic effect of an international agreement depends normally on the approval of the conclusion of the agreement by the proper national authorities. The ECJ limited itself to reviewing the legality of such approval.

3. Acts Susceptible to Interpretation by the ECJ

Quite obviously, where the ECJ has jurisdiction to annul or declare void an act of an EC institution, it also may interpret such act. One of the interesting features of the EC system of judicial review is the preliminary ruling. Pursuant to Article 177 (new Art. 234) EC, an EC Member State court may, or as the case may be, must submit to the ECJ a question of interpretation of the EC Treaty or of secondary EC law or a question of legality of secondary EC law—more precisely 'on the validity and interpretation of acts of the Institutions of the Community'.

(a) Agreements entered into by the EC

In *Haegeman*[22] a Belgian company importing Greek wines sought repayment of countervailing charges exacted from it by Belgium. It argued before a Belgian court that the imposition of those charges was unlawful having regard to the (then) Association Agreement between the EEC and Greece. The Belgian court submitted a number of questions of interpretation of the Association Agreement to the ECJ.

The ECJ examined *in limine* its jurisdiction. It referred to Article 177 (new Art. 234) EC Treaty and went on to state:

The Athens Agreement was concluded by the Council under Articles 228 and 238 of the Treaty as appears from the terms of the decision [of the Council approving the conclusion of the Agreement] of 25 September 1961.

---

[21] [1994] ECR I-3641, Opinion of Tesauro AG, paras 8–11.   [22] [1974] ECR 449.

The Agreement is therefore in so far as concerns the Community, an act of one of the institutions of the Community within the meaning of subparagraph (b) of the first paragraph of Article 177.

The provisions of the Agreement, from the coming into force thereof, form integral part of Community law.

Within the framework of this law, the Court accordingly has jurisdiction to give preliminary rulings concerning the interpretation of this Agreement.[23]

In this case the provision whose interpretation was sought by the Belgian court was not the decision approving the Association Agreement, but a provision of this agreement itself, which, as such, is not listed in Article 177 (new Art. 234) EC among the acts covered by the ECJ's jurisdiction. The ECJ assimilated the Association Agreement to 'an act of an institution of the Community', and considered that its provisions form an integral part of Community law, having found that this agreement had been approved by a Council Decision. It has been argued that the ECJ's argument would be justified only if the EC adopts a strictly dualist approach to international agreements.[24] However under the monist approach, an international agreement must be properly concluded under national constitutional law to have domestic effect.

The ECJ has taken the same view in subsequent judgments.[25]

(b) 'Mixed Agreements'

The EC and its Member States have recourse to the 'mixed agreements' formula 'when it appears that the subject-matter of an agreement or contract falls in part within the competence of the Community and in part within that of the Member States'.[26] This formula has been analysed in the literature to which we refer for further reading.[27] The advantage of the formula is that it allows fudging the issue of the exact demarcation of EC competence. If that issue had to be definitively resolved every time an international agreement was concluded, the process would be even more fraught than it usually is.[28]

The question addressed here is the extent of the ECJ's jurisdiction with respect to mixed agreements. In the literature various views have been put

[23] [1974] ECR 449, paras 3–6.

[24] T. C. Hartley, 'International Agreements and the Community Legal System: Some Recent Developments', 8 ELR (1983), 383 at 390.

[25] *Polydor* [1989] ECR 329; *Kupferberg* [1982] ECR 3641; *Demirel* [1987] ECR 3719; *Greece v Commission* [1989] ECR 3711.

[26] Opinion 2/91 (ILO Convention concerning the Safety in the Use of Chemicals at Work), [1993] ECR I-1061, para. 36.

[27] O'Keeffe and Schermers (eds.), *Mixed Agreements* (Kluwer, December 1983); Bourgeois, Dewost, Gaiffe (eds.), *La Communauté européenne et les accords mixtes. Quelles perspectives?* (P.I.E., Bruxelles, 1997).

[28] A. Dashwood, 'Why continue to have Mixed Agreements at all?' in Bourgeois, Dewost, Gaiffe (eds.), n. 27 above, at 94.

forward. According to some the ECJ may interpret such agreements in their entirety;[29] others take the view that the ECJ's jurisdiction is limited to clauses of a mixed agreement that do not extend beyond the EC's field of operation.[30]

Leaving aside earlier cases the ECJ faced this issue in *Demirel*.[31] The request for a preliminary ruling by the ECJ was made by a German court in which Mrs Demirel, a Turkish national, challenged her expulsion which was ordered on the grounds that her visa, which was only valid for a visit, had expired. Mrs Demirel wanted to remain in Germany with her husband who resided in Germany. Mrs Demirel relied on certain provisions of the Association Agreement between the EEC and Turkey. Two Member States intervened in the proceedings in the ECJ and called the jurisdiction of the ECJ into question.

The ECJ ruled as follows:

However, the German Government and the United Kingdom take the view that, in the case of 'mixed' agreement such as the Agreement and the Protocol at issue here, the Court's interpretative jurisdiction does not extend to provisions whereby Member States have entered into commitments with regard to Turkey in the exercise of their own powers which is the case of the provisions on freedom of movement for workers.

In that connection it is sufficient to state that that is precisely not the case in this instance. Since the agreement in question is an association Agreement creating special, privileged links with a non-member country which must, at least to a certain extent, take part in the Community system, Article 238 must necessarily empower the Community to guarantee commitments towards non-member countries in all the fields covered by the Treaty. Since freedom of movement for workers is, by virtue of Article 48 *et seq.* of the EEC Treaty, one of the fields covered by that Treaty, it follows that commitments regarding freedom of movement fall within the powers conferred on the Community by Article 238. Thus the question whether the Court has jurisdiction to rule on the interpretation of a provision in a mixed agreement containing a commitment which only the Member States could enter into in the sphere of their own powers does not arise.

Furthermore, the jurisdiction of the Court cannot be called in question by virtue of the fact that in the field of freedom of movement for workers, as Community law now stands, it is for the Member States to lay down the rules which are necessary to give effect in their territory to the provisions of the agreements or the decisions to be adopted by the Association Council.

---

[29] E.g. A. Bleckmann, 'Der Gemischte Vertrag im Europarecht', (1976) *Europarecht* 301; H. Krück Ad Art. 177 in Groeben, Thiesing, Ehlerman (eds.), *Kommentar zum EU-/EG-Vertrag*, 5th edn., vol. 4 (Nomos, Baden-Baden, 1997), at 615.

[30] E.g. Schermers and Waelbroeck, *Judicial Protection in the European Communities*, 5th edn., (Kluwer, Deventer, Boston, 1992), at 430; T. Hartley, *The Foundations of European Community Law: an Introduction to the Constitutional and Administrative Law of the European Community* (Oxford University Press, 1994), 186, 273.

[31] *Meryem Demirel v Stadt Swäbisch Gmünd* [1987] ECR 3719.

As the Court held in its judgment of 26 October 1982 in Case 104/81 *Hauptzollamt Mainz v. Kupferberg* [1982] (ECR 3641), in ensuring respect for commitments arising from an agreement concluded by the Community institutions the Member States fulfil, within the Community system, an obligation in relation to the Community, which has assumed responsibility for the due performance of the agreement.

Consequently, the Court does have jurisdiction to interpret the provisions on freedom of movement for workers contained in the Agreement and the Protocol.[32]

It should be noted that whatever may have been the reasons why Member States wanted to conclude this agreement alongside the EC, it could probably have been concluded by the EC alone. Moreover, the clauses of the agreement for whose interpretation the ECJ considered that it had jurisdiction came within the competence of the EC under Article 238 EC. The situation is arguably different with respect to the interpretation of those clauses of mixed agreements that come squarely within the competence of EC Member States

The ECJ's Jurisdiction in Relation to WTO Law

1. The ECJ's Jurisdiction in Relation to the GATT

There have been a series of cases involving the GATT. The point addressed here is whether the ECJ has jurisdiction under Article 177 (new Art. 234) EC to give preliminary rulings on the interpretation of the GATT.

This question was submitted to the ECJ by the Corte Suprema di Cassazione in *SPI*[33] in a dispute between several importers and the Italian Treasury about duties for administrative services levied on imports from GATT contracting parties. Under Italian law the provisions of the GATT were held to create subjective rights for private parties. As it was aware of previous case law of the ECJ interpreting EC law in light of the GATT, the Corte Suprema di Cassazione apparently wanted to avoid a conflict between its own interpretation and that of the ECJ. By the same token it wanted to clarify whether pursuant to Article 177 (new Art. 234) EC the ECJ considered that it had the final say on the interpretation of GATT provisions also where EC Member State courts were asked to rule on the compatibility of EC Member State measures with the GATT.

The Corte Suprema di Cassazione put the question squarely before the ECJ:

---

[32] [1987] ECR 3719, paras 8–12.

[33] *Amministrazione delle Finanze dello Stato v Società Petrolifera Italiana (SPI) and SpA Michelin Italiana (SAMI)* [1983] ECR 801.

As a preliminary point: Since the Community has been substituted for the Member States with regard to the fulfilment of the obligations laid down in GATT and since it negotiated the concessions and bindings made within the framework thereof before 1 July 1968, do the provisions of GATT and the schedules thus negotiated fall (and if so, since when and subject to what limitations) within the measures on the interpretation of which the Court of Justice has jurisdiction to give a preliminary ruling under Article 177 of the Treaty, even where the national court is requested to apply them or to interpret them with reference to relations between parties for purposes other than that of determining whether or not a Community measure is valid?[34]

The ECJ replied as follows:

As the Court had occasion to stress in the judgments cited, it is important that the provisions of GATT should, like the provisions of all other agreements binding the Community, receive uniform application throughout the Community. Any difference in the interpretation and application of provisions binding the Community as regards non-member countries would not only jeopardize the unity of the commercial policy, which according to Article 113 of the Treaty must be based on uniform principles, but also create distortions in trade within the Community, as a result of differences in the manner in which the agreements in force between the Community and non-member countries were applied in the various Member States.

It follows that the jurisdiction conferred upon the Court in order to ensure the uniform interpretation of Community law must include a determination of the scope and effect of the rules of GATT within the Community and also of the effect of the tariff protocols concluded in the framework of GATT. In that regard it does not matter whether the national court is required to assess the validity of Community measures or the compatibility of national legislative provisions with the commitments binding the Community . . .

The answer to be given to the question submitted is therefore that, since as regards the fulfilment of the commitments laid down in GATT the Community has been substituted for the Member States with effect from 1 July 1968, the date on which the Common Customs Tariff was brought into force, the provisions of GATT have since that date been amongst those which the Court of Justice has jurisdiction, by virtue of Article 177 of the EEC Treaty, to interpret by way of a preliminary ruling, regardless of the purpose of such interpretation . . .[35]

It should be noted that the ECJ did not say that the GATT was 'an act of one of the Institutions of the Community' within the meaning of Article 177 (new Art. 234) EC. It relied on the purpose of this provision and on the substitution of the EC for its Member States in relation to commitments under GATT. This ruling has been approved in the literature;[36] it has also been criticized.[37] It

---

[34] [1983] ECR 801, para. 11.   [35] [1983] ECR 801, paras 14–19.

[36] E.g. A. Giardina, 'International Agreements of the Member States and their Construction by the Court of Justice' in Capotorti, Ehlermann, Frowein, Jacobs, Joliet, Koopmans, Kovar (eds.) *Du droit international au droit de l'intégration. Liber Amicorum Pierre Pescatore* (Nomos, Baden-Baden, 1987), 263 at 270.

[37] E.g. T. C. Hartley, n. 24 above.

would seem that, once the ECJ had ruled that the EC had replaced the EC Member States concerning the compliance with the obligations of the GATT, the ECJ could hardly have come to another conclusion in *SPI.*

2. *The ECJ's Jurisdiction in Relation to the WTO*

In view of the 'joint competence' of the EC and its Member States, a specific issue on the ECJ's jurisdiction arises in relation to the General Agreement on Trade in Services (GATS) and the Agreement on Trade-Related Aspects of Intellectual Property Rights (TRIPS).

The issue of the ECJ's jurisdiction has been put to the ECJ by a request for a preliminary ruling in *Hermès International* on Article 50, paragraph 6 of the TRIPS Agreement dealing with procedural rules applying to judicial remedies contemplated by the TRIPS Agreement.

It should be recalled that in its *Opinion 1/94* on the EC competence to conclude the GATS and the TRIPS Agreements the ECJ rejected the European Commission view that the EC had exclusive competence to conclude these agreements. The ECJ also rejected the view of Member States that a number of clauses of the TRIPS Agreement (i.e. those relating to judicial remedies) fall within the exclusive competence of Member States. The ECJ was of the opinion that the EC and its Member States 'are jointly competent to conclude the TRIPS Agreement'.[38]

In his opinion of 13 November 1997 in *Hermès International* Tesauro AG concluded that the ECJ had jurisdiction to interpret Article 50 of the TRIPS Agreement. He relied on the fundamental requirement of a uniform interpretation and application of all provisions of mixed agreements, on the EC's international responsibility (the EC is a party to the TRIPS Agreement alongside its Member States, and this Agreement is, pursuant to Article 228 (new Art. 300) EC Treaty, binding on the EC and its Member States), the duty of the EC and its Member States to co-operate implying the duty to endeavour to adopt a common position, and the EC legal system that seeks to function and to represent itself to the outside world as a unified system.[39]

In its judgment of 16 June 1998[40] the ECJ pointed out the following. The WTO Agreement was concluded by the EC and its Member States 'without any allocation between them of their respective obligations towards the other contracting parties'. When the WTO was signed the EC Regulation on the Community trade mark, which contains provisions on safeguarding the Community trade mark by the adoption of provisional measures, had been in force for one month. The EC is a party to the TRIPS Agreement, which applies to the Community trade mark. EC Member State courts are required, when applying the remedies of the EC Regulation on the Community trade

---

[38] *Opinion 1/94*, [1994] ECR I-5267, para. 105.
[39] [1998] ECR I-3603, 3606, at paras 20–1.   [40] [1998] ECR I-3603.

mark, 'to do so, as far as possible, in the light of the wording and purpose of Article 50 of the TRIPs Agreement.' The ECJ concluded from this that it had jurisdiction to interpret Article 50 of the TRIPS Agreement.

In *Hermès* the ECJ thus managed to avoid the issue of its jurisdiction. It is however bound to face sooner or later the issue of its jurisdiction with respect to clauses of mixed agreements that cannot be regarded as coming within the EC's powers. The consequences that would result from the absence of a uniform interpretation throughout the EC of GATS and TRIPS Agreement provisions are undoubtedly 'undesirable, artificial and perhaps unworkable'.[41] One might add that if the EC, and in particular, in the absence of a determination by the EC political bodies, the ECJ fails to rule on whether and how GATS and TRIPS provisions are to be interpreted uniformly within the EC, a WTO panel or the WTO Appellate Body could very well be called upon to do so.

The challenge for the ECJ is to devise a theory to justify its jurisdiction to interpret the whole of WTO law and not just those provisions that can be regarded as coming within the EC's powers. It seems fairly obvious that such clauses can hardly be assimilated to an 'act of an institution of the Community' within the meaning of Article 177 (new Art. 234) EC.

In *Hermès* Tesauro AG noted that the EC is a party to the TRIPS Agreement *vis-à-vis* the other WTO Members and that an international agreement concluded by the EC is, pursuant to Article 228 (new Art. 300) EC Treaty, binding on *both* the EC Member States and the EC institutions. From this, Tesauro AG concluded that the EC is responsible for each part of the agreement in question. He inferred from that the ECJ's jurisdiction to give a preliminary ruling in order to ensure the uniform interpretation, and thus application, of the international provisions in question within the EC and to protect the EC interest not to be liable for breaches by one or several EC Member States.

In the relations with third countries that probably makes sense. The EC is a rather anomalous phenomenon in international law, i.e. an actor without the entirety of external powers other actors, i.e. states, usually enjoy. Except where, upon the conclusion of a mixed agreement third parties have insisted on, and the EC has accepted to make, some declaration making clear which parts of the agreement are concluded by the EC, third parties will be in a position to call the EC rather than one or several EC Member States to account. Being in part responsible for the uncertainty on who had the power to bind itself for which parts of a mixed agreement, in line with Article 46 of the Vienna Convention on the Law of Treaties the EC would probably be estopped from claiming that under its 'constitution' Member States rather than itself are bound by a given clause of a mixed agreement.

[41] P. Eeckhout, 'The Domestic Legal Status of the WTO Agreement: Interconnecting Legal Systems', 34 CML Rev. (1997) 11 at 20; the point is illustrated by telling examples.

In the relations between the EC and its Member States the ECJ's jurisdiction over clauses of mixed agreements that are not coming within the EC's powers is more difficult to justify.

In *Hermès* the Commission argued that there is no perfect and necessary parallelism between the EC's powers to enter into international agreements and the ECJ's jurisdiction to interpret such agreements. This is right but is subject to limitations. While recourse to Article 164 (new Art. 220) EC may justify the ECJ's jurisdiction to interpret an international agreement that is not binding on the EC,[42] this jurisdiction is incidental; it depends on a question of interpretation or validity of EC law for which the interpretation of such international agreement is relevant.[43] Such jurisdiction is not incidental where a Member State court requests a preliminary ruling by the ECJ on a clause of a mixed agreement that is squarely outside the scope of the EC's external powers in a case in which no EC rule or measure is at stake.

Eeckhout argues that the extension of the ECJ's jurisdiction to such cases could not affect the division of competence between the EC and the Member States.[44] This may very well be, but raises the question of the legal basis of the ECJ's jurisdiction in such cases.

Rosas distinguishes between different types of mixed agreements. He differentiates between 'parallel' and 'shared' competences of the EC and Member States. 'Parallel competence' refers to cases where the EC may adhere to an international agreement with full rights and obligations as any other contracting party, alongside Member States. Rosas cites as an example the Agreement establishing the European Bank of Reconstruction and Development open to states and the EC alike and obliging each contracting party to provide financial assistance to a third state or an international fund. 'Shared' competence refers to some division, between the EC and its Member States, of rights and obligations contained in an international agreement. Rosas cites as an example of this category an agreement containing one chapter on trade in goods and another on military defence. One can further distinguish between mixed agreements with 'coexistent' competence—i.e. containing clauses that fall under the exclusive competence of Member States—and mixed agreements with 'concurrent' competence—i.e. the agreement as a whole cannot be separated into parts covered by EC competence

[42] As in *Burgoa* [1980] ECR 2787; or in *Poulsen and Diva Navigation* [1992] ECR I-6019.

[43] According to Warner AG in *Haegeman v Belgium* [1974] ECR 449 at 473, the ECJ has jurisdiction to interpret an international Agreement only 'where its interpretation is relevant to the question of the validity of an act of a Community institution or to the question of the interpretation to be given to such an act'; in *Opinion 1/91* (First EEA Opinion) [1991] ECR 6079, para. 39, the ECJ limits its interpretation 'insofar as that Agreement is integral part of Community law'. See also the reasoning of the ECJ rejecting the challenge to its jurisdiction to interpret the Eurocontrol Agreement in *SAT v Eurocontrol* [1994] ECR I-43, para. 9.

[44] N. 41 above, at 23–4.

and parts covered by Member States' competence.[45] According to Rosas, the ECJ would be competent to interpret the whole agreement where mixing is of a 'parallel' nature and of a 'concurrent' nature.[46]

Using Rosas's terminology the difficult cases are likely to arise in relation to mixed agreements of a 'concurrent' nature. Two types of cases should be distinguished. A first case arises where neither the Council nor an international document related to the mixed agreement identify those parts of the mixed agreement that are covered by EC competence. A second case arises where Member States insist on the identification of those parts of the agreement that are covered by EC competence or, alternatively, where the EC accepts requests of third countries to that effect.

In the first type of cases the absence of identification of the parts of the mixed agreement that are covered by EC competence and thus of Member States' competence may indicate that Member States' participation is more symbolic than real. In that event there does not seem to be any serious objection to the ECJ's jurisdiction. Alternatively it may indicate that the Council could not agree on where to draw the line between EC and Member States' competences. Arguably that means that ultimately it is incumbent on the ECJ to resolve this issue and by the same token to define whether it has jurisdiction.

In the second type of cases, i.e. where the parts of the agreement covered by EC or Member States' competences are clearly identified, the ECJ could conceivably justify its jurisdiction to interpret the parts of the agreement covered by Member States via the EC Member States Community loyalty duty laid down in Article 5 (new Art. 10) EC. It does not appear inconceivable to infer from Article 5 EC the duty for Member States to apply clauses of mixed agreements uniformly in view of the consequences which would result from disparate interpretations by Member States and thus the ECJ's jurisdiction to ensure such uniform interpretation. This may appear as a second-best remedy[47] but it would be a remedy for difficulties created by the recourse to mixed agreements, which is itself a second-best formula.

The Mandate of Article 164 EC Treaty

Article 164 (new Art. 220) EC provides that:

[t]he Court of Justice shall ensure that in the interpretation and application of this Treaty the law is observed.

[45] A. Rosas, 'Mixed Union—Mixed Agreements' in M. Koskenniemi (ed.), *International Law Aspects of the European Union* (Kluwer Law International, The Hague, London, Boston, 1998), 125 at 129–31.
[46] Ibid., at 141.
[47] Which S. Prechal called 'a magic box; the amalgam of all sorts of obligations which can be pulled out of a hat as one pleases', Note in 29 CML Rev. (1992), 374 at 375.

Article 173 (new Art. 230) EC mentions among the grounds of illegality governing applications for annulment of EC acts: 'infringement of any rule of law relating to the application of the Treaty'. It is generally accepted that these grounds of illegality apply for the other methods of challenging EC acts.[48]

In *International Fruit*,[49] the first case in which it was faced with an alleged conflict between an EC measure and the GATT, the ECJ had to examine whether the 'validity' of the EC measure also referred, within the meaning of Article 177 (new Art. 234) EC, to its validity under international law. The ECJ held that this jurisdiction 'extends to all grounds capable of invalidating those measures' and that:

the Court is obliged to examine whether their validity may be affected by reason of the fact that they are contrary to a rule of international law . . . provided that the EC is bound by that rule of international law.[50]

The ECJ did not refer to Article 164 (new Art. 220) EC, although Mayras AG had done so in his opinion.

The question arises whether in reviewing EC measures as against an international law rule the ECJ is interpreting and applying EC law. Kapteyn, a member of the ECJ, argues that this is the case and that it must be: there is an implicit premise in the ECJ's reasoning i.e. the international law rule is part of EC law and may thus be interpreted and applied by the ECJ.[51]

Another interpretation is however possible in light of Article 164 (new Art. 220) EC. When interpreting and applying EC law, the ECJ is called upon to review it by reference to 'the law'. This 'law' may be the EC Treaty itself or general principles common to the laws of the EC Member States which are considered by the ECJ as part of EC law. As results from Article 164 (new Art. 220) 'the law' to be observed does not necessarily coincide with 'this Treaty'.[52] Members of the ECJ have argued by reference to Article 164 EC that, in seeking to resolve disputes by judicial process the ECJ may take into consideration every relevant legal factor, whatever its nature and sources.[53] Arguably, Article 164 EC does not require that the 'law' to which it refers be part of EC law in order to be relied upon by the ECJ when interpreting and applying EC

---

[48] E.g. Schermers and Waelbroeck, n. 30 above, at 193; with respect to validity see G. H. Krück in Groeben, Thiesing, Ehlermann, n. 29 above; see also M. J. Hahn and G. Schuster, 'Le droit des Etats Membres de se prévaloir en justice d'un accord liant la Communauté' (1995) RGDIP 367 at 369.

[49] [1972] ECR 1219.   [50] Ibid., paras 6 and 7.

[51] 'Quelques réflexions sur les effets des accords internationaux liant la Communauté dans l'ordre juridique communautaire' in *Hacia un nuevo orden internacional y europeo. Estudios en homenaje al Profesor Don Manuel Díez de Velasco* (Technos, Madrid, 1993), 1007 and 1009.

[52] G. H. Krück in Groeben, Thiesing, Ehlermann, n. 29 above, at 374.

[53] P. Pescatore, A. Donner, R. Monaco, H. Kutscher, 'Aspects of the Court of Justice of the European Communities of interest from the point of view of international law' 32 ZaöRV (1972) 239–46.

law. If one takes the monist view defended by Kapteyn that international law binding on the EC is incorporated in EC law,[54] the issue becomes moot.

It is interesting to note that in certain judgments the ECJ interpreted EC law by reference to international law or reviewed EC measures against international law as a matter of course without examining whether such international law was incorporated in EC law. In the *Radio Tubes* case,[55] for the purpose of interpreting Article 234 (new Art. 307) EC, the ECJ referred to a principle of international law that has since then been codified in Article 30 of the Vienna Convention on the Law of Treaties. In the *Woodpulp* case, the ECJ relied on 'the territoriality principle as universally recognized in public international law' to control the EC's jurisdiction to apply its competition rules.[56] In *Opel Austria* the Court of First Instance of the EC considered that 'the principle of good faith, a rule of customary international law, is binding on the Community' and may be relied upon by private parties.[57] It remains to be seen whether the same applies to international agreements binding on the EC.

III THE STATUS OF INTERNATIONAL AGREEMENTS IN EC LAW

The question of the status of international agreements in EC law has two aspects which are not always properly distinguished: on the one hand, the relationship between international law and EC law; on the other, the effect of international law in the EC legal system.

The Relationship between International Law and EC Law

1. The Problem

As is well known, traditionally one distinguishes two approaches to the relationship between international law and national law: the 'monist' and the 'dualist' theories. Basically they relate to the question whether ('monism') or not ('dualism') an international agreement applies as such in the national legal system.

There are intermediate forms; for example, among the EC Member States[58] there are three different approaches. In a first category (e.g. Belgium, France, the Netherlands) an international agreement entered into by the state that has been duly approved by the state and has entered into force in the international

---

[54] Kapteyn, n. 51 above, at 1010.   [55] [1962] ECR 10.

[56] *Åhlström e.a. v Commission*, [1988] ECR 5243.

[57] [1997] ECR II-39, paras 90 and 93.

[58] See F. G. Jacobs, 'Introduction' in F. G. Jacobs and S. Roberts (eds.) *The Effects of Treaties in Domestic Law* (Sweet & Maxwell, London, 1987), XXIII. This analysis referred to the then EC Member States.

plane automatically becomes part of the law of the state, without any separate act of 'incorporation' or 'transformation' being required. In a second category (e.g. Germany and Italy) an international agreement has, of itself, no effect in the internal legal system and requires a legislative act in order to produce that effect. Once such act is passed the international agreement is applicable as such. In a third category (e.g. Denmark and the UK) the effect of an international agreement is dependent upon a process of transformation: an international agreement, as such, has no effect, and the effect is produced only by national rules which purport to incorporate the international agreement.

The dualist approach very often results from theories defended[59] and options taken in a given historical setting and at a time where international agreements dealt mainly with *inter*-state matters. However, the fact that nowadays international agreements deal increasingly with *intra*-state matters may precisely be used as an argument to justify a dualist approach. Such international agreements touch on matters regulated by national law; yet, parliaments are not involved in the treaty-making process. Parliaments may wish to adapt the international agreement to tailor it to national circumstances. They may want to impose their interpretation of the international agreement for the purposes of national law.[60]

There are thus two categories of arguments put forward in favour of a dualist approach: those that are derived from democratic principles and those that relate to the desire of a state to modulate as it sees fit the effect of an international agreement in its national legal system. The arguments of the first category are not entirely convincing. It is possible to involve parliaments at national level in the negotiating process. Moreover, constitutions that do not require specific legislation to incorporate an international agreement in the national legal system provide that certain categories of international agreements are not binding on the state or have no effect in the national legal system in the absence of some form of parliamentary approval. The arguments of the second category are somewhat dubious in that they appear to reserve the possibility of departing from international obligations. If that is the purpose, the right approach is to negotiate a proper clause or to enter reservations to that effect rather than to do so by the back door.

In the EC the situation is at the same time more simple and more complicated. The EC Treaty does not pronounce on the effects of an international agreement in the EC legal system. Under the decision-making process set forth by the EC Treaty, EC Member States have a built-in guarantee that

---

[59] Ch. Sasse recalls the theories put forward by Triepel, Anzilotti, and Kelsen in 'The Common Market: Between International and Municipal Law' 75 *Yale L.J.* (1966), 695 at 712–13.

[60] See J. H. Jackson, 'Status of Treaties in Domestic Legal Systems: A Policy Analysis' 86 Am. J.Int. L. (1992), 310 at 323–5.

their interests will be duly taken into account,[61] since international negotiations are concluded by the Council consisting of representatives of Member States.

One may object that the instances in which international agreements are concluded by the Council acting by qualified majority increase and parliamentary control of the Member States in the minority will not prevent the international agreement from having effect in those Member States. This however is 'compensated' by increased involvement of the European Parliament. The EC Treaty now provides that the European Parliament must be consulted before the conclusion of international agreements (Art. 228(2) (new Art. 300)) (except for international agreements based on Article 113(3) (new Art. 133)) (Art. 228(3)—in practice the European Parliament is usually consulted even on these agreements). Moreover certain types of international agreements now require the assent of the European Parliament (association agreements; agreements establishing a specific institutional framework by organizing co-operation procedures; agreements having important budgetary implications for the EC; agreements entailing amendments of an act adopted under the co-decision procedure) (Art. 228(3)).

It has been said that the European Parliament does not offer an effective substitute as a result of its limited powers, inadequate representativeness, the absence of a European political party system, and the insufficient democratic accountability of its members.[62] One begs to disagree. With respect to international agreements as indicated one can no longer argue that the European Parliament's powers are 'limited' and at any rate that they would be more limited than those of national parliaments. One fails to see in what sense its representativeness is inadequate. As to a European political party system, one wonders whether this is a necessary element: is there really in the USA a political party system similar to those in the EC Member States? Quite obviously the MEPs' democratic accountability could be improved. The question, however, is whether members of national parliaments are more accountable to their constituencies than to their party. Petersmann recognizes this as he pleads for a foreign policy constitution that does not replicate the constitutional failures of nation states.[63]

This having been said, an international agreement that has entered into force and that has been properly 'concluded' by the EC is as such part of EC

---

[61] See e.g. J. H. J. Bourgeois, 'Trade Policy-making Institutions and Procedures in the European Community' in M. Hilf and E. U. Petersmann (eds.), *National Constitutions and International Economic Law* (Kluwer, Deventer, 1993) 175 at 191; see also D. McGoldrick, *International Relations Law of the European Union* (Longman, London and New York, 1997), 89–92.

[62] E. U. Petersmann, 'Proposals for a New Constitution for the European Union: Building Blocks for a Constitutional Theory and Constitutional Law of the EU', 32 CMLRev. (1995), 1123 at 1126.

[63] Ibid., at 1140.

law according to the case law of the ECJ, from *Haegeman*[64] to *Racke*.[65] This approach of the ECJ has been generally approved in the legal literature.[66]

There is a debate in the literature on whether the ECJ is following a dualist or a monist approach. According to Pescatore, the case law analysed by him can only be explained within a pragmatic monistic theory.[67] Other writers consider that the ECJ is tending towards a dualist approach.[68] Still others take the view that it is not possible to provide a general answer to the question of the relationship between EC law and public international law[69] or that recourse to dualist and monist theories is unproductive.[70]

It would seem that the debate rests on a certain view of what monism and dualism mean. In our view, under the monist approach an international agreement is as such part of the EC legal system once the EC's 'constitutional' procedures required for the EC to be bound internationally have been complied with; in other words in order to have effect in the EC legal system the international agreement does not need to be transformed in a regulation or a directive.[71] In that sense, it would seem that the ECJ has followed a monist approach from *Haegeman* to *Racke*. As will be seen, this does not mean that EC international agreements are assimilated without further ado to EC law.

---

[64] [1974] ECR 449: 'the [Association] Agreement [with Greece] was concluded by the Council under Articles 228 and 238 of the Treaty . . . The Agreement is therefore, in so far as concerns the Community, an act of one of the institutions of the Community . . . The provision of the Agreement, from the coming into force thereof, form an integral part of Community law.'

[65] [1998] ECR I-3655: 'An agreement with a third country concluded by the Council in conformity with the provisions of the EC Treaty, is, as far as concerns the Community, an act of Community institutions and the provisions of such Agreement form an integral part of Community law' (para. 41).

[66] See Ch. Tomuschat ad Article 228 in Groeben, Thiesing, Ehlermann, n. 29 above, vol. 4 at 502 and literature cited; *contra* T. Hartley n. 24 above, at 383.

[67] P. Pescatore, 'Die Rechtsprechung des Europäischen Gerichtshofs zur innergemeinschaftlichen Wirkung Völkerrechtlicher Abkommen' in *Völkerrecht als Rechtsordnung, Internationale Gerichtsbarkeit, Menschenrechte—Festschrift Mosler* (Springer, Berlin, 1986) 661–89; this view is shared by E. U. Petersmann, 'Constitutional Principles Governing the EEC's Commercial Policy' in M. Maresceau (ed.), *The European Community's Commercial Policy after 1992: the Legal Dimension* (Martinus Nijhoff, Dordrecht, 1992) 21 at 36; K. J. Kuilwijk, *The European Court of Justice and the GATT Dilemma* (Nexed Editions Academic Publishers, Beunougen, 1996), 84.

[68] E.g. T. Hartley, n. 24 above; A. Th. S. Leenen, *Gemeenschapsrecht en Volkenrecht* (T. M. C. Asser Instituut, den Haag, 1994), 74–5 and literature cited.

[69] E.g. K. Meessen, 'The Application of Rules of Public International Law within Community Law' 13 CML Rev. (1976) 485 at 500–1; P. Verloren van Themaat, 'The Impact of the Case Law of the Court of Justice of the European Communities on the World Economic Order', *Festschrift Eric Stein* 82 Mich. L. Rev. (1984), 1423 at 1435.

[70] U. Everling, 'The Law of the External Economic Relations of the European Community' in M. Hilf, F. Jacobs and E. U. Petersmann, *The European Community and the GATT* (Kluwer, Deventer, 1986), 85 at 95.

[71] See Chapter 3 above.

However, the ECJ has never explained why an international agreement forms an integral part of EC law as a result of the fact that such agreement is concluded by the EC. Pescatore refers to Article 228 (new Art. 300) (E)EC and states: '[a]s a consequence these agreements have to be considered as being an integral part of the law applicable inside the Community'.[72] But Article 228 EC only provides that international agreements are binding on the EC and EC Member States.[73] Article 228 EC is in fact stating the obvious as far as the EC institutions are concerned and it is an application of the Community loyalty clause as far as Member States are concerned.[74] Quite clearly, the act whereby the Council approves the conclusion is not considered by the ECJ as a 'normative act'. In *Bresciani*[75] it held that a private party could rely on the Convention of Yaounde even though its conclusion had been approved by way of a 'decision' rather than by way of a regulation which is by definition 'directly applicable'. Against the background of *Bresciani* the Council has maintained its non-consistent practice of approving the conclusion of international agreements by way of 'decisions' or regulations making at least clear that it considers the type of the legal act as irrelevant for the status of international agreements in the EC legal system.

2. What Does 'Integral Part' of EC Law Mean?

Having seen that according to the ECJ international agreements form an integral part of the EC legal system, the question then arises what 'integral part' means, and what the ECJ has said and not (yet) said about this.

Forming an integral part of the EC legal system may mean becoming EC law. Whether this is the case has divided legal writers.[76] This is not just of academic interest: it has implications for the interpretation of international agreements (EC law methods or international law methods?) and for their hierarchical status in the EC legal system (does the *lex posterior priori derogat* principle apply when an EC legal act of a later date conflicts with the international agreement?). The extent to which an international agreement forms an integral part of EC law depends also on how far it is assimilated to EC law.

---

[72] 'Treaty-making by the European Communities' in F. G. Jacobs and Sh. Roberts, n. 58 above, 171 at 179.

[73] For the same assumption see O. Jacot-Guillarmod, *Droit communautaire et droit international public* (Georg, Librairie de l'University, Genève 1979), 92, who elsewhere refers to 'la forte connotation moniste' of Article 164 EC. But isn't the question precisely whether the 'law' referred to in Article 164 (new Art. 220) EC includes international law?

[74] Ch. Tomuschat ad Art. 228 in Groeben, Thiesing, Ehlermann, n. 29 above, at 501; R. Kovar, 'Les accords liant les Communautés européennes et l'ordre juridique communautaire: à propos d'une jurisprudence de la Cour de Justice' (1974) RMC 345.

[75] [1976] ECR 129.

[76] See literature cited by Jacot-Guillarmod, n. 73 above, at 104–5.

(a) Interpretation

Some of the implications of international agreements 'forming integral part of Community law' became apparent in *Polydor*.[77] RSO Records Inc. and Polydor Ltd., respectively the UK owner and the executive UK licensee of the copyright of a sound recording entitled 'Spirits Having Flown' and featuring The Bee Gees, had brought an action in the UK courts against Harlequin Record Shops Ltd., a retailer. The retailer sold in the UK records reproducing the same song by the same group; these records had been produced and marketed in Portugal—before Portugal's accession to the EC—by two Portuguese licensees of RSO, the UK copyright owner.

As was established during the proceedings, Simons and Harlequin, respectively the importer-wholesaler and the retailer of the Portuguese records, had by their acts infringed section 16(2) of the UK Copyright Act of 1956. That provision, which implements the territoriality principle of the protection of copyrights, provides that a copyright is infringed by any person who, without the licence of the owner of the copyright, imports an article into the UK, if to his knowledge the making of that article constituted an infringement of that copyright, or would have constituted such an infringement if the article had been made in the place into which it was so imported. Harlequin and Simons claimed, however, that under EC law Polydor was not entitled to enforce the rights conferred upon it by section 16(2) of the Copyright Act. To that purpose they relied on the 1972 Free-Trade Agreement between the EEC and Portugal and in particular on two provisions thereof—Articles 14(2) and 23—on elimination of restrictions on trade between the two parties. These provisions are expressed in terms similar to those of the EC Treaty on the abolition of restrictions on trade within the Community (Articles 30 and 36 (new Arts. 28 and 30)). There is no doubt that if the records had as in this case been lawfully produced and marketed by a licensee in one of the EC Member States instead of Portugal, the EC Treaty provisions as interpreted by the ECJ would have prevented the enforcement by RSO Records and Polydor of their UK copyrights.[78]

---

[77] *Polydor v Harlequin Record Shops Ltd* [1982] ECR 329.

[78] In a series of decisions involving industrial and commercial property rights, the ECJ developed the doctrine of 'exhaustion of rights'. Article 36 (new Art. 30) of the EC Treaty, which permits restrictions in intra-Community trade where such restrictions are justified to protect industrial and commercial property rights, does not cover the right under national law to prevent importation from another Member State of products protected by an industrial or commercial property right in the importing Member State, if these products have been lawfully made and sold in the exporting Member State by the holder of the right or with his permission. See, with respect to copyrights, *Dansk Supermarked A/S v A/S Imerco* [1981] ECR 181; *Musik-Vertrieb Membran GmbH v GEMA* [1981] ECR 147; *Deutsche Grammophon Gesellschaft mbH v Metro-SB-Grossmärkte & Co.* [1971] ECR 487.

The ECJ first stressed the structural differences between the EEC Treaty and the Agreement. Referring to its case law interpreting the EEC Treaty provisions, the ECJ emphasized that its scope 'must indeed be determined in the light of the Community's objectives and activities' and recalled that 'the Treaty, by establishing a common market and progressively approximating the economic policies of the Member States, seeks to unite national markets into a single market having the characteristics of a domestic market'.[79] In contrast, the Portugal Agreement, 'although it makes provision for the unconditional abolition of certain restrictions . . . and measures having equivalent effect', does not have the same purpose as the EEC Treaty.[80] Second, there is also, according to the ECJ, an institutional difference. A distinction as to interpretation between EEC Treaty provisions and similarly worded provisions of the Portugal Agreement 'is all the more necessary inasmuch as the instruments which the Community has at its disposal in order to achieve the uniform application of Community law and the progressive abolition of legislative disparities within the common market have no equivalent in the context of the relations between the Community and Portugal'.[81]

This led to the conclusion that, unlike Articles 30 and 36 (new Arts 28 and 30) of the EEC Treaty, concerning intra-Community trade, the similarly worded provisions of the Portugal Agreement do not exclude a prohibition, based on the protection of copyright, on the importation into the EC of a product originating in Portugal.

From the absence of transposition of the case law on EC law provisions, the following general indications may reasonably be inferred. Existing interpretations relating to similarly worded EC law provisions are useful only to the extent that they do not relate to the purpose of the EC Treaty, which seeks to create a single market reproducing as closely as possible the conditions of a domestic market. This is particularly relevant for provisions of international agreements relating to charges on imports other than customs duties, to measures applying specifically to imported products other than import bans or import quotas, to discrimination in taxation and in domestic legislation on manufacturing, marketing, and so on, to competition, and to state aid. To be compatible with an international agreement, it will be sufficient that a measure having a restrictive effect on trade be either justified by an exception or a derogation or pursue an aim which is legitimate under the agreement. Neither the restrictive effect[82] nor the aim[83] of such a measure

---

[79] [1982] ECR 329, para. 16.   [80] Ibid., para. 18.

[81] Ibid., para. 20. Such an approach finds support in international law. See Schermers, *'The Direct Application of Treaties with Third States: Note Concerning the* Polydor *and* Pabst *Cases'* 19 CML Rev. (1982), 563 at 568.

[82] See the distinction between intra-Community trade and trade with third countries made in *International Fruit*, [1971] ECR 1107. See also *EMI* [1976] ECR 811.

[83] In *Polydor* [1982] ECR 329, the injunction restraining the sale and distribution of the

will be weighed against the broader objectives of the agreement. This kind of assessment, in which considerations of expediency have a large part to play, is left to the contracting parties.

In *Polydor*, the ECJ thus made it clear that clauses of international agreements mirroring provisions of the EC Treaty, while 'forming integral part of Community law', were not, for that reason, to be interpreted in the same fashion. In other words, they remain international law for the purpose of their interpretation: they are interpreted by using the customary rules of interpretation of public international law as codified in Articles 31 and 32 of the Vienna Convention on the Law of Treaties. This leads the ECJ in particular to distinguish the EC context from the context of the international agreement entered into by the EC.

Obviously, this does not mean that clauses of international agreements mirroring provisions of the Treaty will never be interpreted in the same fashion.[84]

(b) Hierarchical Ranking of International Agreements

It is now well established that in the event of a conflict between an international agreement and the EC Treaty itself, the international agreement does not take precedence. This has been made clear by the ECJ in *Opinion 1/91* on the Agreement establishing the European Economic Area (EEA) between the EC and EFTA countries. The ECJ found that the jurisdiction conferred on the EEA Court was incompatible with EC law. It was likely to adversely affect the allocation of responsibilities defined, *inter alia*, by the European Communities Treaties and, hence, the autonomy of the EC legal order and the Agreement had 'the effect of introducing into the EC legal order a large body of legal rules which is juxtaposed to a corpus of identically-worded Community rules'.[85] In other words, before the EEA Agreement could lawfully be entered into, the European Communities Treaties had to be amended. The implication is that the Treaties are the 'constitution' of the EC and that international agreements which conflict with the Treaties cannot take precedence over these Treaties. The Maastricht Treaty amended Article 228 (new Art. 300), whose paragraph 6 is to be seen as drawing the formal consequence from *Opinion 1/91*.[86]

---

imported records was tantamount to an import ban. The aim which the restrictive measure pursued, i.e. the protection of the copyright, was accepted; the ECJ did not examine whether this aim and the restrictive effect of the measures outweighed the objectives of the Agreement.

[84] In fact, judgments interpreting such clauses in the same fashion as EC provisions are more numerous from *Bresciani* [1976] ECR 129 to *Opel Austria* [1997] ECR II-39.

[85] [1991] ECR I-60791, paras 35, 36, and 42; for a comment see M. A. Gaudissart, 'La porté des avis 1/91 et 1/92 de la Cour de Justice des Communautés européennes relatifs à la création de l'Espace Economique Européen', (1992) Rev.M.U.Eur 121 (No. 2).

[86] Tomuschat, n. 66 above, at 511.

There are some early *obiter dicta* to the effect that according to the ECJ in case of conflict between an international agreement and EC secondary law the former takes precedence over the latter.[87] As other courts usually do, the ECJ makes every effort to interpret EC law so as to avoid a conflict between an EC measure and international obligations.[88] So far, subject to the cases referred to in the next section, the ECJ has not found a conflict between an EC measure and an international agreement. The prevailing view in the literature is that, in the event of conflict, international rules binding on the EC take precedence over inconsistent EC secondary law.[89] To the extent that one supports a monist approach, the precedence of international rules over inconsistent EC secondary law is a logical consequence. Much depends, however, on the effect recognized to international rules, and more particularly international agreements, in the EC legal system.

The Effect of International Agreements in the EC Legal System

This question is about the various functions which international agreements may have as legal rules under which courts—EC Member State courts and EC courts—review measures of the EC and of its Member States. The effect of international law in the EC legal system, and in any national legal system for that matter, has many aspects which cannot be limited to the sole question whether international law gives rise to individual rights that may be enforced in national courts.[90] The issue addressed here is probably the most important one: once an international agreement forms integral part of EC law, can it be relied upon as such in court or does it have to meet certain requirements in order to be successfully relied upon to challenge the legality of an EC act?

1. Reliance on an EC International Agreement in an EC Member State Court

Quite obviously, there are legal rules that are not as such capable of being applied by courts either on account of their preparatory nature or because their general nature needs further legislation. In order to be relied upon in an EC Member court, an EC law provision must meet certain requirements. In

---

[87] From *International Fruit* [1972] ECR 1219, para. 7 to *Germany v Council* [1994] ECR I-5039, para. 111.

[88] From *Carciati* [1980] ECR 2773, para. 2 to *Poulsen and Diva Navigation* [1992] ECR I-6019, para. 16.

[89] E.g. O. Jacot-Guillarmod, n. 73 above, at 120; J. Krück, n. 29 above, at 386; P. Pescatore, n. 72 above, at 182; H. Schermers in Commission of the EC (ed.), *Thirty Years of Community Law* (OOPEC, Luxembourg, 1981), 241 at 253; Schermers and Waelbroeck, n. 30 above, at 217; C. Tomuschat, n. 66 above, at 512.

[90] See e.g. with respect to WTO rules Eeckhout, n. 41 above, at 13; see also P. Pescatore, who argues that the reality cannot be summarized by the insufficiently qualified questions of whether international agreements are 'applicable' within the EC and whether they are 'directly enforceable'. n. 67 above, at 663.

particular, in order to be capable of regulating the legal position of private parties before an EC Member States court, to create rights which a private party may enforce in an EC Member States court, an EC law provision must have 'direct effect', i.e. it must meet certain technical requirements:

- the provision contains a clear obligation on the Member State
- its content must be such that it can be applied by a court
- no further acts either by the EC or by Member States are required
- the provision is unconditional
- the Member State has no discretion in the implementation of the obligation.

In its landmark judgments *Van Gend en Loos* and *Costa v Enel*, the ECJ determined that where EC law provisions meet such technical requirements, they are as such enforceable in EC Member States courts because the EC 'constitutes a new legal order of international law . . . the subject of which comprise not only Member States but also their nationals'[91] and because 'the EEC has created its own legal system, which, on the entry into force of the Treaty, became an integral part of the legal system of the Member States . . .'.[92]

When the question arose as to the right of a private party to rely in a Member State court on an international agreement entered into by the EC, the ECJ used quite naturally the concept of 'direct effect'. In *Bresciani* the ECJ held that the prohibition in Article 2(1) of the Yaounde Convention on the abolition of charges having equivalent effect to customs duties was 'capable of conferring on those subject to Community law the right to rely on it before the courts' on the ground that 'this obligation is specific and not subject to any implied or express reservation on the part of the Community'.[93] It came to that conclusion having found that Article 2(1) of the Yaounde Convention met the technical requirements making it capable of being applied by a court. Following a similar reasoning as in *Van Gend en Loos* and in *Costa/Enel*, it did not consider that such technical requirements were enough: it also relied on 'the spirit, the general scheme and the wording of the Convention'.[94]

In *International Fruit*,[95] where a private party relied in court on the GATT against an EC measure, the ECJ required that a provision of international law be not only binding on the EC but also 'capable of conferring rights on citizens of the Community which they can invoke before the courts'. What this exactly meant is unclear. According to Kapteyn, this was equivalent to the term 'self-executing'.[96] Schermers criticized the ECJ for introducing an

---

[91] [1963] ECR 1 at 12.
[92] [1964] ECR 585 at 593; in *Opinion 1/91* the ECJ refers to the EEC Treaty as 'the constitutional charter of a Community based on the rule of law' ([1991] ECR I-6079, para. 21).
[93] [1976] ECR 129, para. 25.   [94] [1976] ECR 129, para. 16.
[95] [1972] ECR 1219, para. 8.
[96] 'The Domestic Law Effect of Rules of International Law within the European Community System of Law and the Question of the Self-Executing Character of GATT Rules' 8 *The International Lawyer* (1974), 74 at 76.

additional and unwarranted condition for the application of international law in EC law.[97]

As has been further clarified in subsequent judgments, when defining the relationship between international law (or at least international agreements) and EC law and, through EC law, EC Member State law, the ECJ does not use the same 'direct effect' concept which it developed to define the relationship between EC law and EC Member State law.

In *Kupferberg*,[98] the ECJ analysed Article 21 of the FTA with Portugal on which Kupferberg relied and found that it:

imposes on the Contracting Parties an unconditional rule against discrimination in matters of taxation, which is dependent only on a finding that the products affected by a particular system of taxation are of like nature, and the limits of which are the direct consequence of the purpose of the Agreement. As such this provision may be applied by a court and thus produce direct effects throughout the Community.[99]

However, before examining whether this provision of the Agreement was as such capable of being applied by a court, the ECJ verified whether 'the nature' or 'the structure' of the Agreement 'may prevent a trader from relying on the provisions of the said Agreement before a court in the Community'.[100]

In *Demirel*[101] the ECJ stated this as follows:

A provision of an agreement concluded by the Community with non-member countries must be regarded as being directly applicable when, regard being had to its wording and *the purpose* and *nature* of the *agreement* itself, the provision contains a clear and precise obligation which is not subject, in its implementation or effects, to the adoption of any subsequent measure (emphasis added).

The possibility for a private party to rely on an international agreement depends thus not only on whether the provision relied upon is technically capable of being applied by a court but also on the nature and the structure of the international agreement of which it is part. This approach has been criticized by some writers[102] and approved by others.[103]

Whether there is a real doctrinal difference between the ECJ's concept of 'direct effect' applied to EC law and the concept of 'direct application' or the 'self-executing' character applied to international agreements used by the International Court of Justice and national courts is left aside here.[104] The

---

[97] 'Community Law and International Law' 12 CMLR (1975), 77 at 80.

[98] [1982] ECR 3641.   [99] Ibid.   [100] Ibid., paras 10–22.

[101] [1987] ECR 3747, para. 14.

[102] E.g. P. Pescatore n. 72 above, at 187.   [103] E.g. C. Tomuschat n. 66 above, at 506–10.

[104] No difference: e.g. B. de Witte, 'Retour à Costa. La primauté du droit communautaire au service du droit international' (E.U.I. Working Paper No. 49, 1983) and with qualifications H. N. Tagaras, 'L'effet direct des accords internationaux de la Communauté', 20 CDE (1984) 15 at 24–5; difference: e.g. C. Tomuschat, 'Zur Rechtswirkung der von der Europäischen Gemeinschaft abgeschlossenen Verträge in der Gemeinschaftsordnung' in *Gedächtnisschrift für L.J. Constantinesco* (Carl Heymanns, Köln, 1983), 801 at 803.

practical consequences may be important; when relying on EC law provision a private party needs to demonstrate only that that provision meets the technical criteria of 'direct effect'. When relying on a clause of an EC international agreement, a private party must also demonstrate that the context of this clause, i.e. the agreement, its wording, nature, and purpose, is such as to justify 'direct effect'.

That clauses of an international agreement are as a result denied direct effect while similarly worded EC provisions are granted direct effect is not inconsistent with a monist approach, bearing in mind the different contexts in which they originate. An EC legal provision is given direct effect, regard being had to the EC context. The concept of direct effect of EC law was developed in relation to the inner workings of the EC legal order, both as a legal system of its own right and as a creation of its 'constitution' or its institutions as a 'primary instrument of integration'.[105] The specific purposes of developing this doctrine of direct effect may neither be easily nor appropriately transferred to a creation outside the EC legal system.[106] However, this does not mean, as several ECJ judgments show, that EC international agreements never have 'direct effect', i.e. never give rise to rights that are legally enforceable in EC Member State courts. Except for the GATT and the WTO, the contrary appears to be the rule.

2. Reliance on an EC International Agreement in the EC Courts

When an applicant relies in a direct action in the ECJ or the Court of First Instance of the EC on an EC rule, he need not demonstrate that such rule has 'direct effect'. There is, at any rate, no judgment that states such requirements. This is not surprising. The 'direct effect' concept was developed to define the relationship between the EC legal system and the legal systems of the EC Member States. It has arguably no place within the EC legal system: if, as the ECJ has repeatedly stated, private parties are subjects of that legal system, they are entitled to rely on any provision of that legal system, provided this provision is technically capable of being applied by a court.

The question then arises whether the ECJ would require that, in order to be relied upon in a direct appeal before it, a clause of an EC international agreement meet the same sort of 'direct effect' test as it requires where such clause is relied upon in a national court. Subject to situations in which there has been some form of legislative implementation by the EC (see below), it would seem that the same 'direct effect' test would apply: that is, the enforceability of a clause of an EC international agreement in the ECJ and in the CIF would depend not only on the technical requirements of the clause but also

---

[105] G. Bebr, 'Agreements concluded by the Community and Their Possible Direct Effect', 20 CML Rev. (1983), 35 at 66.

[106] I. Cheyne, 'International Agreements and the European Community Legal System', 18 ELR (1994), 582 at 594.

on its context—i.e. the international agreement (wording, nature, structure) of which it is part.[107] Here again this does not mean that no EC international agreement would ever pass the test. A case in point is *Opel Austria*,[108] in which the applicant challenged in the Court of First Instance a duty imposed on gearboxes manufactured by Opel Austria to counteract subsidies granted by Austria to Opel Austria. The applicant claimed, *inter alia*, that such duty infringed several clauses of the Agreement on the European Economic Area. The CFI applied only the technical test to Article 10 of the EEA Agreement to find that it had 'direct effect'.[109] It apparently took for granted that the EEA Agreement itself, its wording, nature, and purpose justified the direct effect of that Article.

EC Implementing Measures

The cases described so far are to be distinguished from cases where there is some form of legislative implementation by the EC. In *Fediol III*,[110] the applicant claimed that the Commission had misinterpreted a number of GATT provisions when it rejected the applicant's complaint lodged under the EC's so-called New Commercial Policy Instrument. The ECJ held that the applicant could rely on those provisions on the grounds that the New Commercial Policy Instrument defined 'illicit practices' against which private parties may complain, *inter alia*, by reference to the GATT. In his opinion, Van Gerven AG took the view that an international law provision which does not have direct effect *per se* may none the less be transformed within a particular legal order, by a rule of that legal order, into a rule having direct effect.[111]

In a later case, the ECJ has taken a further step. In *Nakajima*, the applicant was questioning in an incidental manner under Article 184 (new Art. 241) EC the applicability of the EC basic anti-dumping regulation by claiming that it was incompatible with Article VI of the GATT and certain clauses of the GATT Anti-dumping Code. The ECJ considered that the applicant could rely on these GATT provisions on the ground that the basic anti-dumping regulation had according to its preamble been 'adopted in order to comply with the international obligations of the Community'.[112] In one of the *Bananas* cases, the ECJ made clear that it will review the legality of an EC act under the GATT 'only if the Community intended to implement a particu-

---

[107] This seems to result clearly from one of the *Bananas* cases. Gulman AG took the view that it is not because a provision does not have direct effect in a Member State court that it may not be relied upon in a direct appeal in the ECJ ([1994] ECR I-4980, para. 135). The ECJ, however, rejected his view and applied the same test in this direct appeal as the test it applied in preliminary rulings for the purposes of application by EC Member State courts ([1994] ECR I-4973, para. 105).

[108] [1997] ECR 39.   [109] Ibid., para. 102.   [110] [1989] ECR 1781.
[111] Ibid., at 1806, fn. 8.   [112] [1991] ECR I-2069, para. 31.

lar obligation entered into within the framework of GATT, or if the Community act expressly refers to specific provision of GATT'.[113]

Thus, where a provision of an international agreement does not as such have 'direct effect', it may none the less acquire it where it is incorporated, even by reference, into EC law or where the EC makes clear when enacting legislation that it intended to implement the international agreement. It has been argued[114] that the latter exception is not logical: if an international agreement does not as such have 'direct effect' as a result of an objective test, why and how could it acquire such direct effect as a result of some statement of the Council of the European Union in an EC legal act that this act is designed to implement that agreement? The counter-argument is that where under the objective test an international agreement has no 'direct effect', this means that contracting parties have no international duty to allow its enforcement by national courts. This does not mean that a contracting party may not do so.

IV THE STATUS OF THE GATT AND THE WTO AGREEMENT IN EC LAW

The purpose of this section is to examine in light of the findings of the previous section the status of the GATT and the WTO Agreement in EC Law.

The Relationship between the GATT, and the WTO Agreement, and EC Law

It may be recalled that the ECJ has avoided stating, unlike it did for other international agreements, that the GATT 'forms integral part of Community law'. This may be due to the fact that the EC was not a contracting party to GATT 1947. The ECJ has, however, avoided this qualification also in relation to WTO Agreements.

(a) Interpretation

In view of the ECJ's stance on the effect of GATT and WTO law in the EC legal system, there is little to say about the question how GATT and WTO law are interpreted by the ECJ and about their hierarchical rank in the EC legal system.

In *Fediol II*[115] the ECJ examined the Commission's interpretation of the term 'subsidy' in light of the GATT and the Tokyo Round Subsidies Code. It

---

[113] *Germany v Council* [1994] ECR I-4973, para. 111.

[114] Ph. Manin, 'A propos de l'accord instituant l'Organisation mondiale du commerce et de l'accord sur les marchés publics: la question de l'invocabilité des accords internationaux conclus par la Communauté européenne' (1997) RTDE 399 at 409.

[115] [1988] ECR 4155, para. 12.

held that 'the Commission was not wrong or arbitrary in concluding that the concept of subsidy . . . presupposes the grant of an economic advantage through a charge on the public account'. In *Nakajima*, in which it accepted that the Tokyo Round Anti-dumping Code could be relied upon in a plea of illegality under Article 184 (new Art. 241) EC, the ECJ compared the EC Anti-dumping Regulation and the relevant international provision. It concluded that the EC Anti-dumping Regulation was in conformity with the international law provision 'inasmuch as, without going against the spirit of the latter provision, it confines itself to setting out, for the various situations which might arise in practice, reasonable methods of calculating the constructed normal value'.[116] In the *International Dairy Agreement* case the Commission brought proceedings against Germany for the latter's breach of obligations under the EC Treaty resulting from its failure to comply, *inter alia*, with the International Dairy Agreement (hereinafter the IDA), one of the agreements concluded in the framework of the Tokyo Round. Germany contended that the IDA did not cover goods imported and exported under inward processing arrangements. The ECJ rejected Germany's interpretation of the IDA on one point on the basis of the text[117] and on another point on the basis of the context of the relevant provision and of 'the general rule of international law requiring the parties to any agreement to show good faith in its performance',[118] together with the purpose of the IDA.[119] It should be noted that Germany did not argue, even in the alternative, that the IDA did not form an integral part of EC law or that it could not otherwise be relied upon by the Commission.

From this limited evidence it seems to follow that when *interpreting* GATT provisions the ECJ follows the same approach as in the case of other international agreements.

(b) Hierarchical Ranking

Although so far the ECJ has not held a provision of secondary EC law illegal for breach of a GATT or a WTO obligation, it has accepted that possibility in *Fediol II* and *Nakajima*. That possibility is, however, very limited in view of the ECJ's stance on the effect of the GATT in the EC legal system. It would very probably take the same stance as regards other WTO agreements.

The Effect of WTO Agreements in the EC Legal System

1. *Reliance on WTO Agreements in EC Member States Courts*

As already indicated, since *International Fruit* the ECJ has held that GATT and GATT agreements cannot be relied upon by private parties in EC Member State courts in order to challenge EC or national measures.

---

[116] [1991] ECR I-2069, para. 37.   [117] [1996] ECR I-3989, paras 21–4.
[118] Ibid., para. 30.   [119] Ibid., paras 31–7.

After *Nakajima,* in which the ECJ set the door to reliance on a GATT agreement ajar, one could have wondered whether the ECJ would display a similar, more open attitude with respect to enforcement of GATT and GATT agreements by Member State courts. Certainly the ECJ no longer needed to be concerned about the risk for the uniform application of EC law if Member State courts were to enforce the GATT and GATT agreements. In *Foto-Frost* the ECJ had held that a Member State court faced with a plea of illegality of an EC measure could only disapply such measures following a preliminary ruling by the ECJ to that effect.[120] The ECJ could thus ensure the uniform application of EC law in light of GATT obligations.

However, subsequent judgments, in particular the main *Bananas* judgment,[121] revealed that uniform application of EC law by Member State courts was not the ECJ's main concern. At any rate, as already indicated, the ECJ's concern about uniform application of EC law by Member State courts and beyond that the integrity of EC law in the face of international obligations acquired a new dimension in the wider WTO context. The EC and the Member States being jointly competent for concluding the GATS and the TRIPS Agreement, it is likely, as the *Hermès* case shows, that some Member State courts, will consider that provisions of these agreements may be relied upon before them and enforced by them. Less than ten days after the ECJ rendered judgment in *Hermès,* another Dutch court in another case specifically submitted to the ECJ a request for preliminary ruling on the direct effect of the same TRIPS provisions.[122] Even if an EC measure is not directly at issue, disparate enforcement by Member State courts of an international agreement, such as the TRIPS, may well have an impact on the movement of goods across Member State lines within the EC.[123]

2. Reliance on WTO Agreements in the EC Courts

As already indicated, when an applicant relies in a direct action in the ECJ or the Court of First Instance on an EC rule, he need not demonstrate that such rule has 'direct effect': this is not the case with international agreements. As has been mentioned, in the main *Bananas* case, the ECJ subjected the possibility to rely on the GATT in a direct appeal to practically the same 'direct effect' test as the test to be used by EC Member State courts for the purposes of applying international agreements.

---

[120] [1987] ECR 4199.   [121] [1994] ECR I-4973.

[122] The Hague District Court on 25 June 1998 in *Parfums Christian Dior v Tuk Consultancy* cited by M. C. E. J. Bronckers, 'The Exhaustion of Patent Rights under WTO Law', 32 JWT (No. 5, 1988), 137 at 141; see also the Dutch Supreme Court on 30 October 1998 in *Assco Holland Steigers Plettac v Wilhelm Lagher GmbH* (OJ 1999 C1/6).

[123] This is one of the reasons why the ECJ interpreted the First EC Directive on Trademarks as excluding the exhaustion theory in relation to goods put on the market by the trademark holder or with his consent outside the EC in *Silhouette* [1998] ECR I-4799.

In this case the ECJ defined the issue as 'assessing the scope of GATT in the Community legal system'. It applied the test based on 'the spirit, the general scheme and the terms of the GATT'.[124] It then stated:

106 It is settled law that GATT which according to its preamble is based on the principle of negotiations undertaken on the basis of 'reciprocal and mutually advantageous arrangements', is characterized by the great flexibility of its provisions, in particular those conferring the possibility of derogation, the measures to be taken when confronted with exceptional difficulties and the settlement of conflicts between the contracting parties.

107 The Court has recognized that those measures include, for the settlement of conflicts, depending on the case, written recommendations or proposals which are to be 'given sympathetic consideration', investigations possibly followed by recommendations, consultations between or decisions of the *contracting parties*, including that of authorizing certain contracting parties to suspend the application to any other of any obligations or concessions under GATT and, finally, in the event of such suspension, the power of the party concerned to withdraw from that agreement.

108 It has noted that where, by reason of an obligation assumed under GATT or of a concession relating to a preference, some producers suffer or are threatened with serious damage, Article XIX gives a contracting party power unilaterally to suspend the obligation and to withdraw or modify the concession, either after consulting the contracting parties jointly and failing agreement between the contracting parties concerned, or even, if the matter is urgent and on a temporary basis, without prior consultation (see Joined cases 21 to 24/72 *International Fruit Company v. Produktschap voor Groenten en Fruit* [1972] ECR 1219, paragraphs 21, 25 and 26; Case 9/73 *Schlüter v. Hauptzollampt Lörrach* [1973] ECR 1135, paragraph 29; Case 266/81 *SIOT v. Ministero delle Finanze* [1983] ECR 731, papragraph 28; and Joined Cases 267 to 269/91 *Amministrazione delle Finanze dello Stato v. SPI and SAMI* [1983] ECR 801, paragraph 23).

It concluded that:

110 The special features noted above show that the GATT rules are not unconditional and that an obligation to recognize them as rules of international law which are directly applicable in the domestic legal system of the contracting parties cannot be based on the spirit, general scheme or terms of GATT.

The end-result is that the GATT cannot be relied upon in the EC courts to challenge the lawfulness of EC measures, be it by private parties or by Member States. The ECJ added that:

it is only if the Community intended to implement a particular obligation entered into within the framework of GATT, or if the Community act expressly refers to specific provisions of GATT, that the Court can review the lawfulness of the Community act in question from the point of view of the GATT rules.[125]

---

[124] [1994] ECR I-4973, para. 105.   [125] [1994] ECR I-4973, para. 111.

Some Comments

The ECJ's case law on the GATT has been abundantly commented on in the literature. The judgment in the main *Bananas* case has likewise prompted many to put forward their views.[126] Some points should be noted in particular at this stage.

From an EC law perspective the ECJ's approach has an obvious dualist flavour: the GATT may only be relied upon against EC measures if the EC political bodies have so decided. This results from the statement in the main *Bananas* case reported earlier.[127] This stands in contrast to *Kupferberg*[128] where the ECJ considered that it was up to the courts to decide on the effect of an international agreement in the internal legal order, where contracting parties to such agreement have not agreed on this effect. By leaving it to the EC political bodies to decide on the effect in the EC legal system of the GATT, the ECJ has effectively introduced some sort of 'sovereignty shield'[129] in the hands of these political bodies against the GATT. The ECJ appears to have bowed in advance to the statement in the preamble of the Council Decision approving the WTO Agreements according to which 'the Agreement establishing the World Trade Organization, including the Annexes thereto, is not susceptible to being directly invoked in Community or Member State courts'.[130] Interestingly, Advocates General have different views on whether this statement is binding on the ECJ.[131]

From an international law perspective, the different outcomes of the 'direct effect' test as applied by the ECJ to the GATT and as applied to other EC international agreements remain puzzling. The distinctions made in the past[132] do at any rate no longer apply since the entry into force of the WTO Agreement.

---

[126] E.g. G. Berrisch, 'Zum Bananen-Urteil des EuGH vom 5.10.1994', (1994) EWR 461; M. Dony, 'L'affaire des Bananes', 31 CDE (1995) 461; F. Castillo de la Torre, 'The Status of GATT in EC Law, Revisited', 29 JWT (No. 1, 1995) 53; P. Eeckhout and S. Coppieters, 'Hoe krom zijn de bananen nu nog?', 46 SEW (1998) 402; U. Everling, 'Will Europe slip on Bananas? The Bananas Judgment of the Court of Justice and National Courts', 33 CML Rev. (1996) 401; M. J. Hahn and G. Schuster, n. 48 above; Ph. Lee and B. Kennedy, 'The Potential Direct Effect of GATT 1994 in European Community Law', 30 JWT (No. 1, 1996) 67; Ph. Manin, n. 114 above; C. Schmid, 'Immer Wieder Bananen; der Status des GATT/WTO-Systems im Gemeinschaftsrecht', (1998) NJW 189 (No. 4).

[127] [1994] ECR I-4973, para. 111.   [128] [1982] ECR 3641, para. 18.

[129] Term used in the EP's *Report on the Relationship between International Law, Community Law and Constitutional Law of the Member States* (PE 220.225/fin).

[130] OJ 1994 L 336/1.

[131] No: Tesauro AG in *Hermès*, n. 39 above; not without relevance; Cosmas AG in *Affish* ([1997] ECR I-4315, opinion para. 127); quoted by Elmer AG in support of denying 'direct effect of GATT' in *T-Port* ([1998] ECR I-1023, opinion para. 28).

[132] In *Kziber* van Gerven AG contrasted the GATT and the Co-operation Agreement with Morocco (much more restricted possibilities for adopting safeguard measures and compulsory settlement of disputes) [1991] ECR I-199.

From a WTO perspective the ECJ did not draw any consequences from the considerable change brought about by the Understanding on Rules and Procedures Governing the Settlement of Disputes (hereinafter the DSU): the settlement of disputes is compulsory and panel and Appellate Body reports are adopted by the Dispute Settlement Body, representing the WTO Members, unless there is a consensus against the adoption. As part of the WTO Agreement the DSU entered into force on 1 January 1995, that is, after the main *Bananas* judgment. However, in *Chiquita Italia* the ECJ gave its preliminary ruling on 12 December 1995 and it repeated its stance in the main *Bananas* case without even mentioning the DSU.[133] If the ECJ is to maintain its doctrine that the GATT does not meet the 'direct effect' test and extends it to other WTO agreements, it will need to devise standards, other than the standards it used up to now to deny 'direct effect' to the GATT and WTO agreements.

A Tentative Assessment

Irrespective of the merits or disadvantages of the ECJ case law on the GATT 1947 and the GATT 1994 from other perspectives, its internal logic cannot be disputed. As other international agreements, the GATT is binding on the EC as an international instrument. Its effect in the EC legal system, or as the ECJ calls it, its 'scope' (*'portée' 'Bedeutung'*), is to be determined according to rules of interpretation of public international law. In order to be relied upon to challenge the legality of EC acts that are in conflict with the GATT, its provisions must meet the requirements of 'direct effect'; that is, the provisions must be clear and unconditional, and the agreement of which they form part must be such as to justify 'direct effect' in light of its wording, nature, and purpose.

This having been said, as already indicated it is remarkable that the outcomes of the same test as applied to a series of EC international agreements and as applied to the GATT 1947 and even more so to the GATT 1994 are fundamentally different. The fairly widespread criticism which the ECJ's approach to the GATT 1947 and to the GATT 1994 met in legal literature prompts the question why, from a legal and a legal policy point of view, the ECJ is bound to, or, as the case may be, ought to accord the GATT 1994 and other WTO agreements the effect in the EC of a rule of law that may be relied upon to review the lawfulness of EC measures; and this, irrespective of whether the EC political bodies have decided to give it such effect.

1. The Legal Point of View

Regard should be had to the GATT and to the EC Treaty in order to verify whether they contain any principle or rule requiring the ECJ to recognize 'direct effect' to GATT rules.

---

[133] [1995] ECR I-4533, para. 26.

(a) Is the Denial of 'Direct Effect' of GATT Rules Inconsistent with the EC's International Obligations?

It has been argued that in denying the possibility of relying on GATT rules to challenge inconsistent EC acts, the ECJ is disregarding, even breaching, international law. One of the most outspoken advocates of this theory is Petersmann.[134] However gallant, Petersmann's efforts are not persuasive *de lege lata*. It is obvious that a number of GATT rules are perfectly capable of being applied by a court of law, as they are applied by WTO panels and the WTO Appellate Body. But this is not the point. Save for a few scattered provisions, the WTO Agreement leaves it clearly to each individual Member to decide how to comply with its obligations or, to coin the phrase used by the ECJ, to determine on its own the 'scope' ('*portée*', '*Bedeutung*') of the various agreements that form part of the WTO Agreement in its internal legal system. The only requirement on each Member is to 'ensure the conformity of its laws, regulations and administrative procedures with its obligations'[135] as provided in the WTO Agreement.

There certainly was no consensus within the WTO membership on the advisability of a clause providing how Members should incorporate WTO rules and even less so on any clause providing for domestic remedies to ensure that their laws, regulations, and administrative procedures comply with WTO obligations. A Swiss proposal made during the Uruguay Round and designed to ensure that the resulting agreements would be capable of having direct effect or some equivalent status in the national law of all participants was rejected by most big players in the negotiations and dropped.[136] Roessler's remark, made in 1990, that the citizen had so far not been seriously considered by the trade negotiators in the GATT as a candidate to enforce GATT rules[137] is still valid.

The negotiations on the dispute settlement system illustrate this. At the end of the dispute settlement process, there can no longer be any doubt about the precise substantive scope of a Member's obligation. Yet, no agreement could

---

[134] See, *inter alia*, 'Darf die EC das Völkerrecht ignorieren?' 8 EuZW (No. 11, 1997) 325; for a reply J. Sack, 'Von der Geschlossenheit und den Spannungsfeldern in einer Weltordnung des Rechts', 8 EuZW (No. 21, 1997) 650; for a rejoinder E. U. Petersmann, 'GATT/WTO—Recht: Duplik', 8 EuZW (No. 21, 1997) 651; for a second reply J. Sack, 'Noch einmal: GATT/WTO und europäisches Rechtschutzsystem', 8 EuZW (No. 22, 1997) 688.

[135] Marrakesh Agreement establishing the World Trade Organization Art. XVI:4 published in WTO, *The Results of the Uruguay Round of Multilateral Trade Negotiations, The Legal Texts* (Geneva, 1995), at 6.

[136] P. J. Kuijper, 'The New WTO Dispute Settlement System: the Impact on the Community' in Bourgeois, Berrod, Gippini-Fournier (eds.), *The Uruguay Round Results. A European Lawyers' Perspective* (EIP, Brussels, 1995), 87 at 106.

[137] F. Roessler, 'The Constitutional Function of the Multilateral Trade Order' in Hilf and Petersmann, n. 61 above, 53 at 62.

be found on a provision entitling the Dispute Settlement Body to recommend to a Member how it should comply in bringing its measures into conformity with WTO rules: a panel or the Appellate Body may only 'suggest' ways to do so.[138] There is thus no GATT/ WTO obligation that would require the ECJ to grant 'direct effect' to GATT/WTO rules.

(b) Denial of 'Direct Effect' and EC Legal Principles

One should distinguish between the position of private parties on the one hand, and that of EC Member States (and conceivably that of EC Institutions) on the other.

As far as *private parties* are concerned, Petersmann has for many years brilliantly and with unceasing determination defended the theory of the 'domestic policy functions of GATT law'.[139] He has argued, *inter alia*, that the EC's GATT obligations on the use of transparent, non-discriminatory and proportionate policy instruments must be taken into account in the interpretation of the foreign trade law of the EC.[140]

Certain constitutional law principles have been laid down in the EC Treaty such as proportionality (Art. 3(b) (new Art. 5), para. 3) and non-discrimination (Art. 6 (new Art. 12)). Are these principles to be construed as requiring the ECJ to enforce, and thus to recognize 'direct effect' to any GATT/WTO obligation? Article 6 EC which lays down the non-discrimination principle does not expressly limit its scope to citizens of EC Member States or to situations within the EC. Yet, so far, the ECJ has held that there exists in the EC Treaty no general principle obliging the EC, in its external relations, to accord to non-member countries equal treatment in all respects.[141] Similarly the ECJ has effectively held that the EC Treaty does not require according national (EC) treatment to non-EC goods.[142] This appears to be right as far as Article 6 (new Art. 12) EC as such is concerned. Relying on this provision as a mandate for the ECJ to interpret it in light of EC international obligations on non-discriminatory treatment is a circular reasoning. It presupposes that the

---

[138] Understanding on Rules and Procedures Governing the Settlement of Disputes, Art. 19:1 published in WTO, *The Results of the Uruguay Round of Multilateral Trade Negotiations* (Geneva, 1995), 404.

[139] E.g. in 'The EEC as a GATT Member—Legal Conflicts Between GATT Law and European Community Law' in Hilf, Jacobs, Petersmann, n. 70 above, 25 at 28.

[140] 'National Constitutions and International Economic Law' in Hilf and Petersmann, n. 61 above, at 20.

[141] *Faust v Commission* [1982] ECR 3745; recently *United Kingdom v Council,* judgment of 19 November 1998 (not yet reported).

[142] E.g. *EMI Records v CBS U.K.* [1976] ECR 811 where the ECJ stated that 'the provisions of the Treaty on commercial policy do not, in Article 110 *et seq.*, lay down any obligation on the part of the Member States to extend to trade with third countries the binding principles governing the free movement of goods between Member States . . .' (para. 17).

international obligation is to be interpreted as creating individual rights which are enforceable in a court of law.

The proportionality principle could possibly come into play in connection with Article 110 (new Art. 131) EC, according to which the aims of the EC's commercial policy are to contribute to the harmonious development of world trade, the progressive abolition of restrictions on international trade, and the lowering of customs barriers. Reliance on the proportionality principle to require the ECJ to enforce compliance with GATT obligations faces several hurdles. First, it implies that GATT obligations are to be subsumed in the aims set forth in Article 110 (new Art. 131) EC as a benchmark to test the proportionality of an EC trade policy measure or, more precisely, the direct objective pursued by that measure. This is far from obvious. Article 110 has been inserted in the EEC Treaty to quieten fears that had been raised in some third countries as a result of the proposal leading to the creation of the EEC.[143] This can, however, hardly be construed as a condition to which the Member States have subjected the transfer of trade policy powers to the then EEC. Second, the possible review of the lawfulness of an EC trade policy measure in light of the aims of Article 110 EC, incorporating compliance with GATT obligations, would involve assessing the proportionality of the balance struck by political bodies weighing conflicting policy objectives. The ECJ has not ruled out such weighing as being non-justiciable.[144] However, the ECJ carries out at best a marginal review. It considers that the lawfulness of a measure can be affected only if the measure is manifestly inappropriate having regard to the objective pursued.[145] The ECJ even lets such decisions stand when challenged as disproportionate in light of certain fundamental rights.[146] When fundamental rights are at stake the ECJ errs probably on the side of caution when applying the proportionality test. It let decisions stand which were arrived at by the EC political bodies with difficulty and after much debate. However, the aims of the EC's trade policy set forth in Article 110

---

[143] A. Sciolla-Lagrange, P. Herzog and Article 110 in Smit and Herzog (eds.) *The Law of the European Economic Community. A Commentary* (Matthew Bender, New York, NY, 1976); cf. U. Everling in Wohlfarth, Everling, Glaesner, Sprang (eds.), *Die Europäische Wirtschaftsgemeinschaft* (Berlin-Frankfurt a.M., 1960); J. Mégret in J. Mégret, J. V. Louis, D. Vignes, M. Waelbroeck (eds.) *Le droit de la Communauté économique européenne*, Vol. 6. (Ed. ULB, 1976), t.1, 393.

[144] E.g. in *ADBHU* ([1985] ECR 531) the ECJ reviewed rules of a Directive on the collection of waste oils in light of the principle of freedom of trade and held that their restrictive effect on that freedom did not 'go beyond the inevitable restrictions which are justified by the pursuit of the objective of environmental protection, which is in the general interest'.

[145] E.g. most recently with respect to quantitative restrictions on imports of toys from China, *United Kingdom v Council*, judgment of 19 November 1998 (not yet reported).

[146] The result in the main *Bananas* case, in which Germany relied, *inter alia*, on fundamental rights, amounts, according to Everling (n. 126 above, at 419), to granting *carte blanche* to the EC political bodies.

(new Art. 131) EC can hardly be assimilated to fundamental rights against which trade policy measures are to be reviewed via the proportionality test.

As far as *Member States* are concerned, the ECJ's ruling that the scope of GATT is such that Member States also cannot rely on its provisions to challenge the legality of an EC act has been criticized in the literature. It has been argued that the ECJ is preventing Member States from protecting themselves against their international liability for breaches of GATT/WTO law.[147] It is, to say the least, debatable that another WTO Member could call EC Member States to account for breaches of WTO rules by the EC in matters for which the EC is the proper WTO Member. In *T-Port,* another *Bananas* case, a *Finanzgericht* thought that as a result of Article 234 (new Art. 307) EC, Germany should have the power to fulfil its obligations under GATT law which takes precedence over the EC common organization of the banana market of a later date. The ECJ considered the question as irrelevant, as Ecuador, the country from which the bananas were imported, was not a party to the GATT 1947. In its opinion Elmer AG was quite rightly of the view that claims arising from GATT 1994 can only be addressed to the EC and not to the various Member States.[148] According to some writers EC Member States are acting in an '*amicus curiae*' capacity; they may be defending their own interests but they may also do so to seek to ensure that the law is observed by the EC.[149] To the extent that the ECJ would in the main *Bananas* case have assimilated Germany's *ius standi* to that of a private party, Everling's criticism would be justified. Denying a Member State the right to challenge an EC measure on account of its inconsistency with WTO law, as the ECJ did in the main *Bananas* case, while allowing the European Commission to challenge a Member State measure on account of its inconsistency with GATT law, as the ECJ did in the *IDA* case, is on balance not satisfactory, if one considers that the two situations are comparable.[150] It is true that both cases involved a breach of GATT obligations of the EC. In EC law terms both cases involved a breach of Article 228 (new Art. 300), paragraph 7 EC. They can however be distinguished. The main *Bananas* case was about the enforcement of an obligation of the EC *vis-à-vis* the GATT while the *IDA* case was about enforcement of a Member State obligation primarily *vis-à-vis* the EC. The rationale of *IDA* seems to be that it cannot be left to a Member State to appreciate autonomously whether or not to respect an obligation under the GATT.

---

[147] Everling, n. 126 above, at 423; Hahn and Schuster, n. 48 above, at 374; M. Hilf, 'The Role of National Courts in International Trade Relations' in Hilf, Petersmann, n. 61 above, 559 at 575.

[148] [1998] ECR I-1023, opinion, para. 16.

[149] Everling, n. 126 above, at 422; Hahn and Schuster, n. 48 above, at 375, Schmid, n. 126 above, at 193; doubtful: P. Manin, n. 114 above, at 409, fn. 31.

[150] See, *inter alia,* C. Schmid, n. 126 above, at 192; in the *IDA* case Tesauro AG expressed his 'misgivings' as to this approach ([1996] ECR I-3992, para. 23).

In the main *Bananas* case the rationale appears to be that the decision whether or not to respect an obligation under the GATT should be reserved for the EC.[151] Alternatively, in both cases the ECJ upholds EC law rather than international law. In *Bananas* it denies a Member State the right to challenge an EC measure as being inconsistent with an international obligation of the EC. In *IDA* it accepts the right of the Commission to challenge a Member State measure as being inconsistent with the EC decision to comply with an international obligation of the EC.

As an aside it would seem that the ECJ's stance with respect to review of trade policy decisions in general, of which its stance with respect to the exclusion of the GATT as grounds for reviewing EC trade policy measures could be one example, is not in effect out of line with the position of the judiciary in at least some of the Member States that follow a monist approach. In France the application of the '*actes de gouvernement*' doctrine[152] could very well lead to the same result. In Germany courts tend to interfere only where an individual may be affected directly by an individual executive act rather than by an international treaty, and in the field of foreign trade law courts do recognize that their own expertise in the evaluation of notions like 'public interest', 'general welfare', and others is not better than that of the Parliament or the executive.[153]

2. The Legal Policy Point of View

As far as the position of private parties is concerned, the arguments found in the literature in favour of permitting private parties to rely on GATT, now WTO, rules to challenge EC measures are attractive. One may leave aside the economic and political economy justifications;[154] they are a matter of political choice beyond the remit of the ECJ. There is however a legal policy argument. GATT and WTO law is made by states for states, but it is also made for private parties. Notwithstanding respectable arguments to the contrary,[155] at the end of the day there is something wrong with a system that on the one hand generates rules designed to regulate international trade, even it if is to regulate what states are supposed to do or not to do in matters of trade, but, on the other, denies people, affected by what states do or do not do in matters of trade, the possibility of relying on these rules to protect their interests.

---

[151] See C. Timmermans, 'The Implementation of the Uruguay Round by the EC' in Bourgeois, Berrod, Gipppini-Fournier, n. 133 above, 501 at 507.

[152] For a short description see E. Zoller, 'EEC Foreign Trade Law and French Foreign Trade Law' in Hilf, Petersmann, n. 61 above, 265 at 268.

[153] M. Hilf, 'Treaty-making and Application of Treaties in Germany', in Hilf, Petersmann, n. 61 above, 211 at 230.

[154] As some of the arguments put forward by C. J. Kuilwijk, n. 67 above, at 263–333 and by F. L. Abbott, 'Regional Integration Mechanisms in the Law of the United States: Starting Over' I *Ind. J. Global Leg. Stud.* (1993), 155.

[155] E.g. J. H. Jackson, n. 60 above.

The opposing legal policy consideration has to do with the position of EC governments. Clearly, many Member States would not welcome a review by the ECJ of EC measures against GATT/WTO rules at least at the request of private parties. In *Kupferberg* several Member States intervened in the proceeding to urge the ECJ to reply in the negative to the *Bundesfinanzhof*'s question on the direct effect of the EEC–Portugal Free Trade Agreement.[156] Interestingly, in that case the German government referred to its observations in *Polydor*, in which, alongside the Danish, French, Netherlands, and UK governments, it had supported Polydor's argument against direct effect of the EEC–Portugal Free Trade Agreement. The German government added that the structure of the Agreement and the intentions of its authors were such that infringements of a provision of the Agreement were to give rise to consultations between the two contracting parties; in view of that, it would, according to the German government, be contrary to the general scheme of the Agreement to confer direct effect on provisions of this type.[157] The message conveyed to the ECJ by the EC Member States intervening in *Kupferberg* was clear: this was a matter for governments not for courts. While in the main *Bananas* case two Member States intervened to support Germany's application, other Member States intervened in support of the Council's defence that the GATT could not be relied upon by Germany to challenge the lawfulness of the import rules for bananas. It may be recalled that when approving the conclusion of the WTO Agreement, the Council, and thus (at least a qualified majority of) Member States, stated that this agreement and the agreements forming part of it are not susceptible to being directly invoked in EC or Member States' courts. This reflects the view traditionally held by most governments of EC Member States that trade policy, as part of foreign relations, is the preserve of governments and that interference by courts is to be avoided in order to pursue fully the possibilities of resolving disputes by negotiation.

With respect to the GATT and more generally the WTO, the main policy argument why it is thought preferable not to have 'direct effect' and thus keep the EC's hands free is well known. As long as other Members do not allow private parties to rely on WTO rules in their courts, their political bodies keep their hands free. Should courts in the EC enforce GATT/WTO rules for the benefit of private parties—or Member States—the EC political bodies would have their hands tied behind their backs. This argument has, however, become significantly less persuasive. The much-vaunted flexibility of the GATT is no more. The new WTO dispute settlement system, while leaving room for negotiated settlements before the Dispute Settlement Body adopts

---

[156] As aptly recalled by P. Mengozzi, 'The Marrakesh DSU and its Implications on the International and European Level' in Bourgeois, Berrod, Gippini-Fournier (eds.), n. 133 above, 115 at 126.

[157] [1982] ECR 329 at 340.

a panel report—which it does absent a consensus against adoption—is for all practical purposes adjudication. Once a panel report—or, as the case may be, an Appellate Body report—has been adopted, discussion about who is legally right or wrong is no longer possible. The only flexibility left is about remedies; that is, comply or pay with new trade concessions.

Another policy argument put forward against 'direct effect' of GATT and more generally WTO rules is that in none of the other main WTO Members can these rules be directly enforced in national courts. This is the case, *inter alia*, in the USA and in Japan. In the USA the 'political question' doctrine[158] could be relied upon to exclude review of US laws or measures against WTO rules, if this were not excluded *de plano* by Congress. In Japan there is a general negative attitude of the courts towards arguments relying directly upon treaties and alleging conflicts between Japanese law and treaties.[159] 'Direct effect' of these rules in the EC would, it is argued, upset the balance of rights and obligations within the WTO.[160] Whether as a result the EC would necessarily be worse off from a general economic point of view is questionable. The fact is that from a political point of view a stricter enforcement of GATT/WTO rules by the EC is perceived as detrimental to the EC's interests.

From an EC Member State perspective, there is conceivably an additional policy reason why Member States should not be permitted to challenge EC trade policy measures on the grounds that they are inconsistent with the GATT and more generally the WTO. To the extent that such policy measures are decided by the Council of the European Union by qualified majority voting, EC Member States may want to avoid giving outvoted Member States a second bite at the cherry, i.e. the possibility of overturning a qualified majority decision by a judicial challenge based on the GATT or more generally the WTO, which would make compliance by the EC with its international obligations into a device protecting Member States against qualified majority decisions prejudicial to their interests. Yet, as the example of Germany's legal challenge in the main *Bananas* case shows, this is not (or no longer) a unanimous view. Germany was supported by Belgium and the Netherlands. That challenge has been followed by a challenge by the Netherlands of an EC Directive on the Legal Protection of Biotechnological Inventions on the grounds, *inter alia*, that a provision of this Directive is in breach of the TRIPS Agreement and of the WTO Agreement on Technical Barriers to Trade.[161]

---

[158] F. L. Morrison and R. E. Hudec, 'Judicial Protection of Individual Rights under the Foreign Trade Laws of the United States', in Hilf, Petersmann, n. 61 above, at 112–14.

[159] Yuji Iwasawa, 'Implementation of International Trade Agreements in Japan', in Hilf, Petersmann, n. 61 above, 299 at 344.

[160] See *inter alia* P. Kuijper in Bourgeois, Berrod, Gippini-Fournier, n. 133 above, 87 at 105 and Ph. Lee and B. Kennedy, n. 126 above.

[161] Case C 377/98 (OJ 1998 C 378/13).

Whatever may be the underlying reasons, attitudes of governments of at least some EC Member States are changing. They are obviously concerned about the possibility for them (as opposed to private parties) to rely on GATT and more generally on WTO rules in the ECJ. Yet once it is accepted that WTO obligations of the EC are relevant for the lawfulness of EC measures within the EC legal system, it is difficult to see how they would be relevant only where they would be relied upon by Member States.

3. The WTO Perspective

From a WTO perspective, as already indicated, it appears safe to assume that governments of most WTO Members are not ready to enter into commitments on enforcement of WTO rules by national courts. Yet, there is increasing pressure for more direct involvement of private parties in WTO dispute settlement proceedings. Although the WTO Dispute Settlement Understanding does not provide it, the Appellate Body considered in *Shrimp*[162] that panels could accept and consider submissions of non-governmental organizations. Moreover, in the literature there now are calls for granting private parties access to WTO dispute settlement proceedings.[163]

Leaving other considerations aside, it would seem more appropriate to grant private parties the possibility of invoking WTO rules in national proceedings than to allow private parties access to a WTO dispute settlement system that is already now overburdened. It would also be more sensible to leave it to national courts, where possible, to handle disputes about the application of WTO rules: they are better equipped to deal with the facts and are the natural forum for citizens.[164]

There is in the wider WTO context a case to be made for a change in the ECJ's approach. The main WTO Members have manoeuvred themselves into a deadlock. Everybody expects someone else to make a move with the result that nobody moves. Many years ago the ECJ faced the issue of the *ius standi* of third country exporters in direct appeals against regulations imposing anti-dumping measures. The European Commission pleaded in favour of a broad interpretation by referring to the fact that EC exporters could challenge US anti-dumping measures in the Federal Court of International Trade. The ECJ held that third country exporters had standing, even though Article 173 (new Art. 230) EC does not provide for such appeals by private parties.[165] It would obviously be naïve to think that, likewise, should the ECJ recognize 'direct effect' to WTO rules, courts in other WTO Members would as a result start

---

[162] WT/DS58/AB/R of 12 October 1998, para. 106.

[163] 'Is the WTO Dispute Settlement Mechanism Responsive to the Needs of Traders? Would a System of Private Action by Private Parties Yield Better Results?' Panel discussion, 32 JWT (No. 2, 1998), 147.

[164] *Contra*: Eeckhout, n. 41 above, at 50; Tagaras, n 104 above, at 50.

[165] *Allied Corporation* [1984] ECR 1005.

allowing private parties to rely on WTO rules. However, such a decision of the ECJ would reverberate beyond the EC borders. It would have repercussions in those WTO Members where pressure for change exists. It would break the deadlock.

Elements of a Possible New Approach

The main legal policy considerations that obviously led the ECJ to continue denying 'direct effect' to GATT provisions and would normally lead it to do so for the provisions of WTO agreements in general, weighty as they are, are counterbalanced by other legal policy considerations in favour of recognizing such effect to those provisions where they are, as such, capable of being enforced judicially.

The *Nakajima* doctrine is a step in this direction. Even though it may be characterized as an 'indirect effect',[166] it opens the door to judicial enforcement with respect to EC legislative measures intended to bring EC law in line with WTO agreements and, conceivably, to EC legislative measures in areas covered by WTO agreements, except where EC political bodies have explicitly excluded judicial enforcement.

Reassessing the general issue of the status and effect of WTO agreements in the EC legal system can at any rate not be avoided by the ECJ even if it were to maintain the stance it took in the main *Bananas* case. As illustrated by the request of a preliminary ruling by the Netherlands Supreme Court on the TRIPS Agreement[167] and the application for annulment of provisions of the EC Directive on protection of biological inventions filed by the Netherlands on the grounds, *inter alia*, of inconsistency with the same TRIPS Agreement and the WTO Agreement on Technical Barriers to Trade,[168] it is difficult to see how the ECJ could escape the dilemma it is facing. It could not even escape it where WTO agreements provisions are concerned with respect to which it held in *Opinion 1/94* that the EC and its Member States were jointly competent: it cannot simply declare that it has no jurisdiction, if it wants, as it should, to prevent the interference with the functioning of the internal market that would result in the event that these provisions are enforced judicially in certain Member States and not in others.

There is also some truth in the point made by Cottier that the dual membership of the EC and the Member States is perhaps the most important policy argument in favour of reassessing judicial policies in the EC: the costs of denying direct effect to GATT provisions amount to a real risk of turmoil within the EC legal order.[169] Cottier referred to the bananas debate in

---

[166] Eeckhout, n. 41 above, at 45–6.   [167] OJ 1999 C1/6.

[168] OJ 1998 C378/13.

[169] *The Relationship of WTO Law, National and Regional Law*, Discussion Paper. ILA International Trade Law Committee (June 1997).

Germany. In other Member States not only courts but also policy makers are of the view that judicial enforceability of WTO agreements cannot be rejected across the board. On the other hand recognizing direct effect to WTO agreements would probably also cause turmoil in other EC Member States.

Two further aspects of the issue of the status and effect of WTO agreements on the EC legal system deserve some comments: reciprocity and the relationship between EC judicial enforcement and WTO dispute settlement.

1. Reciprocity

The ECJ has dealt in the past with the reciprocity argument in connection with 'direct effect' of international agreements. In *Kupferberg* it considered that the fact that the courts of one party to an agreement do not recognize direct application, whereas the courts of the other party do so, is not in itself such as to constitute a lack of reciprocity in the implementation of the agreement.[170] The ECJ left the door ajar by using the term 'in itself'. It has been argued that national courts do not normally take reciprocity into account when interpreting international agreements or when considering the effect of international agreements in their legal system,[171] and that where they do so, as in France, they enter into almost inextricable difficulties.[172] Yet it does not seem out of order for a court to take into account possible manifest and substantial non-performance by the other party that would upset the balance of an agreement. As Mengozzi argued, in examining the *bona fide* performance of an agreement by another State, a court must not only have regard to the lack of direct effect but also more broadly to the overall behaviour of that State.[173]

There are, however, considerable practical difficulties in applying a non-reciprocity doctrine to a multilateral agreement such as the GATT or another WTO agreement. Some conclude from this that non-reciprocity should not stand in the way of enforceability by the ECJ.[174] Considering that a substantive non-performance by a contracting party to a multilateral treaty may not always permit the suspension of the EC's obligations, others are of the view that the ECJ may be much more reticent on the issue of accepting that multilateral treaties may have direct effect.[175] Montañà I Mora proposed applying the 'equilibrium principle'. This would entail a more analytical test; that

---

[170] [1982] ECR 3641, para. 19.

[171] Decaux, *La réciprocité en droit international* (C. Rousseau, Paris, 1980), *passim*.

[172] J. Groux, 'L'invocabilité en justice des accords internationaux des Communautés européennes' RTDE (1983), 203 and 212.

[173] N. 156 above, at 131.

[174] E. U. Petersmann, 'Application of GATT by the Court of Justice of the European Communities', 20 CMLRev. (1983), 397 at 433.

[175] N. Neuwahl, 'Individuals and the GATT: Direct Effect and Indirect Effects of the General Agreement on Tariffs and Trade in Community Law' in Emiliou and O'Keeffe (eds.), *The European Union and World Trade Law* (J. Wiley & Sons, Chichester, 1996), 313 at 320.

is, whether or not the granting of 'direct effect' to a precise and unconditional provision of such an agreement would substantially impair the balance of rights and obligations of the EC.[176] Such a test would obviously not be easy to apply, as it would involve assessing whether the legislation and the practice of other Members are in compliance with their WTO obligations. However, much would depend on how this test would be carried out. First, it does not seem necessary to apply the test on an individual WTO Member basis in order to verify whether, with respect to goods imported from a given WTO Member, that particular WTO Member complies with its WTO obligations. Denying enforceability of a WTO rule selectively *vis-à-vis* single WTO Members would hardly be consistent with the MFN treatment provided by the great majority of the WTO agreements. The test would rather be designed to verify whether enforcing a WTO rule would on the whole upset the balance of the EC's rights and obligations. This could be done by limiting the exercise to the EC's major trading partners. The Council of the European Union took a similar position by stating in the preamble of the Anti-dumping Regulation and the Anti-subsidy Regulation that 'in applying the rules it is essential, in order to maintain the balance of rights and obligations which the GATT Agreement establishes, that the Community take account of how they are interpreted by the Community's major trading partners'.[177]

Second, the exercise should be limited to the WTO agreement in question. This is not only to make the test more workable. It is also more appropriate: the issue is whether a provision of a given WTO agreement should be judicially enforced in light of the question whether this would upset the balance of the EC's rights and obligations. In this regard rights and obligations under other WTO agreements are hardly relevant.

In view of this a 'reciprocity' assessment should not face the ECJ with insuperable difficulties, in particular if it were requesting the defendant Council or Commission, or, as the case may be, the Commission intervening in Article 177 (new Art. 234) EC proceedings, to state why granting 'direct effect' to a provision of a given WTO agreement would upset the balance of the EC's rights and obligations under that agreement.

2. Relationship between EC Judicial Enforcement and WTO Dispute Settlement

What Eeckhout called 'connecting the judicial operators'[178] raises certain issues. He illustrated this by referring to the *Bananas* case with its various developments under the (old) GATT and subsequently under the WTO[179]

---

[176] 'Equilibrium: A Rediscovered Basis for the Court of the European Communities to Refuse Direct Effect to the Uruguay Round Agreements?', 30 JWT (No. 5, 1996), 43 at 53–4.

[177] Regulation (EC) 384/96 (OJ 1996 L 56/1); Regulation (EC) 3284/94 (OJ 1994 L 349/22) contains comparable language.

[178] N. 41 above, at 48.   [179] N. 41 above, at 31–2 and 53.

and wonders whether and when it was up to the ECJ to intervene and to state that Germany could rely on the GATT to challenge the EC import rules on bananas and, one might add, to state that private parties could also do so.

One should make several distinctions: first, between panel and Appellate Body reports adopted by the Dispute Settlement Body in general and such reports where they find that the EC breached WTO rules and, second, between pending WTO dispute settlement proceedings on alleged breaches by the EC of WTO rules and the subsequent, adopted panel or Appellate Body reports.

(a) Panel and Appellate Body Reports in General

Adopted panel and Appellate Body reports in general interpret WTO rules. It is still debated whether such interpretations are part of the WTO *'acquis'* and are binding on Members other than the parties to the dispute. In practice, however, a Member will take such interpretations into account if it wants to avoid a dispute settlement proceeding in which a panel or the Appellate Body will rely on such interpretations.

In its *Opinion 2/91* on the EEA Agreement the ECJ accepted that the EC could enter into an international agreement establishing a court with jurisdiction to settle disputes between the parties to that agreement and that such decisions of such a court would be binding on the EC, including the ECJ.[180] One could argue that where the ECJ held that GATT does not have 'direct effect', interpretations of the GATT under the dispute settlement system cannot have 'direct effect' either. This is probably correct as far as these interpretations would be relied upon to challenge the lawfulness of EC measures.[181]

(b) WTO Disputes on EC Measures

The issue of enforceability of a WTO rule in the EC legal system against an EC measure may arise at different stages: absent, pending, or after a WTO dispute settlement proceeding on such an EC measure.

In the absence of a dispute settlement proceeding, the ECJ could maintain its stance on the non-enforceability of the WTO rule on which a private party or a Member State relies to challenge an EC measure allegedly in breach of that WTO rule, arguably by using the reasons it gave in the main *Bananas* case. At that stage, in the face of another Member's allegations of a breach of a WTO rule, the EC has a number of avenues open to it: it can seek a negotiated solution with that Member; under the GATT it can request a waiver; it can 'unbind' customs duties; it can, if the conditions are fulfilled, take a safeguard measure under one of the escape clauses, etc. A good argument could be made that it would be premature for the ECJ to recognize enforceability of the WTO rule in the EC legal system with the normal consequence that it would declare the EC measure unlawful.

---

[180] [1991] ECR I-6079.   [181] *Acc.* Eeckhout, n. 41 above, at 52.

When a dispute settlement proceeding is initiated, as the respondent Member the EC still has many avenues open to it to find a solution to avert the subsequent adoption by the Dispute Settlement Body of an adverse panel or Appellate Body report. There is a possible additional argument against the ECJ enforcing at this stage the WTO rule against the EC measure: the need to avoid conflicting decisions of two adjudicating bodies where both are seized by cases in which the lawfulness of the same measure is called into question. This argument is less persuasive. It would not seem impossible for the ECJ to stay the proceedings pending the outcome of the WTO dispute.[182]

Once a panel or an Appellate Body report finding that an EC measure is in breach of a WTO rule is adopted by the Dispute Settlement Body, there still are arguments *pro* and *contra* enforceability of the relevant WTO rule within the EC legal system. One of the arguments is derived from EC law: a declaration by the ECJ that an EC measure is unlawful operates as a rule *ex tunc*. However, compliance with WTO law does not require this. The Member, whose measure is found to be inconsistent with a WTO agreement, is bound to bring the measure into conformity with the agreement:[183] decisions of the Dispute Settlement Body are prospective. The ECJ could rely on Article 174(2) (new Art. 231) EC and decide likewise.

Even assuming that the 'pay' option is not a measure of last resort, once a breach of a WTO rule is established by the Dispute Settlement Body that option can no longer justify denying enforceability of the WTO rule in the EC legal system. If that were the case, hardly any international agreements, would be enforceable in the EC legal system. Moreover, in the event that the ECJ wanted to take the option into account, it could probably do so by ruling pursuant to Article 174(1) (new Art. 231) EC that the effects of the EC measure are maintained pending the exercise by the EC of that option.

SOME CONCLUSIONS

The ECJ faces a series of challenges with respect to GATT and WTO agreements in general.

The first challenge is about the jurisdiction. As a result of both the mixed WTO membership of the EC and its Member States and the 'joint competence' of the EC and the Member States for most of the matters covered by the General Agreement on Trade in Services (GATS) and the Agreement on Trade-Related Aspects of Intellectual Property Rights (TRIPS), the ECJ will face squarely—without being able to avoid it as in *Hermès*—the issue of its

---

[182] See for some cases K. P. E. Lasok, *The European Court of Justice, Practice and Procedure*, 2nd edn. (Butterworth, London, 1994), at 72.

[183] *Understanding on Rules and Procedures Governing the Settlement of Disputes*, Art. 19(1) in WTO, *The Uruguay Round Results. The Legal Texts* (Geneva, 1995), 404.

jurisdiction over matters which justified, or even required, according to conventional views, Member States' participation in so-called mixed agreements and with respect to which EC rules have been enacted. There are two options for the ECJ.

The first option is to take a narrow approach: the ECJ could declare it has no jurisdiction whatsoever over GATS and TRIPS provisions coming within the scope of Member States' powers and leave it to the Member States and the EC political bodies to sort out the rather messy situation both within the EC and *vis-à-vis* other WTO Members. The ECJ could conceivably make a distinction between situations that are purely internal to a Member State and those that are not, and not exercise jurisdiction in the former type of situations. The result would be that provisions of GATS and TRIPS would be interpreted differently depending on the situation. Apart from the fact that this would be hardly conducive to legal certainty, one may wonder how a different meaning to one and the same provision of the GATS or the TRIPS could work where implementation within the EC context and in a purely national context may be inextricably linked. An additional drawback of this option is that it would be up to the ECJ to draw the line dividing EC and Member States' external powers. This would be a difficult but more importantly a politically controversial exercise. The EC political bodies and Member States find the mixed agreements formula convenient. It is a solution of creative ambiguity that avoids talmudic discussions and difficult decisions. It also allows escape from casting in stone the division of external powers which needs to be flexible enough to cater for evolving policy requirements.

The second option is for the ECJ to take jurisdiction without, however, on the one hand, calling into question its *Opinion 1/94* on the results of the Uruguay Round and, on the other, pre-empting a decision of the EC political bodies, under paragraph 5 of Article 113 (new Art. 133) on trade in services and on intellectual property rights (once this amendment to Article 113 EC inserted by the Amsterdam Treaty to that effect enters into force). This would mean exercising jurisdiction over Member States' legislation and their international obligations in cases where the ECJ is not able to link Member State legislation to EC legislation or to rely on a substitution of Member States by the EC. Although it would be skating on thin legal ice, the ECJ could exercise jurisdiction via a broad interpretation of Article 5 (new Art. 10) EC laying down the Community loyalty principle. Without referring expressly to Article 5 EC, in *Opinion 1/94* the ECJ identified a duty of 'close cooperation' which extends to 'the fulfilment of the commitments entered into'. Such close co-operation could also apply to Member States' courts and imply for them a duty to seek preliminary rulings under Article 177 (new Art. 234) EC.

The second challenge which GATT 1994 and more generally the WTO agreements present to the ECJ is that of their enforceability in the EC legal system. Quite obviously the rationale for denying 'direct effect' of GATT 1947 can no longer be sustained. If the ECJ is to maintain its stance, it will need to have recourse to another rationale. The fundamental aspect of this challenge, however, is whether or not to recognize a degree of enforceability to GATT 1994 and more generally to WTO agreements where they contain provisions that are as such capable of being enforced judicially. Within the EC there no longer seems to be a consensus among Member State governments against judicial enforceability of GATT 1994 and other WTO agreements as a matter of principle; alternatively there no longer is passive acceptance by some of a majority view. The ECJ will not be able to avoid a decision and whatever its decision it will test the acceptability by some EC Member States, as it will touch on traditionally held views on the effect of international agreements and on their perceived interests in a globalizing world economy. Steps could and ought to be taken in this direction. '*A vivre sans péril, on triomphe sans gloire.*'

5

On Kith and Kine (and Crustaceans): Trade and Environment in the EU and WTO

JOANNE SCOTT*

INTRODUCTION

This chapter is about cattle and their calves. It tells two stories highlighting recent controversies over the manner in which these animals are reared, and the quality of the meat which they produce. The theme of the chapter is trade and environment, with the latter being broadly conceived to include animal welfare and public health issues.

The first of these bovine case studies begins by examining issues surrounding the export of live veal calves in the European Union. This highlights questions of Community law, exemplifying in a Community context the theme which has formed the focus for the trade/environment debate in international law. This is often conceived either in the language of 'extra-territoriality' or, perhaps more usefully, in terms of a distinction between the application of domestic 'product' and 'process' standards *vis-à-vis* imported goods. The GATT/WTO approach to this issue will be examined in the context of the recent 'shrimp' reports of a GATT panel and WTO Appellate Body. The second case study considers the Community's 'hormones' regime and its associated prohibition on the importation of beef from cattle to which hormones have been administered for fattening purposes. This focuses upon the WTO Agreement on the Application of Sanitary and Phytosanitary Measures (SPS Agreement), and the manner in which this has been construed in recent panel

* Reader in EU Law, Queen Mary and Westfield College, University of London and Jean Monnet Fellow (1998/9), European University Institute, Florence. This paper is based on a lecture given at Harvard Law School within the framework of Professor Joseph Weiler's seminar on the EU, NAFTA, and the WTO. Many thanks to Joseph Weiler for this invitation and for his comments on the paper. Earlier versions were also presented at the European University Institute at the invitation of Professors Joerges, Ladeur, and Snyder. Many thanks to them for their help, and to Alec Stone-Sweet for his comments as discussant. Thanks also to Gráinne de Búrca, Michael Doherty, Carole Lyons, Wade Mansell, and Ellen Vos for their helpful comments along the way. The usual disclaimers apply.

reports, and by the WTO Appellate Body (AB). In this sense, the second case study takes shape at the contested interface between EU and WTO law.

While this is a paper about trade and environment it does not purport to be comprehensive. The aim of the paper is neither to provide an exhaustive exposition of the rules applicable in the two legal orders under consideration, nor to present an exhaustive comparative survey. Its aims are more modest. It seeks merely to highlight a small number of the important questions and themes arising in the sphere of trade and environment at a time of rapid evolution in European and international approaches to free trade. The cases under discussion highlight a number of complex and contested issues, relating in particular to the scope of the relevant environmental exceptions to free trade, and the circumstances in which states (or groups of states) may justify departure from the free movement objective. The cases not only highlight the challenges posed by regulatory diversity in the EU and WTO, but also the difficulties associated with looking outside the law for a 'meta-legal' mechanism for the normative assessment of domestic environmental preferences. Such difficulties—exemplified here within the framework of the SPS Agreement which is predicated upon the application of scientific rationality—may be thought to militate in favour of the adoption of procedural rather than substantive tools for judging the legality of domestic standards in an international trade setting. This is an issue which is highlighted in the conclusion of the chapter.

CASE STUDY 1: COMPASSION IN WORLD FARMING AND CALVES IN CRATES

Towards the end of 1995 the High Court of England and Wales referred to the European Court for a preliminary ruling in the case *R v Minister of Agriculture, Fisheries and Food, ex parte Compassion in World Farming*.[1] This reference arose in the context of an action for judicial review of a ministerial decision *refusing* to restrict the export of veal calves from the United Kingdom to other Member States of the European Union. The minister's decision was predicated upon legal as well as policy considerations. In particular, his refusal to institute an export ban reflected his concern to comply with the requirements of Articles 29 and 30 (formerly Articles 34 and 36) of the EC Treaty. The action before the High Court was brought by a public interest association, acting against a backdrop of heightened public opposition in the United Kingdom to the 'veal crate system', or the raising of calves 'in individual box-like structures where they remain until they are removed for slaughter approximately five months later'.[2] This system is deployed in a number of the

---

[1] Case C-1/96 [1998] ECR I-1251.   [2] Ibid, para. 23.

Member States in the European Union, notably in France.[3] Public opposition in the United Kingdom was manifested in widespread protests and demonstrations at the seaports and airports through which exports of veal calves were routed. Public antipathy was further reflected in the introduction of a prohibition on the use of the veal-crate system in the United Kingdom and Northern Ireland.[4]

The veal-crate system is not entirely unregulated at a European level. In 1976 a *European Convention on the Protection of Animals kept for Farming Purposes* (the Convention) was adopted within the framework of the Council of Europe. It was approved on behalf of the European Community in 1978.[5] A Recommendation concerning cattle was promulgated pursuant to this Convention in 1988. More recently, following intervention by the European Parliament, the Community adopted a directive laying down minimum standards for the protection of calves.[6] The first question referred to the European Court in the case under discussion related to the validity of this directive, and specifically to its compatibility with the Convention and subsequent Recommendation. The Court disposed of this issue rapidly, finding that 'consideration of the Directive has disclosed no factor of such a kind as to affect its validity'.[7] This reflects both the breadth of discretion which states enjoy under the Convention, and the non-binding nature of the Recommendation.

The second question referred raised issues of more profound significance, concerning the construction of Community rules on the free movement of goods. Specifically, the High Court sought to ascertain whether Member States might rely upon the Article 30 EC exception (formerly Article 36) in order to justify an export ban which, the parties accepted, constituted a quantitative restriction within the meaning of Article 29 EC (formerly Article 34).[8] The Court decided that they could not. It did so exclusively on the basis of its construction of the 1991 directive, without passing comment upon the scope of the relevant Treaty rules. At one level, the Court's ruling is unremarkable in view of the (unusual) terms of the directive, Article 11(2) of

---

[3] See, by way of background, Elworthy, S., 'Crated Calves and Crazy Cows: Live Animals and the Free Movement of Goods' in Holder, J., *The Impact of EC Environmental Law in the United Kingdom* (Wiley, 1997).

[4] This entered into force in 1990. See, for the measures currently in force, *Welfare of Livestock Regulations* (SI 1994 No. 2126) and *Welfare of Livestock Regulations (Northern Ireland)* (SR 1995 No. 172).

[5] Council Decision 78/923/EEC OJ 1978 L323/12.

[6] Council Directive 91/629/EEC OJ 1991 L240/28.   [7] N. 1 above, para. 37.

[8] In an earlier case the High Court had highlighted difficulties in determining whether Article 29 (formerly Article 34) applies to an export ban in the light of the *Groenveld* case (Case 15/79 [1979] ECR 3409). This limited the scope of Article 29 (formerly Art. 34) to discriminatory measures, c.f. Article 28 (formerly Art. 30). See *R v Minister of Agriculture, Fisheries and Food, ex parte Roberts* [1991] 1 CMLR 555 and Jarvis, M., *The Application of EC Law by National Courts* (OUP, 1998) ch. 4, for a full discussion of this point.

which provides that Member States may, from a specified date, subject to the general rules of the Treaty and an obligation to inform the Commission, maintain or apply *within their territories* stricter rules for the protection of calves than those laid down in the directive. Thus, in this case, the directive itself explicitly establishes territorial limits to the application of more stringent Member State standards. It established 'a right for Member states to impose [only] *on their own undertakings* standards which are higher, without the possibility to oppose free movement',[9] on the basis of the failure of trading partners to comply with these higher standards. In this respect *Compassion in World Farming* may be compared to the *Gallaher* case.[10] In *Gallaher* it was held that while the United Kingdom could lawfully impose higher standards on its own undertakings it could not block the importation of goods from other Member States, where these complied at least with the minimum standards laid down by the directive on tobacco labelling. This similarly followed from the text of the directive itself which, having been based on Article 95 (formerly Article 100a), contained a 'market access' clause. This provides that Member States may not, for reasons of labelling, prohibit or restrict the sale of products which comply with the directive.

While relatively (legally) uncontentious in terms of outcome, the veal calves case highlights an issue of enormous significance for the trade/environment debate. This concerns the legal capacity of states to restrict trade with a view to protecting environmental resources situated outside of their territory. Almost invariably this issue arises in a context of the application of domestic 'process' as opposed to 'product' standards; standards pertaining not to the characteristics of the product itself but to its manner of production. This is exemplified by the veal calves case, in that the environmental issue arising concerned not the quality of the veal produced, but the quality of the conditions under which the calves were raised. Yet this case not only highlights this issue (albeit in circumstances which are unusual, concerned as it is with exports rather than imports, and with a directive which is unusually explicit in its territorial scope). It also offers an important insight into how it is that the European Court has avoided addressing this crucial issue in the context of the EC Treaty environmental 'exceptions'.[11]

---

[9] Bernard, N., 'The Future of European Economic Law in the Light of the Principle of Subsidiarity' (1996) 33 CMLRev. 633, at 646.

[10] Case C-11/92, *R v Secretary of State for Health, ex parte Gallaher, Imperial Tobacco Ltd., Rothmans Tobacco Ltd.* [1993] ECR I-3545.

[11] I place the word 'exceptions' in inverted commas because here I have in mind both Article 30 (formerly Art. 36), which is an explicit exception to the Treaty prohibition on quantitative restrictions on imports and exports and measures with equivalent effect, and the concept of mandatory requirements developed by the Court in its construction of Article 28 (formerly Art. 30). Properly speaking (if one wants to be pedantic) this concept is relevant in defining the scope of the rule and hence does not represent an exception to that rule. This discussion of the

The 1991 veal calves directive lays down minimum standards. Minimum harmonization is a legislative technique frequently employed by the Community today. In some areas, such as environmental policy, the Community only enjoys competence to enact minimum standards.[12] Even in other areas '. . . consideration should be given to setting minimum standards, with freedom for Member States to set higher standards . . . where this would not conflict with the objectives of the proposed measure or with the Treaty'.[13] It has been said of minimum harmonization measures that they establish a 'floor' of obligations below which Member States may not sink. The 'ceiling', circumscribing the legitimate scope of more stringent measures introduced by Member States, is constituted by the EC Treaty and in particular (in the context of goods) by Articles 28–30 (formerly 30–6) thereof.[14] This may be illustrated by a recent case in the area of trade and environment, *Aher-Waggon GmbH v Bundesrepublik Deutschland.*[15] The facts of this case were as follows.

In 1992 the German Federal Office of Aviation refused to grant registration for a propeller-driven aircraft previously registered in Denmark. It did so on the basis that the aircraft did not comply with domestic German standards regulating noise emissions. The aircraft did, however, comply with the minimum standards laid down in the relevant Community directives. The company which owned the aircraft sought judicial review of this decision and the national court hearing the action referred to the European Court for a preliminary ruling. Significantly, for the purposes of the present discussion, the European Court noted that the Community directive at issue 'merely lays down minimum requirements' and 'allows Member States to impose stricter noise limits'.[16] However, in keeping with Weatherill's conception of minimum harmonization above, the Court went on to observe that Member State autonomy above the 'floor' established by the Community directives on aircraft emission limits is not unconstrained. It is that the more stringent national standards enacted be consistent with other provisions of Community law,[17] and in particular with the Treaty provisions on the free movement of goods. In this respect the Court observed:

National legislation of the kind at issue . . . restricts intra-Community trade since it makes the first registration in national territory of aircraft previously registered in a

territorial scope of the environmental 'exceptions' in a trade context is relevant also in the context of the application of Article 95(4) and (5) (formerly Art. 100a(4)).

[12] Article 176 (formerly Art. 130t).

[13] *Conclusions of the Edinburgh Economic Council,* Annex I to Part A (EC Bulletin 12–1992), 15.

[14] Weatherill, S., 'Beyond Preemption? Shared Competence and Constitutional Change in the European Community' in O'Keeffe and Twomey, *Legal Issues of the Maastricht Treaty* (Wiley Chancery, 1994), 25.

[15] Case C-389/96, [1998] ECR I-4473.

[16] Ibid, para. 15.   [17] Ibid, para. 16.

Member State conditional upon compliance with stricter noise standards than those laid down by the Directive, while exempting from those standards aircraft which obtained registration in national territory before the Directive was implemented.[18]

Consequently, prima facie, the measures were deemed to fall within the scope of Article 28 (formerly Article 30). However, the European Court went on to conclude that such measures were susceptible to justification on the basis of considerations relating to public health and environmental protection, both of which constitute mandatory requirements recognized by Community law. The German measures were, the Court observed, neither disproportionate nor more restrictive of trade than necessary. It is significant in this respect that the German rules merely preclude the new registration of aircraft in Germany where these do not comply with the more stringent noise emission standards laid down in domestic law. They do not preclude aircraft registered in other Member States, but not complying with German law, from being used in German airspace or on German territory.[19]

While *Aher-Waggon* raises some interesting issues concerning the scope of the Community free-movement provisions, in terms of the manner in which the Court characterizes the Community directive, and the relationship between the directive and the Treaty, its approach is consistent with traditional conceptions of minimum harmonization. In this it may be distinguished from the veal calves case. Here the European Court, while recognizing the 'minimum' nature of the obligations laid down in the 1991 calves directive, insists that this directive is such as to lay down 'exhaustively common minimum standards'.[20] As the directive is deemed to constitute an exhaustive harmonization measure (albeit one laying down minimum standards) the Court, in keeping with previous jurisprudence, concludes that Member State recourse to Article 30 (formerly Article 36) is precluded. The legality of the national measures falls for determination in the light of the directive, this being characterized in such a way as to represent both 'floor' and 'ceiling' in terms of Member State obligations.

It is thus apparent, in my view paradoxically, that according to the European Court, minimum harmonization may be exhaustive in nature. Indeed in one earlier case the Court (bizarrely in my view) specifically cites

---

[18] Ibid, para. 18.

[19] Ibid, paras. 19–26. It is noteworthy that the Court does not consider whether the German rules were discriminatory in that they treated aircraft previously registered in Germany before implementation of the directive differently from those registered in another Member State prior to this implementation date. This is important because only 'indistinctly applicable measures' are susceptible to justification on the basis of 'mandatory requirements' rather than on the basis of Article 30 (formerly Art. 36). The list laid down in Article 30 (formerly Art. 36) is exhaustive. While public health is included, environmental protection is not. See generally, Scott, J., *EC Environmental Law* (Longmans, 1998), ch. 4.

[20] N. 1 above, para. 56.

the existence of a minimum harmonization clause in a directive as evidence of the fact that the measure is such as to exhaustively regulate Member State powers in the field, and to exclude the application of stricter national standards *vis-à-vis* imported goods, though in this case the directive did not contain a market access clause.[21] Again, by so doing, the Court succeeds in side-stepping the issue of whether the national measure in question was compatible with the Treaty rules on free movement. Interestingly, and perhaps significantly, this case also concerned a national measure restricting trade with a view to protecting an environmental resource situated *outside* of the territory of the regulating state.[22] Specifically it concerned a Dutch ban on the marketing of 'dead red grouse', a bird species not native to the Netherlands and hunted in the United Kingdom in accordance with the minimum standards laid down in the Wild Birds Directive.[23]

While there is always a danger of reading too much into a small number of cases, there does appear to be a propensity on the part of the Court to characterize environmental directives laying down minimum standards as exhaustive in nature, where the national measure is concerned to promote environmental protection outside of the territory of the regulating state,[24] even where (cf. *Compassion in World Farming* and *Gallaher*) the directive does not expressly establish the territorial limits to stricter national measures.

[21] Case C-169/89 *Gourmetterie van den Burg* [1990] ECR 2143, para. 9.

[22] Cf. Advocate General van Gerven in *Gourmetterie* who examines the legality of the measure in question from the perspective of the Treaty rules on free movement of goods. In his view the measure goes further than is permitted by the Article 30 (formerly Art. 36) 'ceiling' in that it may not be regarded as proportionate to the objective being pursued. In this, the Advocate General adopts a traditional 'floor'/'ceiling' approach to minimum harmonization measure.

[23] Council Directive 79/409/EEC OJ 1979 L103/1.

[24] See also Case C-5/94 *R v Ministry of Agriculture, Fisheries and Food, ex parte Hedley Lomas (Ireland) Ltd.* [1996] ECR I-2553. Here again the Court found that the existence of a harmonizing directive was such as to preclude recourse to Article 30 (formerly Art. 36) in the context of UK restrictions on the export of live sheep to Spain. Its finding in this respect is less controversial here given the absence of a minimum harmonization clause in the directive concerned. However, this case establishes that recourse to this article is precluded even where it is alleged (or presumably established) that the directive has not been properly applied by the trading partners concerned. A Member State may not 'unilaterally adopt, on its own authority, corrective or protective measures designed to obviate any breach by another Member State of rules of Community law' (para. 20). On the contrary they 'must rely on trust in each other to carry out inspections on their respective territories' in order to ensure the application and effectiveness of Community law' (para. 19). See also the recent important decision of the European Court in Case C-203/96 *Dusseldorp* [1998] ECR I-4704, where again the Court does not address the issue of 'extra-territoriality'—arising in this case as a result of a prohibition on the export of certain waste. The Court found the measure to be contrary to the EC Treaty as there was no evidence that exportation would pose a threat to the life or health of humans. In keeping with previous case law the Court also rejected arguments of an economic nature put forward in seeking to justify the ban.

While the reasoning of the Court seems supremely contrived in the context of the wild birds directive, in that this contains an explicit minimum harmonization clause, this approach has enabled the Court to avoid addressing the politically contentious question of the territorial scope of Article 30 (formerly Article 36) and of the concept of mandatory requirements.

It should be observed that *Gourmetterie* was in one respect at least a more difficult case than *Compassion in World Farming*. Whereas the calves directive explicitly delimits the territorial scope of application of stricter national measures, the wild birds directive does not. Consequently, there was, in respect of the latter, considerable room for doubt as to whether the Dutch ban was compatible with the directive. It is significant that the Court found that it was not. The Court held, having regard to the objectives pursued by the directive, that stricter measures could be enacted only in respect of bird species occurring within the territory of the regulating state, or in respect of species which are endangered or migratory which (according to the preamble of the directive) constitute 'a common heritage of the Community'.[25] Again, this construction may be criticized as being textually strained, and misleading in that the directive establishes a general system of protection for all wild birds.[26] It does, however, hint at a scepticism on the part of the Court as regards the legitimacy of trade restrictions adopted with a view to protecting 'foreign' environmental goods, at least in so far as these are not conceived as 'shared'—representing part of the common heritage of humankind. In this way, just as 'the protection of consumers in other Member States is not, as such, a matter for the Netherlands authorities',[27] so too environmental interests may be conceived as territorially bounded, except in the case of those defined as concerning common or shared resources.

The above discussion has exemplified the uncertainty which continues to characterize the Community law approach to the issue of 'extra-territorial protection' in the context of the trade/environment debate. It is testimony to the creativity of the Court's reasoning that, as yet, it has not clarified the territorial scope of the EC Treaty environmental 'exceptions'. The reticence of the European Court on this point is not matched by a similar degree of restraint on the part of various GATT panels.[28] This issue lay at the heart of

[25] N. 21 above, para. 11.

[26] See Krämer, L., *European Environmental Law: Casebook* (Kluwer, 1993), 152–9.

[27] See Case C-384/93 *Alpine Investments v Minister van Financien* [1995] ECR I-1141, para. 43.

[28] There is a huge literature studying the subject of trade and environment within the framework of the GATT/WTO. For an excellent account of the issues see Esty, D. C., *Greening the GATT: Trade, Environment and the Future* (Institute for International Economics, 1994). See also a recent special issue of RECIEL (Vol. 6, Issue 2, 1997) for a discussion of recent controversies and debates. Generally, the *Journal of World Trade* carries many articles on this subject. Those individual contributions upon which I have relied most heavily will be cited in the footnotes which follow.

the two tuna/dolphin panel reports[29] and arose again, more recently, in the context of the 'shrimp' panel and AB reports.[30] It is to the latter that this paper will now turn.

United States Restrictions on the Importation of Shrimp

The recent 'shrimp' report of a GATT panel arose against a backdrop of concerns in the United States about the incidental capture and drowning of sea turtles by shrimp trawlers. This forms a significant source of mortality for sea turtles (as does tuna fishing for dolphins), all species of which are listed as endangered or threatened pursuant to the US Endangered Species Act. Such concerns led, in 1987, to the enactment in the United States of regulations concerning, *inter alia*, the deployment of Turtle Exclusion Devices (TEDs) by shrimp fishermen.[31] In 1989 the United States enacted further legislation. This so-called Section 609 provided that:

. . . shrimp harvested with technology that may adversely affect certain sea turtles protected under US law may not be imported into the United States, unless the President annually certifies to the Congress that the harvesting country concerned has a regulatory programme governing the incidental taking of such sea turtles that is comparable to that of the United States, that the average rate of that incidental taking by the vessels of the harvesting country is comparable to the average rate of incidental taking of sea turtles by United States vessels in the course of such harvesting, or that the fishing environment of the harvesting country does not pose a threat of incidental taking to sea turtles in the course of such harvesting.[32]

Whereas, initially, Section 609 was applied only to countries of the Caribbean/ Western Atlantic, its application was extended to all countries in 1996, pursuant to a ruling of the US Court of International Trade. At this time also, the new guidelines established that all imports of shrimp or shrimp products into the United States must be accompanied by a declaration providing *either* that the shrimp originated in a certified country, or that they had been harvested under conditions that did not adversely affect sea turtles. Hence, at this time, the United States legislation permitted the importation of specific batches of shrimp from non-approved countries so long as that

---

[29] *United States Restrictions on Imports of Tuna* 30 ILM (1992) 1598 [*Tuna/Dolphin I*] and 33 ILM 839 (1994) [*Tuna/Dolphin II*].

[30] *United States—Import Prohibition of Certain Shrimp and Shrimp Products.* All panel and Appellate Body Reports are now published on the WTO internet site. See http://www.wto.org. It is notable that the AB at least sought to avoid characterizing the issue in terms of extra-territoriality, finding a sufficient nexus between the United States and the turtles. See n. 55 below.

[31] These are defined in the panel report as a grip trapdoor installed inside a trawling net that is designed to allow shrimp to pass to the back of the net while directing sea turtles and other unintentionally caught large objects out of the net.

[32] N. 30 above, Section VII, Findings, para. 3.

batch had been captured in a manner deemed appropriate by the United States. This changed in 1996, again pursuant to a ruling of the US Court of International Trade. Henceforth shrimp harvested with commercial fishing technology would be permitted access to the US market only in the event that it originated in a state certified by the President under Section 609.[33] Thus, at this point, the United States shifted to a state of origin based approach to market access, and it is with the legality of this approach that the panel report is concerned.

As a starting point it should be observed that the GATT panel found that the US measures under consideration amounted to a 'prohibition or restriction' on the importation of shrimp and hence constituted a violation of GATT 1994, Article XI.1.[34] Before proceeding to examine the panel's construction of the GATT's environmental exceptions it is important to say a few words about this initial finding. The structure of the GATT is arguably such that measures which comply with Article III are 'saved' and will not fall for consideration under the GATT Article XI prohibition on quantitative restrictions.[35] Article III.4 lays down the principle of national treatment, providing that:

The products of the territory of any contracting party imported into the territory of any other contracting party shall be accorded treatment no less favorable than that accorded to like products of national origin in respect of all laws, regulations and requirements affecting their internal sale, offering for sale, purchase, transportation, distribution or use . . .

At first sight it might appear as though the US measures might be justified on this basis, so long as they are genuinely even-handed, implying neither direct nor indirect discrimination.[36] However, the question of whether a given mea-

---

[33] A later judgment of this Court clarified that its judgment did not apply to shrimp harvested by manual methods which do not harm sea turtles, by aquaculture, or in cold water.

[34] N. 30 above, Section VII, Findings, para. 17.

[35] See Schoenbaum, T. J., 'International Trade and Protection of the Environment: The Continuing Search for Reconciliation' (1997) 91 AJIL 268, at 273. He notes that the 'mutual exclusivity of Articles XI and III often presents difficulty, and can be understood only in the context of the correct methodology for applying the tests of the two articles. The measure in question should *first* be analysed as to whether it is protected by Article III. If it fails the tests of Article III, Article XI is automatically applicable and, unless it falls under one of the narrow exemptions . . . in that article, it will fail'. This construction is by no means uncontested but is rather simply one way of making sense of existing panel reports. One could equally argue that the full implications of Article XI in the sphere beyond discriminatory measures had not been fully appreciated until recently. Hence where a measure was held to be consistent with the principle of national treatment underpinning Article III, it was assumed to be consistent with Article XI, even though the latter might be argued to adopt an 'obstacle' as opposed to a discrimination-based approach (see Weiler, n. 80 below).

[36] On the treatment of 'facially neutral measures' (indirect discrimination) under the GATT, see Farber and Hudec, 'GATT Legal Restraints on Domestic Environmental Regulations' in Bhagwati and Hudec, *Fair Trade and Harmonization: Prerequisites for Free Trade?*, Vol. 2, 'Legal Analysis' (The MIT Press, 1996), 70–80.

sure is discriminatory depends upon the construction of 'like' for the purposes of comparing domestic and imported goods. The issue of when one product is 'like' another is viewed by GATT panels as an issue of policy rather than as a straightforward issue of fact. 'Likeness' is conceived as, in part, contingent upon the aim and effect of the measure and whether it is such as to afford protection to domestic product. Thus, the concept of 'like' is conceived against a backdrop of consideration of the overall legitimacy of the measure in terms of its regulatory purpose or protectionist aim or effect.[37] Moreover, various GATT panels have attached considerable significance to a Note to GATT, Article III.4 which provides:

The *products* of the territory of any contracting party imported into the territory of any other contracting party shall be accorded treatment no less favourable than that accorded to *like* products of national origin.[38]

On this basis it has been consistently held that Article III requires a comparison between products, and not a comparison between the policies or practices of the importing state and the state of origin.[39] Products which are intrinsically comparable will (subject to the teleological reasoning noted above) be considered as 'alike', regardless of differences in the manner in which they have been produced or harvested. One batch of shrimp is like any other, regardless of how many turtles died in the course of their capture. Consequently, to treat one batch of shrimp (or tuna) differently from another on the basis of differences in harvesting technique is, where this prejudices the imported product, to offend the principle of national treatment. This is a crucial point. The concept of national treatment has been construed in such a way as to permit the application of domestic *product* standards to imported goods. However, the application of domestic *process* standards to imported goods will amount to less favourable treatment and hence derive no protection under Article III. While *de jure* the principle of national treatment is preserved, because of the manner in which 'like' is construed, *de facto* it has been undermined in the case of process standards.

This issue is not addressed by the AB. Its report focuses rather upon principally one legal question; namely the scope of the GATT, Article XX environmental exceptions. The relevant paragraphs of this article provide:

Subject to the requirement that such measures are not applied in a manner that would constitute a means of arbitrary or unjustifiable discrimination between countries where the same conditions prevail, or a disguised restriction on international trade,

---

[37] See ibid. and for a clear recent example of this *United States—Taxes on Automobiles* 33 ILM (1994) 1937. It should be noted that the European Court has also on occasion manipulated the concept of 'like' in order to facilitate a given policy outcome. See, especially, Case C-2/92 *Commission v Belgium* [1992] ECR I-4431.

[38] Emphasis added. [39] See, especially, *Tuna/Dolphin II*, n. 29 above.

nothing in this Agreement shall be construed to prevent the adoption or enforcement of measures:

. . . (b) necessary to protect human, animal or plant life or health;

. . . (g) relating to the conservation of natural resources if such measures are made effective in conjunction with restrictions on domestic production or consumption.

The scope of these exceptions is by no means free from doubt. Over the years GATT panels have adopted a restrictive approach which has been much criticized.[40] On the issue under consideration here however, namely the application of domestic process standards to imported goods, there is consistency in terms of result though not in terms of reasoning. While the reports of GATT panels have become more nuanced on this point over time, culminating in the decision in the shrimp case, there none the less remains a high degree of scepticism regarding such measures.[41]

   In the shrimps case the panel concludes that the US measures do not fall within the scope of Article XX, and specifically that they are not compatible with the '*chapeau*' to that article, representing an example of 'unjustifiable discrimination between countries where the same conditions prevail'. It does so on the basis of reasoning which is contextual as well as teleological, placing particular emphasis upon the object and purpose of the WTO Agreement as a whole, of which GATT 1994 forms only one part. The panel insists, having regard to the preamble to the WTO Agreement, that the 'central focus of that agreement remains the promotion of economic development through trade', while acknowledging that 'environmental considerations are important for the interpretation of the WTO Agreement'.[42] It stresses the multilateral nature of the trading system which that Agreement seeks to construct and the need to consider whether any measure restricting imports is capable of undermining this multilateral approach. In addressing this issue it observes the importance of assessing the effect not only of the measure under consideration, but also the effect that would arise were other states to follow this example and adopt similar restrictive measures. In this respect it observes:

----

[40] For a forceful critique see Schoenbaum, n. 35 above.

[41] The second *Tuna/Dolphin* report (by way of contrast to *Tuna/Dolphin I*) did not accept that there was any territorial limitation inherent in GATT, Article XX. It found that parties are entitled to protect an environmental resource situated beyond its territorial jurisdiction. None the less it posited the need for a direct causal connection between the measure and the environmental objective pursued. Where a measure is capable of achieving its desired effect only were it to be followed by changes in the policies of the exporting state, it cannot fall within the parameters of the GATT environmental exceptions (see n. 29 above, (*Tuna/Dolphin II*), esp. at 894 and 898). Although, ostensibly, this represents a retreat from the first *Tuna/Dolphin* report, in practice it is difficult to conceive of circumstances in which such a direct connection would exist in the case of process standards, other than in the case of 'drifting pollution' caused by production techniques deployed in one state spilling over physically to the territory of the regulating state.

[42] N. 30 above, Section VII, Findings, para. 43.

. . . if an interpretation of the chapeau of Article XX were to be followed which would allow a Member to adopt measures conditioning access to its market for a given product upon the adoption by the exporting Members of certain policies, including conservation policies, GATT 1994, and the WTO Agreement could no longer serve as a multilateral framework for trade among Members as security and predictability of trade relations under those agreements would be threatened . . . This follows because, if one WTO Member were allowed to adopt such measures, then other Members would also have the right to adopt similar measures on the same subject but with differing, or even conflicting, requirements. If that happened, it would be impossible for the exporting Members to comply at the same time with multiple conflicting policy requirements. Indeed, as each of these requirements would necessitate the adoption of a policy applicable not only to the export product (such as specific standards applicable only to goods exported to the country requiring them) but also to domestic production, it would be impossible for a country to adopt one of those policies without running the risk of breaching other Members' conflicting policy requirements for the same product and being refused access to those other markets . . . Market access for goods could become subject to an increasing number of conflicting policy requirements for the same product and this would rapidly lead to the end of the WTO multilateral trading system.[43]

In the light of this, and in view of the fact that the US measures render importation contingent upon the adoption of satisfactory conservation policies on the part of the exporting state, the panel makes a provisional finding that the measures constitute unjustifiable discrimination within the meaning of the Article XX *chapeau*. Following consideration of additional arguments submitted by the United States, the panel confirms this conclusion. Its finding in this respect is not predicated upon the extra-territorial nature of the measures at hand, but upon their unilateral nature. The panel expresses a clear preference for multilateral (negotiated) solutions to transboundary or global environmental problems, stressing the failure of the United States to commence negotiations on an agreement on sea turtle conservation techniques which would have included the complainants, before the imposition of the import ban. In this regard it observes that 'the risk of a multiplicity of conflicting requirements clearly is reduced when requirements are decided in multilateral fora'.[44] None the less, by way of qualification the panel insists that its findings regarding Article XX 'do not imply that recourse to unilateral measures is always excluded, particularly after serious attempts have been made to negotiate; nor do they imply that, in any given situation, they would be permitted'.[45] The intention is clearly that the issue must fall for determination on a case by case basis, having regard to the circumstances and background of individual measures. Significantly, therefore, the panel does not exclude in principle the possibility of such measures being exempted under

---

[43] Ibid, para. 45.   [44] N. 30 above, Section VII, Findings, para. 60.
[45] Ibid, para. 61.

Article XX. Equally, the tone of the report is such as to suggest that where such measures are adopted pursuant to internationally agreed standards, a more permissive attitude would be adopted.

This, of course, provides an interesting contrast to experience in the EU, where the existence of (exhaustive) international standards, far from serving to legitimate restrictions on trade, operates to facilitate free movement and to preclude recourse to the generally available environmental exceptions. This is especially apparent (cf. *Aher-Waggon*)[46] where the standards concerned are conceived, in terms of legal basis, as facilitating realization of the internal market. It might be supposed further to reflect the spirit of mutual trust or 'mutual confidence', 'which governs relations between Member States when they give effect to a Community directive in their national law',[47] and the range and effectiveness of the enforcement mechanisms which underpins the Community legal order.

It will be readily apparent from the above that the shrimp panel report is far from conclusive on the issue under discussion. As already noted its stance is less deterministic than that of previous panels. Its findings will inevitably be controversial, especially as regards the supposed failure of the United Sates to engage in serious multilateral negotiations, but overall the brilliance of the report, from a public relations perspective, lies in its capacity to represent all things to all people. In particular the panel is scrupulous in its endeavour to carefully delimit the scope of its findings. It is particularly important to note in this respect that the panel's report is concerned only with the situation in which one nation restricts imports on the basis, not of the manner in which a particular batch of a given product has been produced or harvested, but on the basis of a failure on the part of the exporting state to comply generally with the policies of the importing state. It observes in this respect:

> . . . we are limiting our finding to measures—taken independently of any such international obligation—conditioning access to the US market for a given product on the adoption by the exporting Member of certain conservation policies. In this regard, we note that banning the importation of a particular product does not *per se* imply that a change in policy is required from the *country* whose exports are subject to the import prohibition. For instance, a Member may ban a product on the ground that it is dangerous, and accept a similar product that is safe. This is clearly different from adopting a policy pursuant to which only countries that adopt measures restricting all of their production to products considered safe by a particular Member may export to the market of that Member.[48]

---

[46] N. 15 above.

[47] See *Hedley Lomas*, n. 24 above, opinion of the Advocate General. This contrast rests upon the assumption that the logic of *Hedley Lomas* would have applied even had the United Kingdom adduced *evidence* of Spain's failure to comply with the Community standards laid down by the directive. My reading of this case suggests that this would be the case, though the issue is far from having been conclusively settled.

[48] N. 30 above, Section VII, Findings, para. 50.

It is important that here the panel brings to mind the issue of product as opposed to process standards. The question of whether a given item is safe or dangerous will depend upon intrinsic product quality and not upon production process. That, of course, is not to deny that the two may be related, with production process impinging upon product quality. Indeed this is the case in the second of our case studies below. None the less the panel, by virtue of its choice of illustration, leaves open (perhaps deliberately) the question of the legitimacy of applying domestic process standards in the case of imported goods, but on a *batch by batch* basis, rather than a country-wide basis, having regard to the processes underpinning production of the particular item(s) concerned. It is apparent that this kind of measure would not definitively undermine the multilateral nature of the trading system as different batches of goods could be produced according to different methods, according to the process standards prevailing in the market for which they are destined. None the less, such measures would present practical difficulties both for the state of production and, in terms of compliance, for the importing state. Equally, such measures would tend to negate many of the economic benefits associated with a multilateral approach to trade, premised as this is upon considerations of comparative advantage and economies of scale. Then again, the same might be said in the case of product standards which differ widely from state to state but whose application to imported goods is sanctioned, subject to the principle of national treatment.

Turning now to the 'Shrimp' report of the AB: The AB is strongly critical of the panel's approach, reversing its findings in a number of important respects. That said, while it begins with an analysis of the scope of Article XX(g), and accepts that the US measures, in terms of their structure and design, 'relate to the conservation of exhaustible natural resources' and are made effective in conjunction with restrictions on domestic production or consumption, ultimately it concludes that the measures, in view of the manner in which they have been applied, fall foul of the Article XX *chapeau*. Hence, whereas the AB does not accept that it is possible to exclude *a priori* a general category of measures from the scope of measures permitted under the *chapeau*, such are the circumstances surrounding the application of the measures in question that they are found to constitute unjustifiable and arbitrary discrimination between countries where the same conditions prevail. For the purposes of this paper it is necessary merely to highlight those factors which, taken cumulatively, were conceived by the AB as supporting this conclusion.

First, the AB emphasizes the 'rigid and unbending standard by which United States officials determine whether or not countries will be certified', and the manner in which the flexibility which characterized the measures as conceived by Congress evaporated over time at the hands of various administrative and judicial actors. In practice certification is contingent upon the adoption of a regulatory programme which is not merely comparable, but

essentially the same, as that applied in the United States. 'Other specific policies and measures that an exporting country may have adopted for the protection and conservation of sea turtles are not taken into account, in practice,
by the administrators making the comparability determination'.[49] The result
of this is that not only are differences in the conditions prevailing in other
states not taken into account, resulting in discrimination on the basis that the
same treatment is accorded in different circumstances, but also that 'shrimp
caught using methods identical to those employed in the United States have
been excluded from the United States market solely because they have been
caught in waters of countries that have not been certified by the United
States'.[50] This leads the AB to the conclusion that the measures in question
are 'more concerned' with inducing a change of policy on the part of the
exporting state, than with their stated objective of protecting and conserving
sea turtles.

Second, like the panel, the AB attaches considerable importance to the failure of the United States to conduct 'serious, across-the-board negotiations
with the objective of concluding bilateral or multilateral agreements . . .
before enforcing the import prohibition . . .'.[51] That the United States negotiated seriously with some, but not all, Members is presented as further evidence of unjustifiable discrimination. Likewise, the existence of differential
'phase-in' periods for different states, in terms of the application of the United
States measures, offers further evidence of their discriminatory nature and
impact. It is important to observe that, for the AB, this failure to negotiate
was not the only procedural type of obligation which the United States had
failed to respect. In concluding that the measures gave rise not merely to
unjustifiable discrimination, but also to arbitrary discrimination, the AB
attaches considerable weight to the 'singularly informal and casual' manner in
which the certification process is conducted, resulting in a denial of 'basic fairness and due process'.[52] This process is characterized by a lack of transparency
and predictability, offering no opportunity for the applicant to be heard, or to
respond to arguments, or to appeal against, or seek review of, the certification
decision adopted. Remarkably, applicants receive no formal, written notice of
the decision adopted, and no reasons are proffered in support of that decision.
The AB notes in this respect that:

---

[49] *United States—Import Prohibition of Certain Shrimp and Shrimp Products—Report of the
Appellate Body* (Issues Raised in this Appeal: Appraising Section 609 Under Article XX of the
GATT 1994) 12 October 1998, para. 21. See http://www.wto.org. (The number of para-
graphs in the AB report is confusing. Prior to the findings and conclusions (two paragraphs)
there is a section consisting of 44 numbered paragraphs, starting with the heading 'If such
Measures are Made Effective in conjunction with Restrictions on Domestic Production or
Consumption'. The citations which follow are found within these pages at the paragraph indicated.)

[50] Ibid, para. 23 (emphasis removed).   [51] Ibid, para. 24.   [52] Ibid, para. 39.

The provisions of Article X:3 of the GATT 1994 bear upon this matter. In our view, Section 609 falls within the 'laws, regulations, judicial decisions and administrative rulings of general application' described in Article X.1. Inasmuch as there are due process requirements generally for measures that are otherwise imposed in compliance with WTO obligations, it is only reasonable that rigorous compliance with the fundamental requirements of due process should be required in the application and administration of a measure which purports to be an exception to the treaty obligations of the Member imposing the measure and which effectively results in a suspension *pro hac vice* of the treaty rights of other Members. It is also clear to us that Article X:3 of the GATT 1994 establishes certain minimum standards for transparency and procedural fairness in the administration of trade regulations which, in our view, are not met here.[53]

The decision of the AB in the shrimp case represents an important watershed in the evolution of WTO law in the area of trade and environment. This case represented the first opportunity for the AB to address the contentious question of the status of measures adopted by one state (in this case the United States) with a view to promoting a change in the regulatory policies of other states. It is, however, notable that the AB constructs the fact situation in such a way as to avoid confronting the territorial scope of Article XX. It does so by asserting the existence of a 'sufficient nexus between the migratory and endangered marine populations involved and the United States for the purposes of Article XX(g)'.[54] The decision of the AB is predicated upon a generous construction of Article XX(g), particularly as regards its light touch approach to the application of the concept of proportionality,[55] and upon recourse to the Article XX *chapeau* as a mechanism for preventing the abuse or misuse of this exception, and as a means of maintaining a proper equilibrium between the rights and duties of WTO Members. This approach is politically expedient, offering succour both to the trade and to the environment lobbies. Whereas

---

[53] Ibid, para. 40.

[54] Ibid, para. 133. The basis of this claim is not entirely clear. The AB notes that the sea turtle species at stake here is known to occur in United States waters, albeit that it acknowledges that not all populations of these species migrate to, or traverse, waters subject to US jurisdiction. It then adds that none of the parties to the case claim any rights of exclusive ownership over sea turtles, while they are swimming freely in their natural habitats. Add to this the AB's characterization of the species as migratory or endangered and we find that three factors in total have been cited which might be viewed separately, or cumulatively, as lending support to the 'sufficient nexus' thesis.

[55] It is important to note in this respect that the AB, in construing paragraph g, finds that the measures in question are not disproportionately wide in scope, and that the means deployed are reasonably related to the ends pursued. The relationship is observably a close and real one. In this it seeks support from its earlier decision in the *United States—Gasoline* case where it promulgated the test of whether the measures may be regarded as merely incidentally or inadvertently aimed at the conservation of the resource in question. Later on, as noted above, in its construction of the *chapeau*, the AB goes on to observe that the measures are 'more concerned' with influencing the policies of its trading partners than with conservation.

in principle measures of the kind under consideration are legitimate within the framework of the GATT, environmental protection representing a significant objective, in this case, in view of specific circumstances surrounding the *application* (rather than structure or design) of the measures, the measures were not upheld. For the future, the legitimacy of such measures will be adjudged not only on the basis of procedural considerations, including the obligation to negotiate seriously, but also in the light of their responsiveness to the particular circumstances prevailing in a given state, and their flexibility in acknowledging the equivalence or comparability of different conservation policies adopted by their trading partners. It may be anticipated that measures premised upon a batch-by-batch approach, as distinguished from an overall national policy based approach, may have a higher chance of success in the years to come.

Case Study 1: Crated Calves and Trapped Turtles: Concluding Comments

This case study has examined the approach of the European Court and GATT panels to the single issue in the trade/environment debate which has most excited the wrath of environmentalists. This is concerned with the question of whether (and in what circumstances) states may introduce restrictions on trade which are predicated not upon the intrinsic environmental quality of the goods themselves, but upon their manner of production and the negative environmental consequences associated with this. This debate is often framed in the language of extra-territoriality because trade restrictions reflecting concerns about production processes are usually motivated by anxieties over environmental impact, not in the state imposing the restriction, but in the territory of the state from which the goods originate or (in the case of exports) for which they are destined. More often today this debate is conceived in terms of a distinction between product standards on the one hand, and process standards on the other. The latter conception is useful. Framed in these terms, the issue becomes one of the extent to which one state (State A) may restrict trade on the basis of the failure of a trading partner (State B) to comply with either its (State A's) domestic product standards or its (State A's) domestic process standards. This characterization sheds light upon the question of why this issue has proved more contentious in international law than in Community law. Indeed, as noted above, in Community law the issue has not yet been resolved.

Put simply (no doubt too simply), the premises underpinning these two legal orders have traditionally been distinct in terms of their approaches to trade in goods. Whereas Community law is predicated upon the concept of 'mutual recognition' of standards (subject to exceptions), the GATT rests upon a foundation of 'national treatment' (again subject to exceptions). None the less, as seen above, the GATT effectively (*de facto*) departs from this principle of national treatment, in favour of mutual recognition, when it comes to the issue of the application of process standards. Hence the issue of process standards implies, in the context of the GATT, a *de facto* paradigm shift in terms of its foundational premise. While in certain respects Community law might treat product and process standards differently, the consequences of this are less pronounced in terms of the premises underlying the system.

There are, of course, other reasons as to why this issue has proved more contentious, and the debate more heated, in an international as opposed to a Community context. Most obviously, the Community's enhanced capacity for harmonization of standards, including those pertaining to production processes, is of crucial practical and conceptual significance in easing the path from national treatment to qualified mutual recognition. In areas such as environmental policy and social policy, mutual recognition of process standards in the Community operates against a backdrop of a shared regulatory framework constituted at Community level. None the less economic ideology and the Community's 'legitimacy crisis' have combined to ensure that this framework is partial in its coverage and increasingly flexible in its scope.[56]

It will be apparent that this debate about process standards is underpinned by a broad range of considerations: environmental, economic, and moral. Central to it is the well-worn thesis that the capacity of states to regulate in areas such as the environment is contingent, in practice, upon their capacity to demand compliance with these standards on the part of their trading partners. The reasons for this are conceived as economic in nature. This thesis rests upon the assumption that social regulation, including environmental regulation, imposes costs upon economic actors and that economic actors will re-locate (or at least threaten to do so) where production can be more cheaply achieved in another state, without threatening market access. It is no longer only the wind which 'bloweth where it listeth'. This argument is captured by the concept of a regulatory race towards the bottom.[57] This thesis is less fashionable than it once was and certainly it has been applied, by some, in a manner which is excessively deterministic and insufficiently context specific. None the less, it is a thesis which is hard to interrogate in empirical terms as it is difficult, if not impossible, to ascertain the extent to which social regulation is eschewed on the basis of competitiveness concerns. In the Community at least

---

[56] See generally Somsen, H. (ed.), *Yearbook of European Environmental Law* (OUP, 2000 forthcoming).

[57] See Poiares Maduro, M., *We, the Court: the European Court of Justice and the European Economic Constitution* (Hart Publishing, 1997), ch. 4, for a discussion of the phenomenon of 'competition between rules'. Maduro cites much of the relevant literature pertaining to this debate. See also, for an excellent overview of this debate, and its empirical basis in a social policy context, Barnard, C., 'EC Social Policy' in Craig, P. and de Burca, G., *The Evolution of EU Law* (OUP, 1999 forthcoming).

the need to harmonize conditions of competition continues to provide a rationale (albeit contested) for Community-level regulation.[58]

While this debate has tended to be couched in the language of economics and the dangers associated with a de-regulatory 'competition between rules', the cases under discussion in this case study do not reflect exclusively, or arguably even principally, economic or competitiveness concerns. Rather, they bear testimony to the moral dimension of humankind's relationship with nature. In this, and in so far as they reflect the diversity of human values and of the norms giving expression to them, these cases pose a formidable challenge to international trade. The Dutch government's ban on the marketing of dead red grouse speaks not to economic realism but to an abhorrence of the practice of hunting wild birds for commercial gain. The *Compassion in World Farming* case arose against a backdrop of moral outrage as regards the functioning of the veal-crates system. A United Kingdom ban on the export of live calves would serve to prejudice rather than reinforce Britain's economic interests. For the United States the 'incidental' capture of sea turtles is conceived as an issue worthy of moral engagement, and no less so because the turtles concerned are 'foreign'.

In this, their moral dimension, the cases discussed above appear to be quite distinct from that to be examined in the second case study below. Here the trade restriction introduced is presented as having been predicated upon the physical impact of the imported goods on the health of consumers in the importing states. None the less, in so far as physical impact is not established, this case also returns us to the theme of 'right' and 'wrong' in terms of production process, rather than 'good' or 'bad' in terms of physical impact. It is a theme to which we will return in the conclusion of this chapter.

CASE STUDY 2: HORMONES IN BEEF

The Community's hormones regime was established in 1981, extended in 1988, and further extended and consolidated in 1996.[59] As it currently stands it prohibits, subject to certain derogations, the use in stockfarming of certain substances. This prohibition extends to categories of hormones which are naturally occurring and to those which are synthetically produced. The regime prohibits further, again subject to derogations, the placing on the market or the slaughter for human consumption of farm or aquaculture animals which contain the prohibited substances, or to which such substances have been administered. The derogations concern the administration of such substances

[58] It is significant that even the Treaty of Amsterdam Protocol on the Application of the Principles of Subsidiarity and Proportionality recognizes this.

[59] See Council Directive 96/22/EC OJ 1996 L125/3, which represents an extension and consolidation of the previous legislation.

for therapeutic or zootechnical purposes, and are subject to a range of substantive and procedural safeguards.

This hormones regime has always been controversial within the European Community. It came to form the subject matter of a number of cases before the European Court. These were brought variously by non-governmental organizations representing business and agricultural interests,[60] by companies manufacturing and distributing animal 'health' products,[61] and by the government of the United Kingdom, supported by Denmark.[62] While the majority of such cases were found to be inadmissible pursuant to Article 173(4) EC, the Court addressed the substantive issues posed in the direct action brought by the United Kingdom and in *Fedesa* which came before it by way of a preliminary ruling. While, in the former, the Court annulled the directive at issue, as being in breach of an essential procedural requirement, in neither case did the Court question the substantive legality of the measures. Thus, in *Fedesa*, the Court observed that:

Even if it were to be held . . . that the principle of legal certainty requires any measure adopted by the Community institutions to be founded on a rational and objective basis, judicial review must, having regard to the discretionary power conferred on the Council in the implementation of the common agricultural policy, be limited to examining whether the measure in question is vitiated by a manifest error or misuse of powers, or whether the authority in question has manifestly exceeded the limits of its discretion.[63]

It is particularly important to note that the Court did not seek to assess the accuracy of the applicants' claim based on the existence of scientific evidence demonstrating the safety of the hormones at issue. Rather, in upholding the measure, the Court stressed not only the divergent appraisals of the Member States on the question of the safety of hormones, but also the negative position adopted by the European Parliament, the Economic and Social Committee and a number of consumer organizations, each of which had expressed strong opposition to an earlier Commission proposal to relax the Community's hormones regime. Thus, '. . . in view of the divergent appraisals which had been made, traders were not entitled to expect that a prohibition on administering the substances in question to animals could be based on scientific data alone'.[64] The Court's refusal to evaluate the scientific basis of the

---

[60] Case 160/88 *Fédération européenne de la santé animale and others v Council* [1988] ECR 6399; Case 160/88R *Fédération européenne de la santé animale and others v Council* [1988] ECR 4121; Case 34/88 *Cooperative agricole de l'Anjou et du Poitou and others v Council* [1988] ECR 6265.

[61] Case 376/86 *Distrivet SA v Council* [1988] ECR 0209; Case C-331/88 *R v Secretary of State for Health ex parte Fedesa and others* [1990] ECR I-4023.

[62] Case 68/86 *United Kingdom of Great Britain and Northern Ireland v Council* [1988] ECR 0855.

[63] N. 60 above, *Fedesa*, para. 8.   [64] Ibid, para. 10.

directive reflects both its 'light touch' approach to the review of legislative acts adopted within the framework of the CAP,[65] and also the multiple aims pursued by the directive. The recitals to the directive refer not only to considerations relating to human health, but also to the Community interest in preventing competitive distortions and barriers to intra-Community trade. Reference is also made to 'consumer anxieties and expectations' and to the capacity of this harmonizing measure to bring about an increase in the consumption of the product concerned. Social and political conceptions of risk thus find voice before the European Court in assessing the validity of this legislative measure. An obligation attaching to the Commission (pursuant to the 1981 directive) to take account of scientific developments 'does not pre-empt the conclusions which may be drawn therefrom by the Council in the exercise of its discretion'.[66]

Hormones in Beef and the WTO

Almost a decade after the first hormones case law before the European Court, the Community's hormones regime came to form the subject matter of WTO dispute settlement proceedings, following complaints submitted by the United States and Canada.[67] These complaints related specifically to the EC ban on the importation of meat and meat products from cattle treated with six particular hormones for growth promotion purposes. Although separate panels were established to consider the two complaints, they both considered the same measures, comprised the same members, and were assisted by the same scientific experts. Joint meetings were held with the experts appointed, although in view of claims of prejudice submitted by the Community, the Community was allowed to address the meeting twice, first following the submissions of the United States, and again following those of Canada. Though the panel reports are not identical in every detail, they are practically so.[68] They reach the same conclusions and make the same recommendations. The panels requested the Community to bring its hormones regime into conformity with its obligations under the WTO Agreement on the Application of Sanitary and Phytosanitary Measures (SPS Agreement).[69] The Community, and the United States and Canada, chose to appeal from certain issues of law

[65] For a discussion of this see Craig, P. P., 'Legality, Standing and Substantive Review in Community Law' (1994) 14 OJLS 507.

[66] N. 60 above, *Fedesa*, para. 10.

[67] *EC Measures Concerning Meat and Meat Products (Hormones)*. The two panel reports and the report of the Appellate Body can be found on the WTO website, n. 30 above. See also the Arbitration Award of 29 May 1998 (WT/DES26/15 and WT/DS48/13).

[68] Throughout this chapter reference will be made to the panel reports. Where precise paragraph references are given these relate to the Canadian report.

[69] OJ 1994 L336/40.

and legal interpretation in the panel reports. The Appellate Body issued a single report. The aim of this paper is to consider the findings of these dispute settlement bodies. It is not, however, intended to offer a summary of each and every point or argument considered in the course of this lengthy and complex dispute, but rather to highlight some of the most important issues arising. It will focus principally (though not exclusively) on the report of the Appellate Body (AB).

Both the panels and the AB accepted that the SPS Agreement was applicable to the dispute. The EC measures were deemed to constitute sanitary measures within the meaning of Annex A of this Agreement, and to affect international trade. They agreed, moreover, that the application of this Agreement was not excluded on the basis that the Community measures, though still extant, had been enacted prior to the Agreement's entry into force. The definition of SPS measures laid down in Annex A is interesting and important in a number of respects. First, a measure will be defined thus only where it is applied with a view to protecting human, animal or plant life or health. The ostensible objective of the measure is critical to determining its status as an SPS measure. Thus, had the European Community sought to justify the hormones regime in terms other than those relating to the protection of the life or health of humans or animals, the measures would have fallen for consideration under a different part of the WTO Agreement. Second, the definition of SPS measures is explicit in its territorial scope. Measures will be considered pursuant to this Agreement only where they seek to protect the relevant interests *within* the territory of the state adopting the measure. Third, the definition of SPS measures is broad. It includes regulations pertaining both to product and process standards (subject to the territorial caveat above), as well *inter alia* as packaging and labelling requirements directly related to food safety. This latter point should be borne in mind as the following analysis proceeds. Labelling requirements in respect of hormone treated beef would be subject to the same discipline as an import ban predicated upon a failure to comply with Community standards. While labelling is clearly by nature less restrictive of trade, this would be relevant only in assessing a measure's compatibility with Article 5.6 of the SPS Agreement which obliges WTO Members to adopt measures which are no more trade-restrictive than required to achieve the appropriate level of SPS protection. Where, and as will be seen below this appears to be the case, labelling requirements are deemed incompatible with other parts of the SPS Agreement, they cannot be 'saved' by Article 5.6.[70]

---

[70] The panels declined to address the compatibility of the EC measures with Article 5.6, deeming this unnecessary in view of its earlier findings of a breach of other parts of the Agreement. The AB accepted that the panel had demonstrated appropriate 'judicial economy'. See paras 8.249–8.250 of the panel report and paras 247–52 of the AB report, n. 67 above.

As a starting point it is important to note that the AB, like the panels, found the EC measures to be incompatible with the SPS Agreement. However, and this is crucially important, the AB, unlike the panels, did not accept that there had been a breach of Article 5.5. While the AB accepted that the European Community's different treatment of the six hormones under consideration on the one hand, and two other substances on the other (carbadox and olaquindox), did represent an 'unjustifiable distinction' within the meaning of Article 5.5, it did not accept that this resulted either in discrimination or a disguised restriction on trade. The panel's conclusion in this respect was, according to the AB, supported neither by the 'architecture and structure' of the hormones directives and the later carbadox and olaquindox directives, nor by the evidence submitted by the United States or Canada.[71] The panel's finding in this respect was held to be unjustified and erroneous as a matter of law. While one might quibble with the emphasis placed by the AB on the subjective intentions of the Community in enacting this regime, it remains the case that the EC measures were held to be incompatible with the SPS Agreement, *despite* the fact that the regime was not found to result in discrimination, nor to constitute a disguised restriction on international trade.[72] The reasoning of the AB was as follows.

The fundamental tenet of the SPS Agreement is laid down in Article 2.2. This is viewed by the AB as constituting the basic obligation and as informing and imparting meaning to the other parts of the Agreement. Article 2.2 recognizes that Members have a right to enact such SPS measures as are necessary for the protection of the life or health of humans or animals. However, these measures must be based on scientific principles and must not be maintained without sufficient scientific evidence.[73] It is crucial to an understanding of this Agreement to appreciate the emphasis which it places upon science

---

[71] N. 67 above, para. 246 (AB).

[72] This is an important point in the context of risk assessment because it raises the issue of the need to ensure comparability of regulatory regime as between different products; in this case hormones for which a no residue level had been established, and carbadox and olaquindox in respect of which no maximum residue limit had been established. Yet if, as is argued later in this chapter, risk assessment and risk management is about more than responding 'rationally' to 'objective' scientific truths, but reflects also, for example, cultural conceptions of risk and science, then it may well be justified on the basis of political considerations to establish different regimes for different products. In the AB report considerations relating to consumer anxieties and the objective of internal market integration were allowed to enter the equation only in considering whether the measures in question gave rise to discrimination or a disguised restriction on trade, and not in considering whether the distinction could be 'justified' under Article 5.5. Article 5.5 is certain to be highly significant and contentious in the future. See, for example, the recent decision of the AB in *Australia—Measures Affecting Importation of Salmon* (paras 139–78) 28 October 1998 at http://www.wto.org/

[73] Article 2.2 is explicitly subject to Article 5.7 which provides for the *provisional* adoption of SPS measures even where there is insufficient scientific evidence. This is a point to which we will return.

and scientific reason. Measures, broadly defined in Annex A, in order to be compatible with the Agreement, must be susceptible to justification in the language of science. The legitimacy of SPS measures will be evaluated, in part, in terms of the credibility of their basis in science. It is to this issue of scientific rationality, and what it implies in the context of the SPS Agreement, that this chapter will now turn. Looking first at Article 3.3 of the Agreement. This provides:

Members may introduce or maintain sanitary or phytosanitary measures which result in a higher level of sanitary or phytosanitary protection than would be achieved by measures based on the relevant international standards, guidelines or recommendations, if there is a scientific justification, or as a consequence of the level of sanitary or phytosanitary protection a Member determines to be appropriate in accordance with the relevant provisions of paragraphs 1 through 8 of Article 5 . . . Notwithstanding the above, all measures which result in a level of sanitary or phytosanitary protection different from that which would be achieved by measures based on international standards, guidelines or recommendations shall not be inconsistent with any other provision of the Agreement.

This provision, the AB observes, 'is evidently not a model of clarity in drafting and communication'.[74] In particular, on the basis of its language, it appears to identify two situations in which Members may maintain or introduce higher standards; first where there is scientific justification for so doing and second, where these higher standards are deemed appropriate by the Member concerned. It is, however, only in respect of the second of these that an explicit obligation to comply with Article 5.5 SPS is established. Nevertheless, the AB, like the panels, accepted that for a measure to comply with either of these two categories identified by Article 3.3, it must also comply with the strictures of Article 5, including (crucially as will be seen) Article 5.1 on risk assessment. The AB justifies this conclusion on the basis of the final sentence of Article 3.3 and in the light of a footnote to this. This footnote provides that there is a scientific justification for a higher standard only 'if, on the basis of an examination and evaluation of available scientific information in conformity with the relevant provisions of this Agreement, a Member determines that the relevant international standards . . . are not sufficient to achieve its appropriate level of sanitary or phytosanitary protection'. This finding, in my view justified on the basis of the text, is of critical importance. There can be no scientific justification in the absence of risk assessment and unless the higher standards are based on that risk assessment. This concept of risk assessment lies at the heart of the various reports of the dispute settlement bodies and, as elsewhere, there is wide disparity between the panels' approach and that of the AB. The latter is decidedly more nuanced, and undeniably more politically astute. Before turning, in some detail, to the

---

[74] N. 67 above, para. 175 (AB).

theme of risk assessment, it is however important to stress one further point in relation to the construction of Article 3.3, especially having regard to its relationship with Article 3.1.

As noted above, Article 3.3 talks of SPS standards achieving a higher level of protection. 'Higher' in this context refers by way of comparison to the level of protection that would be achieved had the Member in question based their measures on existing international standards, guidelines, or recommendations. Article 3.3 is viewed by the panels as constituting an exception to Article 3.1. The latter provides that Members shall base their SPS measures on international standards etc. where these exist except as otherwise provided for in this Agreement, and in particular in paragraph 3. According to the panels an SPS measure may be said to be 'based on' international standards where it achieves the same level of protection as those standards. Where a domestic measure is based on international standards in this sense, such measures are viewed by the panels as conforming to such standards and hence are (rebuttably) presumed to be compatible with the SPS Agreement and the GATT. It is for the complaining party to rebut this presumption. Where on the contrary such international standards exist but the domestic measures in question are not based on them (conforming with them) the initial burden of proving that they are justified under the Article 3.3 'exception' rests upon the party introducing the measures.

The AB is critical of the panels' approach to the question of the role of international standards within the framework of the SPS Agreement. First, it does not accept the existence of a rule/exception relationship between the first and third paragraphs of Article 3.[75] Article 3.3, it insists, represents an 'autonomous right' and not an exception.[76] Consequently, even where there are international standards, and even where domestic measures are not based on these, the initial burden of demonstrating prima facie that these are inconsistent with Article 3.3 rests upon the complaining party. A prima-facie case is defined as one which, in the absence of effective refutation by the defending party, requires a panel, as a matter of law, to rule in favour of the complaining party . . .'.[77] Second, the AB rejects what it takes to be the panels' equation of the terms 'based on' (in Articles 3.1 and 3.3) and 'conform to' (in Article 3.2), on the basis that the latter implies 'much more' in terms of the relationship between the measures than the former. A measure which conforms to an international standard will be based upon it. However, a measure which is based upon an international standard may not conform with it, even

[75] N. 67 above, paras 104, 106, and 157 (AB).   [76] Ibid, para. 172 (AB).
[77] Ibid, para. 104 (AB). Though the panels erroneously required the EC to bear the burden of proof in respect of those hormones for which international standards existed, the AB found that, 'after careful consideration of the panel record' the United States and Canada had succeeded in discharging their burden to make a prima-facie case that the Community measures were inconsistent with Article 3.3 (see footnote 180 AB).

though it is founded or built upon it.[78] It justifies this conclusion on the basis both of language and purpose. It expresses its concerns in this respect strongly:

To read Article 3.1 as requiring Members to harmonize their SPS measures *by conforming those measures with international standards . . . in the here and now*, is, in effect to vest such international standards . . . (which are by the terms of the Codex *recommendatory* in form . . .) with *obligatory* force and effect. The Panel's interpretation of Article 3.1 would, in other words, transform those standards . . . into binding *norms*. But . . . the *SPS Agreement* itself sets out no indication of any intent on the part of the Members to do so. We cannot lightly assume that sovereign states intended to impose upon themselves the more onerous, rather than the less burdensome, obligation by mandating *conformity* or *compliance with* such standards . . .[79]

It has been argued, and this will be borne out further below, that the AB 'clawed back' some of the more 'audacious' aspects of the panel reports.[80] Nowhere is this more clearly the case than in relation to the role of international standards. There was a certain logic to the panels' approach, at least in so far as it would have created an incentive for Members to conform to international standards by virtue of the shift in the burden of proof which this would provoke. This is consistent with the aim of the Agreement to harmonize SPS measures 'on as wide a basis as possible',[81] 'desiring to further the use of harmonized sanitary and phytosanitary measures between Members, on the basis of international standards . . .'.[82] Pursuant to the AB's conclusions, where domestic SPS measures conform to international standards, the initial burden rests with the complaining state. Where domestic SPS measures do not conform to such standards, and where they achieve a higher level of protection than would be achieved by measures based on these standards, the initial burden still rests on the complaining party. It remains to be seen if there is anything to be gained from conforming to international standards.[83] It is, of course, possible that in the future the strength of the burden resting on the complaining party will be greater (than prima facie) in the event of such conformity. Wisely, however, in view of the considerable controversy surrounding the nature of international standards and the manner in which they are agreed (for example within the Codex), the AB refrains from addressing this point. It is worth noting that the rule/exception relationship posited by the panels smacks clearly of the approach which characterizes traditional

---

[78] Ibid, para. 163 (AB).   [79] Ibid, para. 165 (AB).

[80] Weiler, J., 'The Constitution of the Common Marketplace: Text and Context in the Evolution of the Free Movement of Goods' in Craig and de Burca, n. 51 above.

[81] Article 3.1, SPS Agreement.   [82] Recital 6, Preamble, SPS Agreement.

[83] Note, however, Article 5.6 which imposes a least trade-restrictive means obligation on Members. This is explicitly 'without prejudice' to Article 3.2; the implication being that where measures do conform to international standards they shall not be susceptible to evaluation in the light of this test.

conceptions of minimum harmonization within the EU.[84] It would, however, be a mistake to dismiss international standards as irrelevant in the context of the SPS Agreement as a result of the more deferential approach exhibited by the AB on this point. Analysis of the scope of the risk assessment obligation attaching to states will serve to demonstrate just how crucial the existence of international standards, underwritten by internationally recognized scientific findings, may prove to be.

Article 5.1 provides: 'Members shall ensure that their sanitary or phytosanitary measures are based on an assessment, as appropriate to the circumstances, of the risks to human, animal or plant life or health, taking into account risk assessment techniques developed by the relevant international organizations'.[85] It is perhaps on this issue of risk assessment that the report of the AB departs most dramatically from those of the panels. Thus, for example, the AB is critical of the panels' insistence on distinguishing between risk assessment and risk management. According to the panels, the former involves a purely scientific examination of data and factual studies and does not encompass policy, or social value, judgments as to the nature of the risk as conceived by political bodies.[86] The AB stresses that this distinction has no basis in the Agreement and hence the distinction 'which it apparently employs to achieve or support what appears to be a restrictive notion of risk assessment, has no textual basis'.[87] Somewhat related to this, though not explicitly so, is the AB's understanding of the range of factors which may be taken into account in the context of a risk assessment. Having regard to the list in Article 5.2 of the Agreement, the AB notes that it is not legitimate 'to exclude from the scope of risk assessment . . . all matters not susceptible of quantitative analysis by the empirical or scientific laboratory methods commonly associated with the physical sciences'.[88] Somewhat nebulously, and a tad theatrically, the AB observes: '. . . the risk that is to be evaluated in a risk assessment . . . is not only risk ascertainable in a science laboratory operating under strictly controlled conditions, but also risk in human societies as they actually exist, in other words, the actual potential for

---

[84] See case study 1 above.

[85] See also Annex A(3)(4) SPS for a definition of this concept and Articles 5.2 and 5.3 laying down factors which shall be taken into account in the context of a risk assessment. In view of the AB's approach to risk assessment these lists should not be regarded as exhaustive in nature. Thus whereas the panel excludes consideration of 'non-scientific factors' in risk assessment, such as those arising from difficulties of control, inspection, and enforcement of the requirements of good veterinary practice and the dangers of abuse in the use of hormones, the AB concludes that it is a 'fundamental legal error' to exclude such risks on an *a priori* basis. Nevertheless, the AB finds that the Community 'did not actually proceed to an assessment, within the meaning of Articles 5.1 and 5.2, of the risk arising from the failure of observance of good veterinary practice combined with problems of control of the use of hormones for growth promotion purposes' (para. 209 AB). See generally paras 203–9 (AB).

[86] N. 67 above, para. 8.97 (AB).   [87] Ibid, para. 181 (AB).

[88] Ibid, para. 187 (AB).

adverse effects on human health in the real world where people live, work and die'.[89]

This scepticism regarding the limits to quantitative analysis is reflected moreover in the AB's construction of the second part of paragraph 4 of Annex A to the SPS Agreement. Here the AB is strongly critical of the panel's conflation of the terms 'probability' and 'potential', speaking as it does of the former where only the latter is to be found in the Agreement.[90] This, the AB notes, 'creates a significant concern'.[91] Potential, the AB observes, relates to possibility and not probability and these two terms mean different things, with the latter implying 'a higher degree of threshold of potentiality or possibility'.[92] As a result, the panel wrongly imports a quantitative dimension into the notion of risk assessment. This, according to the AB, is also reflected in the panel's recourse to the language of 'scientifically identified risk' and 'identifiable risk'. '[T]o the extent that the Panel purported to require a risk assessment to establish a minimum magnitude of risk' the AB reiterates that 'the imposition of such a quantitative requirement finds no basis' in the SPS Agreement.[93]

In the same spirit, the AB is also critical of the panels' construction of the expression 'based on' in Article 5.1. Whereas for the panels this is taken to imply the existence of a procedural obligation to demonstrate that the results of a risk assessment were actually taken into account when the SPS measure was enacted or maintained, for the AB this merely implies an obligation to demonstrate the existence of a reasonable or rational relationship between the SPS measure in question, and the risk assessment; namely a substantive rather than a procedural obligation.[94] The AB goes on to examine the scope of this substantive obligation to ensure an 'objective', 'reasonable', or 'rational' relationship between the risk assessment and the relevant SPS measure. In their reports the panels had adopted a three-prong approach in construing the substantive obligation in Article 5.1. First, it is necessary to identify the scientific

---

[89] Ibid.

[90] This defines risk assessment as 'the evaluation of the potential for adverse effects on human or animal health arising from the presence of additives, contaminants, toxins or disease-causing organisms in food, beverage or feedstuffs'.

[91] N. 67 above, para. 184 (AB).   [92] N. 67 above, para. 184 (AB).

[93] Ibid, para. 186 (AB). In the more recent *Salmon* case (n. 72 above), the AB was required to construe the other definition of risk assessment laid down in Annex A, para. 4. This definition (cf. n. 90) provides for an 'evaluation of the likelihood . . .' rather than 'of the potential . . .'. Looking to the OIE (*Office International des Epizooties*) definition of risk and risk assessment and guidelines, the AB found that 'likelihood' as opposed to 'potential' could be conflated with 'probability' and hence that risk assessment here necessitates an evaluation of the likelihood or probability of the entry, establishment, or spread of the relevant disease, etc. Again, however, the AB emphasized that this likelihood may be expressed qualitatively or quantitatively (see paras. 120–4).

[94] Ibid, para. 189 (AB).

conclusions reached in each of the scientific studies referred to by the Community. Second, it is necessary to identify the scientific conclusion reflected in the SPS measure in dispute. Third, and finally to yield a result, it is necessary to determine whether the latter can be considered as being in conformity with the conclusions reached in the former.[95] The reaction of the AB in this respect is somewhat laconic. While it accepts, in principle, that such an approach is useful, it goes on to stress that while 'the relationship between those two sets of conclusions is certainly relevant; they cannot, however, be assigned relevance to the exclusion of everything else'.[96] Article 5.1, the AB stresses, when read alongside and informed by the basic obligation in Article 2.2, requires 'that the results of the risk assessment must sufficiently warrant—that is to say reasonably support—the SPS measure at stake'. It is careful to emphasize that the SPS measure need not be supported by the majority of the relevant scientific community, and that divergent or non-mainstream views could legitimately form the basis for such a measure. 'Responsible and representative governments may act in good faith on the basis of what, at a given time, may be a divergent opinion coming from qualified and respected sources'.[97] Where an SPS measure is based upon divergent or minority opinion this will not necessarily operate to negate the reasonableness of the relationship between the measure and the risk assessment. This, the AB emphasizes, is especially the case 'where the risk involved is life-threatening in character and is perceived to constitute a clear and imminent threat to public health'.[98] In this respect the AB's report is thoroughly infused with an appreciation of the reality of scientific uncertainty. This further reflects the AB's more nuanced approach to the relevance of the precautionary principle in the context of the SPS Agreement. Though this has been 'incorporated and given a specific meaning in Article 5.7', causing the panels to conclude that it could not override the explicit wording of Articles 5.1 and 5.2,[99] the AB found that 'there is no need to assume that Article 5.7 exhausts the relevance' of this principle.[100] This principle is further reflected in the preamble (recital 6) and in Article 3.3 of this Agreement. The AB report is consequently infused with the language of scientific uncertainty and precaution and prudence.

The above discussion merely gives a flavour of the gulf separating the panel and AB reports in terms of interpretative approach and tone. The language of the AB is such as to imply considerable self-restraint and a high degree of deference to the proper autonomy of WTO Members in exercising sensitive policy choices in the interests of public health. None the less the AB accepted that, under the terms of the SPS Agreement, there must be limits to Member State discretion and that the Community had in fact exceeded these limits in the construction of its hormones regime. The AB agreed finally with the pan-

---

[95] N. 67 above, paras 8.120–8.141 (panel).   [96] Ibid, para. 193 (AB).

[97] Ibid, para. 194 (AB).   [98] Ibid.   [99] Ibid, para. 8.160 (panel).

[100] Ibid, para. 124 (AB).

els that the European Community had acted inconsistently with Article 5.1 and that the SPS measures at hand could not be said to be based on a risk assessment within the meaning of Article 5.1. Its bark may be muted, but its bite is strong. Two factors in particular explain the conclusions of the AB in this respect.

First, the AB's eschewal of a quantitative dimension to risk assessment—the need to establish a certain magnitude or threshold level of risk—is more equivocal than at first it appears. In particular, the AB, like the panels, acknowledges that 'theoretical uncertainty' as to the existence of risk is 'not the kind of risk which, under Article 5.1, is to be assessed'.[101] A hypothetical possibility of risk, arising from the failure of scientists to demonstrate with absolute certainty that there is no risk either now or in the future, is not capable of rationally grounding an SPS measure. While it is incumbent on the complaining party to demonstrate a prima-facie breach of the Agreement, the burden resting on this party is not such as to require conclusive proof of the absence of any risk. The initial burden having been discharged, it is for the party adopting the SPS measure to put forth positive evidence of risk, such as is capable of reasonably sustaining the measure. Scientific uncertainty thus works both ways: 'if science is not able to prove the causal relationship leading to possible damage, then symmetrically it may also be unable to divert the possibility of its existence. In other words, requiring proof of the absence of risk is asking for something that science is not able to provide.'[102] This is a lesson which the AB has taken to heart.

Second, the AB's eschewal of a quantitative dimension to risk assessment (subject to the proviso above) is matched by its willingness to import a qualitative dimension.[103] This is apparent in two respects: (a) in its willingness to countenance measures adopted on the basis of divergent or minority scientific opinion, where this comes from 'qualified and respected sources';[104] and (b) in its assessment of the scientific evidence presented by the European Community and by the experts appointed to assist the panels and AB. In this respect it is important to observe at the outset that evidence was submitted to the dispute settlement bodies which classified 'oestrogens as agents which are

---

[101] Ibid, para. 186 (AB).

[102] Godard, O., 'Social Decision-Making under Conditions of Scientific Controversy, Expertise and the Precautionary Principle' in Joerges, Ladeur and Vos, *Integrating Scientific Expertise into Regulatory Decision-Making* (Nomos, 1997), 68.

[103] See also, in this respect, the more recent *Salmon* case (n. 72 above) where the AB did not accept the panel's conclusion that the measures in question were based on a risk assessment under Article 5.1. While it accepted that the lengthy report submitted by Australia satisfied the first stage in the risk assessment process (identification of the disease etc.), it failed to satisfy the second and third (the probability dimension discussed in n. 93 above). It concluded that 'some' evaluation of likelihood or probability was not sufficient to constitute a proper risk assessment within the meaning of Article 5.1 (see paras 112–38).

[104] N. 67 above, para. 194 (AB).

carcinogenic meaning that there is sufficient evidence of carcinogenicity in humans; androgens as agents which are probably carcinogenic; and progestins as agents which are possibly carcinogenic'.[105] The AB had the following to say in response:

The 1987 Monographs and the articles and opinions of individual scientists submitted by the European Communities constitute general studies which do indeed show the existence of a general risk of cancer; but they do not focus on and do not address the particular kind of risk here at stake—the carcinogenic or genotoxic potential of the residues of those hormones found in meat derived from cattle to which the hormones had been administered for growth promotion purposes—as required by paragraph 4 of Annex A of the SPS Agreement. Those general studies are, in other words, relevant but do not appear to be sufficiently specific to the case at hand.[106]

Moreover, at a joint meeting held with the appointed scientific experts,[107] a certain Dr Lucier expressed the following view:

For one in every million women alive in the United States, Canada, Europe today, about every 110,000 of those women will get breast cancer. This is obviously a tremendous public health issue. Of those 110,000 women getting breast cancer, maybe several thousand of them are related to the total intake of exogenous oestrogens from every source, including eggs, meat, phyto-oestrogens, fungal oestrogens, the whole body burden of exogenous oestrogens. And by my estimates one of those 110,000 would come from eating meat containing oestrogens as a growth promoter, if used as prescribed.[108]

This, the AB observes, would, assuming it to be accurate, imply (in a European Union of 371 million) that there could be up to 371 persons who would get cancer as a result of eating meat containing oestrogens used as a growth promoter. None the less, the AB notes that this opinion does not purport to be the result of scientific studies carried out by Dr Lucier, nor under his supervision, focusing specifically on residues of hormones in meat from cattle fattened with such hormones:

Accordingly, it appears that the single divergent opinion expressed by Dr Lucier is not reasonably sufficient to overturn the contrary conclusions reached in the scientific studies referred to by the European Communities that related specifically to residues of the hormones in meat from cattle to which hormones had been administered for growth promotion.[109]

These extracts are not intended to mislead as to the nature of the scientific evidence presented. They are intended rather to illustrate the willingness of the AB to engage in a qualitative assessment of that evidence, and its propen-

[105] This evidence is drawn from the 1987 IARC Monographs upon which the EC placed 'particular emphasis' (n. 67 above, para. 8.129 (panel)).

[106] N. 67 above, para. 200 (AB).

[107] A transcript of this is contained in an annex to the AB Report.

[108] N. 67 above, footnote 181 (AB).   [109] Ibid, para. 198 (AB).

sity to demand a high degree of specificity in the research underpinning SPS measures. The Community measures could not be said to be based upon risk assessment where the only evidence purporting to rationally sustain these measures was insufficiently focused upon the precise issue at hand; namely the dangers arising from residues in meat from animals to which the hormones concerned had been administered.

It is thus apparent that under the SPS Agreement, as construed by the AB, it is not rational, and hence not lawful, for a Member to guard against a 'merely' theoretical or hypothetical risk where to do so would affect international trade. Until, and unless, the 'more than merely theoretical' threshold is reached, only the language of science will resonate in the application of this Agreement.[110] In this sense, the world of the SPS Agreement is a world inhabited by experts, in which authority to distinguish right and wrong is the preserve of the 'qualified and respected' scientist. It is a world of technocracy. It is a world in which the contingency of scientific knowledge is denied, and in which the values which enter law through science remain obscured. It is a world in which hypothetical risk must be endured, regardless of the nature of the risk-generating activity and the social worth attaching to it. Context, as well as culture,[111] is silenced in this unidimensional world of scientific rationality. This is a world in which law is the servant of science in the name of free trade; a world in which law as an instrument of other values—social order, public confidence, trust, community, rights, democracy, or deliberation—has no role. It is a world in which the language of power is science and in which one can be heard only in these terms.

Over the past years much attention has focused upon the role of science in law, spawning a large body of literature by lawyers, scientists, philosophers, sociologists, and cultural theorists.[112] Theoretically sophisticated,

---

[110] Subject, as noted above, to the application of Article 5.7 which allows for the provisional adoption of measures pending review within a 'reasonable time'.

[111] For an influential and entertaining take on 'risk' from the perspective of cultural theory see Adams, J., *Risk* (UCL Press: London, 1995). Adams observes that those assessing and managing risk often cast aspersions on the rationality of those who disagree with them. Cultural theory, however, teaches that it is not the case that one is rational and the other not. Rather the participants may be arguing from different premises. Responses to risk will depend, *inter alia*, on personality: are you an individualist who views nature as stable and robust and capable of shrugging off the insults of humankind and rarely 'biting back'? Or are you an egalitarian clinging to the view of nature as fragile and precarious and desirous that we tread lightly on the earth?

[112] For a taste of this see Joerges, Ladeur and Vos, n. 102 above; Jasanoff, S., *Science at the Bar* (Harvard UP, 1995); Jasanoff, S., *The Fifth Branch: Science Advisers as Policymakers* (Harvard UP, 1990); Jasanoff, Markle, Petersen and Pinch (eds.), *Handbook of Science and Technology Studies* (Sage, 1995); Lash, Szerszynski and Wynne (eds.), *Risk, Environment and Modernity* (Sage, 1996); Hess, D. J., *Science Studies* (New York UP, 1997). David Hess's 'advanced introduction' to this subject contains an excellent bibliography and 'additional information' on sources.

multi-disciplinary, and practically important, the future of science studies within the academy seems secure. One of the central premises of much of this literature—though to varying degrees—has been a rejection of positivistic conceptions of science as capable of revealing an objective truth; a version of reality untainted by politics, ideology or exogenous values. There is a wide-spread acceptance of the socially constructed nature of scientific knowledge. As Sheila Jasanoff, an influential voice in law and science studies, notes:

Although pleas for maintaining a strict separation between science and politics continue to run like a leitmotif through the policy literature, the artificiality of this position can no longer be doubted . . . Studies of scientific advising leave in tatters the notion that it is possible, in practice, to restrict the advisory process to technical issues or that the subjective values of scientists are irrelevant to decision-making. The negotiated and constructed model of scientific knowledge, which closely captures the realities of regulatory science, rules out the possibility of drawing sharp boundaries between facts and values or claims and context . . .[113]

As this conception of science as contingent and uncertain has taken root, and as public awareness of the 'failures' of regulatory science has increased, a democratic impulse has emerged as a counterweight to the 'technocratic view'.[114] This is not new, as the accessible yet pioneering work of the North American sociologist Dorothy Nelkin demonstrates.[115] Demands for 'more and better science' in policy-making are matched by demands for participation and deliberation in the adoption of 'technical' decisions. Such demands rest not only upon a belief in the capacity of the public to develop sufficient expertise to engage in the language of science, but also in the 'validity' of 'lay' knowledge,[116] and in the salience of values imported from beyond the world of scientific reason.[117] Alongside initiatives intended to assess the credibility of scientific findings, there have emerged initiatives designed to foster public participation in a wide variety of forms.[118] Such experiments may be pursued in the name of a democratic ideal, and/or they may reflect the political interest in producing social consensus around public decisions and in defusing controversy—something which the application of scientific reason has conspicuously failed to do. To the extent that such experiments result in the adoption of decisions which do not find support in at least a version of scientific truth, they are today under threat from the supremely technocratic world view endorsed by the SPS Agreement, even as it is construed at the hands of the more politically circumspect AB.

[113] Jasanoff, S., *The Fifth Branch* (n. 112 above), 231.   [114] See generally ibid, 15 ff.
[115] *Technological Decision and Democracy* (Sage, 1977).
[116] See, for example, Wynne, B., 'May the Sheep Safely Graze? A Reflexive View of the Expert–Lay Knowledge Divide' in Lash *et al.*, n. 108 above.
[117] See Nelken, D., 'The Truth about Law's Truth' (EUI Working Paper Law No. 90/1).
[118] See ibid. and Sklove, R., *Democracy and Technology* (Guilford, 1995) and for the work of his 'Loka Institute': http://www.amherst.edu/~loka

Hormones in Beef: Concluding Comments

The above discussion has focused upon the hormones dispute with a view to exemplifying the significance and nature of the SPS Agreement. It is clear that this agreement marks an important step in the evolution of international law regulating trade between states. It rests upon an expanded conception of the 'basic rule', taking us beyond a discrimination based approach to international trade, and upon a restrictive interpretation of the exception to the rule. As regards the latter, the Agreement elaborates rules for the application of the GATT, Article XX(b) exception. The elaboration which it provides is both territorially restrictive (in the sense discussed above in the veal calves case study) and epistemologically closed in its tendency to privilege scientific rationality.[119]

It may, however, be argued that the AB's approach merely reflects the Agreement itself and, in particular, the very definition of SPS measures contained therein. As noted above, this definition is narrow. If the measure in question purports to protect the health or life of humans, animals, or plants *outside* of its own territory then that measure does not fall within the scope of the definition in the Agreement. Equally, were the measure in question to be justified on the basis of moral or ethical considerations, rather than on the basis of a putative threat to the life or health of humans, animals, or plants, again the measure will not be classified as being SPS in character. In either case the measure will fall for consideration under another part of the broad WTO regime, of which the SPS Agreement constitutes only one part. It may thus appear that criticisms of the SPS Agreement, and of the AB's interpretative approach, which rest upon their unwillingness to contemplate values other than those relating to life/health is to overlook the substantive scope of the Agreement. Indeed, it was the case that the Community did not seek to justify its measures other than in terms of the life or health of humans.[120] It may consequently be argued that it was the way in which the EC packaged and presented its measures that led inexorably to the conclusions outlined above. By claiming that the measures were necessary to protect human life/health, the Community quite reasonably was required to demonstrate some objective

---

[119] This raises an interesting point and one which may be argued before the AB in future cases. Article 2(4) of the SPS Agreement provides that SPS measures which conform with it shall be presumed to be in accordance with the relevant parts of the GATT, and in particular Article XX(b) thereof. There would be no need to rely upon the GATT Article XX exceptions in cases where the principle of national treatment is not infringed. In such cases measures would enjoy the blanket of protection offered by the GATT, Article III 'national treatment' rule. It might then be possible to argue that unless a measure is in breach of a relevant GATT norm, hence necessitating reliance on Article XX(b), the discipline of the SPS Agreement does not apply.

[120] N. 67 above, para. 8.276 (panel).

basis for this and, again quite reasonably, precluded from invoking ethical rather than physical concerns.

While such observations based on the text of the Agreement, and specifically the definition of SPS measures contained therein, go some way to explaining the approach of the AB, it is none the less important to recall that the AB was required to establish an evidential threshold in order to apply its rationality test. The threshold which it constructed requires evidence of a more than merely theoretical risk, having regard to scientific studies focusing on the precise issue at hand. This threshold remains the same regardless, for example, of the intensity of the theoretical risk, and of the cultural sensibilities or filters which mediate a society's relationship to risk. The threshold remains the same regardless of citizen preferences, and regardless of the scale or nature of the benefits which would be foregone as a result of measures introduced to mitigate that theoretical risk. In essence it is the unwillingness of the AB to countenance the possibility that an SPS measure might be rational below this threshold, having regard to social and political culture and context, that gives rise to the criticisms put forth in this paper. In the event that science neither proves the existence of risk, nor proves that there is no risk, there is scope for 'rational' debate as to whether this theoretical risk should be tolerated. But it is a debate which will inevitably transcend scientific rationality, thus shattering the fragile illusion of objectivity and universal commensurability, and reducing the potential for 'scientific universalism . . . [to be] used to overcome the particularism of legal systems'.[121]

It is apparent from the above discussion that the European Court exhibited greater deference than the WTO dispute settlement organs in reviewing the scientific basis of Council acts prohibiting hormones in beef.[122] It should, however, be stressed that the reluctance of the Court to second-guess legislative policy choices occurred in the context of an act conceived as facilitating rather than impeding market integration. Indeed, had the measures not been enacted, the different approaches adopted by the Member States to the administration of hormones in farming might have resulted in market fragmentation as a result of Member State recourse to the Article 30 EC exception (formerly Article 36).[123] In construing this provision the European Court has held that it is not enough for the measure in question to claim to

---

[121] Joerges, C., 'Scientific Expertise in Social Regulation and the European Court of Justice: Legal Frameworks for Denationalized Governance Structures' in Joerges *et al.*, n. 102 above.

[122] *Fedesa* n. 60 above. For evidence of the European Court's different approach to review of Community measures, rather than Member State measures, see ibid.

[123] This point is stressed by the Court in assessing the proportionality of the Community measures: 'Since the Council committed no manifest error in that respect, it was also entitled to take the view that, regard being had to the requirements of health protection, the removal of barriers to trade and distortions of competition could not be achieved by means of less onerous measures such as dissemination of information to consumers and the labeling of meat' (n. 60 above, para. 16). See also the opinion of the Advocate General in this case.

be necessary to protect consumer health. Thus, in the context of a Belgian prohibition on the marketing of bread and other bakery products with a salt content higher than the maximum laid down in domestic law, the Court found that '[g]eneral conjecture', as to the risk posed to consumer health, does not amount to proof of a risk for public health:

. . . the fact that there is a risk to consumers is sufficient to make legislation of the kind at issue compatible with the requirements of Article 36 [new Article 30]. However, the risk must be measured, not according to the yardstick of general conjecture, but on the basis of relevant scientific research.

Hence, when the measure in question is such as to impede free movement, the Court manifests a higher propensity to assess the credibility of claims made, and to do so on the basis of scientific rationality.[124] None the less, strict consumer protection measures may be justified in the case of substances which

[124] The topic of risk before the European Court is vast and multi-faceted, and generally beyond the scope of this chapter. See especially Vos, E., *Institutional Frameworks of Community Health and Safety Regulations* (Hart Publishing, 1999). For a recent example in the context of a Commission Decision prohibiting exports of beef from the United Kingdom in the context of the BSE ('mad cow') debate, see Case C-180/96 *United Kingdom of Great Britain and Northern Ireland v Commission* [1998] ECR I-2265. Here the European Commission was entitled to adopt safeguard measures pursuant to powers granted by two Community directives where there is an 'outbreak . . . of any zoonoses, diseases or other cause likely to constitute a serious hazard to animals or human health'. As in its hormones case law the Court emphasized the wide measure of discretion enjoyed by the Commission and restricted itself to reviewing whether the exercise of such discretion is vitiated by a manifest error or a misuse of powers, or whether the Commission did not clearly exceed the bounds of its discretion. Here the European Court adopted a broadly precautionary approach in assessing the legality of the Commission's (temporary) safeguard measures: 'Where there is uncertainty as to the existence or extent of risk to human health, the institutions may take protective measures without having to wait until the reality and seriousness of those risks become fully apparent' (para. 99). The language of the Court, in upholding the legality of the Commission decision, is not dissimilar to that of the AB. It emphasized that the link between BSE and Creutzfeldt-Jakob (CJ) disease had 'ceased to be a theoretical hypothesis' and had become a 'possibility'. Indeed, it noted that, according to the Spongiform Encephalopathy Advisory Committee (SEAC—an independent scientific body advising the UK government) 'the most likely explanation' for CJ was exposure to BSE before the introduction of the specified ovine offal ban in 1989 (para. 52). Later the Court speaks of a 'probable link' (para. 61). The Court accepted that the Commission had been prompted to adopt the provisional measures after examining the measures adopted by the UK, and after consulting the relevant scientific committees (Scientific Veterinary Committee and the Standing Veterinary Committee—on which see Vos, cited above). It is interesting to note that the scientists consulted did not merely accept that it was impossible to prove (or disprove) the existence of a link but also that there was no 'direct evidence of a link, on current data'. None the less, the SEAC was prepared, in the absence of any credible alternative, to assert that exposure to BSE was the most likely explanation (para. 9). This attests extraordinarily clearly to the willingness of the European Court (cf. the panels or AB) to accept scientific conclusions without seeking to evaluate qualitatively the data upon which these are premised. It also attests to the propensity of state actors (or suprastate actors) to take stringent steps to protect against an arguably small risk of something particularly dangerous happening.

are '*per se* dangerous' and which generally—as a category—constitute a major risk to human and animal health and to the environment.[125] Given that there is scientific evidence that oestrogens are carcinogenic in humans, that androgens are probably carcinogenic, and that progestins are possibly carcinogenic, it seems unlikely that the European Court would regard them as other than *per se* dangerous. Hence while the language of science resonates both before the European Court and the WTO organs, when it comes to evaluating justifications for restricting trade, the qualitative threshold for establishing the existence of risk appear to be lower in a Community context, at least in so far as substances which are generally accepted as dangerous are concerned.[126]

TRADE AND ENVIRONMENT IN THE EU AND WTO: CONCLUSIONS

In his recent book examining the free-movement case law of the European Court from a perspective of economic constitutionalism, Miguel Poiares Maduro explores a fundamental dilemma.[127] On the one hand, 'discrimination or protectionist effects tests are seen as inefficient in fighting protectionism because they allow too many protectionist measures to escape judicial consideration'.[128] On the other hand, 'a balance test', such as that represented by the European Court's proportionality-based approach, implies, 'to a great extent, making it [the Court or other dispute settlement body] responsible for defining appropriate regulatory policy'.[129] Not only are courts structurally ill-equipped for this task, but this gives rise to profound issues of legitimacy which ultimately, 'have consequences for the acceptance of their decisions and their authority'.[130] While it is not possible here to do justice to the richness of Maduro's insights, nor the impressive clarity of his expression, Maduro argues convincingly that, in the context of balancing, the search for a 'meta-national' mechanism of substantive assessment is bound to fail. Ultimately, the task of balancing the costs and benefits associated with any given measure will reflect the values, and institutional context, of those endowed with authority.

Maduro's thesis in this respect is nowhere more convincing than in the area of environmental policy. In an area which encompasses, but transcends, physical impact, what is reasonable (proportionate) or 'rational' in terms of policy

[125] See, especially, Case 94/83 *Criminal Proceedings against Albert Heijn BV* [1984] ECR 3263, paras 13–17.

[126] For a more detailed discussion of this case law see Vos, n. 124 above, Joerges, n. 121 above, and Hession and Macrory, 'Balancing Trade Freedom with the Requirements of Sustainable Development' in Emiliou and O'Keeffe, *The European Union and World Trade Law* (Wiley, 1996).

[127] N. 57 above.   [128] Ibid, 53.   [129] Ibid, 59.   [130] Ibid.

response is necessarily contingent.[131] This reflects not merely the uncertainty which characterizes costs and benefits in a context of unknown (unknowable) risk, but also post-positivist conceptions of science, and economics, as capable of constructing merely *a* version of the 'truth' which, like any other, has its roots in the premises, methodologies, and values of the system within which it is articulated. To take a single example, drawn from the first case study above, in *Gourmetterie*[132] Advocate General van Gerven (unlike the European Court) approached the Dutch ban on the marketing of 'dead red grouse' from the perspective of proportionality. He notes in this respect that:

The restriction of intra-Community trade resulting from an absolute prohibition of imports . . . is out of proportion, in my view, to the small contribution which such a prohibition is capable of making in concreto—by discouraging the killing of the bird species in question in the United Kingdom—the achievement of the objective pursued, namely the improvement of stocks of bird species which is not endangered and whose protection is not a priority under Community law. That is so particularly since the measure under consideration and the obstacle to trade resulting therefrom are intended to protect a bird and thus, contrary to the principle of mutual confidence between States, to take effect on the territory of another Member State; moreover, the measure was adopted on the basis of a unilateral appraisal of the interests involved, that is so say without taking into account of interests which may warrant or justify the hunting of that species.

The Advocate General is clearly conscious here that application of the proportionality principle is a matter of judgment. In his view, having regard to the physical objective which he perceives as underlying the national measure, the import prohibition is not proportionate.[133] The objective of the measure

---

[131] It is important to observe that the 'rationality' test of the AB in the hormones case is, as it was expressed there, less intrusive in terms of national policy than a fully fledged proportionality test as applied by the European Court, especially in its review of national measures. In practice, of course, the European Court's test ranges from the strict to a more hands-off 'not manifestly disproportionate standard'. The *Danish Bottles* (Case 302/86 *Commission v Denmark* [1988] ECR 4607) case provides a good example of what I mean by a fully fledged proportionality test, as does the definition of Advocate General van Gerven in the dead red grouse case, n. 21 above. In the context of the SPS Agreement, once the minimum threshold (more than a merely theoretical risk) has been reached the AB said nothing to imply that it would go further in balancing the costs and benefits of the measure in question (subject of course to the least restrictive means test). None the less recourse to the language of rationality or reasonableness, upon which the AB report is predicated, clearly lends itself to the application of a proportionality-style test. It remains to be seen whether, in the future, in the context of an established risk, the AB will develop the concept of a rational relationship in this way.

[132] N. 21 above, para. 10.

[133] The limited physical impact of the measure reflects its extra-territorial nature. The ban may have no impact whatsoever. Grouse may continue to be hunted in the United Kingdom on the same scale. It may be necessary for new markets to be found, whether at home or abroad, but the link between the measure and its physical objective is tenuous. In this, the Advocate General echoes the approach of the GATT panel in the second of the

at hand may, however, be viewed in terms which are not physical. The Dutch interest in the ban may lie not merely in its concern to promote a decline in the hunting of the bird species in question in the United Kingdom, but also in the value which that society attaches to knowing that it is not participating, through trade, in practices which it considers to be wrong. The ban may reflect ethical concerns and seek to protect the moral autonomy of this society. In this sense, it might be considered comparable to a ban on the importation of pornographic or racist literature introduced, not on the basis of evidence of a resulting rise in racism or abuse of women or children, but on the basis quite simply that it is wrong. As in a context of scientific uncertainty, concepts of proportionality or rationality emerge as striking in their subjectivity when they confront the moral, rather than physical, spillovers associated with international trade. It is no doubt for this reason that the European Court has accorded Member States such a broad margin of discretion when confronted with cases concerning the protection of public morality.[134]

This, however, is not the only reason for citing Advocate General van Gerven above. Among the reasons which he provides for his scepticism regarding the legitimacy of the Dutch ban is the fact that the measure was adopted without taking into account the interests of the United Kingdom in hunting red grouse. In this sense the Advocate General is concerned with what Maduro calls 'national bias' in policy-making in Member States. By this Maduro is referring to the 'over-representation of national interests' at the expense of 'out-of-state interests'; 'decisions of Member States that affect the free movement of goods can thus be seen as affecting interests not normally represented in the national political process'.[135] This leads Maduro in a particular direction. He proposes the adoption of a procedural rather than a substantive approach by the European Court in its assessment of the legitimacy of national regulatory measures under Articles 28–30 (formerly 30–6). '[T]he Court of Justice should not second-guess national regulatory choices, but should instead ensure that there is no under-representation of the interests of nationals of other Member States in the national political process'.[136] It is thus the quality of the political process, in terms of interest representation and participation, which is viewed as providing the basis for the evaluation of national measures, rather than the substantive merits of the decision from the perspective of the actor enjoying the power of review.

Maduro's recent contribution does not stand alone. It is indicative of a widespread 'procedural' turn in Community law, an approach which conceives legitimacy in terms of process rather than substantive outcome. This is

Tuna/Dolphin reports. Here the measures were condemned on the basis that they were contingent in their effect upon their occasioning a change of policy on the part of the exporting state.

[134] See, for example, Case 34/79 *R v Henn & Derby* [1979] ECR 3795.
[135] N. 57 above, at 169–75.   [136] N. 121 above, at 173.

perhaps most clearly identified with the work of Christian Joerges and his col-laborators, focusing upon the concept of deliberation in constitutionalizing governance through comitology.[137] Important also in this respect is Karl-Heinz Ladeur's 'network' approach predicated upon decision-making within a framework of 'co-operative', 'a-centric', and 'heterarchical' relations between heterogeneous actors.[138]

Maduro's thesis is resonant also of ongoing debates in political and legal theory concerning the democratic foundations of constitutional adjudication, notably in the United States and Germany. It is resonant in particular of the writings of those who propose a procedural as opposed to a substantive approach to judicial review, and who conceive the authority of the judiciary in terms of the sustenance which this institution might offer to the democra-tic process. Thus, for example, John Hart Ely famously propounded a theory of judicial review which is 'representation-reinforcing'.[139] This focuses upon the role of courts in policing access to the political process, especially in terms of participation by minority groups. This, as Ely would have intended,[140] has been seized upon by those writing within the tradition of civic republicanism, albeit that in this tradition the value of deliberation is highlighted along with participation in defining the democratic ideal.[141]

As Habermas reminds us, procedural perspectives on judicial review demand the elaboration of a specific theory of democracy; something which Habermas purports to do in articulating his conception of 'deliberative poli-tics'.[142] Thus, in so far as judicial review is viewed as process based, it requires that the procedural parameters of legitimate decision-making be identified; a far from simple task even within a nation state as the normative claims of lib-eral, republican, proceduralist and communitarian conceptions of democracy compete for space. At the level of an international organization (such as the WTO), comprising authoritarian as well as liberal democratic states, and eco-nomically developed and developing country members, no more than a 'thin' conception of procedural propriety may realistically underpin adjudication in this setting. It is perhaps for this reason that Maduro's procedural perspective, elaborated for the EU, is closer to that of Ely than Habermas, focusing as it appears to do upon 'representation' of out-of-state interests, rather than upon

[137] See generally, Joerges and Vos, *EU Committees: Social Regulation, Law and Politics* (Hart Publishing, 1999 forthcoming).

[138] See 'Towards a Theory of Supranationality—The Viability of the Network Concept' (1991) 3 ELJ 33 and his contribution to ibid.

[139] *Democracy and Distrust* (Harvard UP, 1980).

[140] See generally Ely, J. H., *On Constitutional Ground*, ch. 1, for a discussion of the politi-cal context and underpinnings of his theory of judicial review and its relevance for a republi-can analysis.

[141] See generally the special issue of the *Yale Law Journal* on republicanism, (1988) 97/8 *Yale LJ*, and especially the contributions by F. Michelman and C. Sunstein therein.

[142] *Between Facts and Norms* (MIT, 1996), especially chs 6 and 7.

the communicative processes according to which these are formed, received, and mediated.

That said, it is interesting to note that in both of the WTO 'cases' under discussion, the dispute settlement bodies, in different ways, looked to process as a tool for assessing the legitimacy of the measures in question. In the 'hormones' case the panels construed Article 5.1 of the SPS Agreement as imposing a minimum procedural obligation to undertake a risk assessment. While the AB reversed this finding,[143] it did so in a manner which was somewhat equivocal. Thus while the AB insisted that it is not necessary for a Member to undertake its own risk assessment, it did none the less require that there be a risk assessment, as well as a reasonable relationship between the results of that assessment and the measures at stake. Thus, in relation to one of the substances in question (MGA), the AB highlighted the almost complete absence of evidence on this in the panel proceedings, and upheld the panels' findings that there had been 'no risk assessment with regard to MGA'.[144] Consequently, the Community measures prohibiting the administration of MGA could not be said to be based upon a risk assessment within the meaning of the SPS Agreement.

In the shrimp case, as noted above, both the panel and the AB emphasized the failure of the United States to engage seriously in across-the-board international negotiations prior to the introduction of the regime in question, the latter noting that this bears heavily in its appraisal under the *chapeau*. Equally, in condemning the United States measures according to the terms of the Article XX *chapeau*, 'due process' considerations in the certification process were highlighted, including the 'singularly informal and casual' nature of the process, the lack of transparency and predictability which characterized it, the absence of a right to be heard, or even to receive reasoned notification of outcome, and the lack of any structure for appeal against, or review of, a certification decision adopted.

Here specific procedural criteria, over and above those explicitly laid down in the WTO Agreement,[145] are identified as underpinning the agreement,

---

[143] It is interesting to note that the AB appears to adopt a different approach to the language of 'based on' in Article 3.1 (concerning international standards) and Article 5.1. Whereas in the case of the former it is taken to mean 'build upon' rather than 'conform to', it is taken to imply a stricter standard of conformity in the latter. It should be observed that this chapter is not arguing that scientific evidence is irrelevant in decision-making, but merely that it is one factor and one perspective which should be required to feed into the policy process; but one of many.

[144] N. 67 above, para. 201.

[145] It is noteworthy in this respect that there is much in the Agreement which would offer succour to those who conceive legitimacy in procedural terms, and in particular for those who posit the value of deliberation at the centre of their theory of democracy. See, for example, in the context of the SPS Agreement, Article 7 on Transparency, Article 11 on consultations between states and Article 12 establishing an SPS committee to provide a regular forum for

and hence as relevant to an assessment of legality, thus sowing the seeds of a process based approach to adjudication in the WTO. As things stand, of course, these procedural considerations inform, rather than supersede, the application of the relevant substantive obligations. None the less their significance should not be understated, conceptually or practically. Not only do they offer a vision of dispute settlement in the WTO which is such as to nourish rather than thwart the democratic process, but they also promise to structure decision-making in such a way as to render it more responsive to the global context and consequences of domestic decisions. It is to be hoped that this in turn might serve both to avert disputes between states, and to facilitate the informal resolution of those which do arise.

consultations. This committee shall arrive at its decisions by consensus. See generally, *The WTO Dispute Settlement Procedures: A Collection of Legal Texts* (WTO, 1995) for the relevant materials, and especially Articles 4, 5, and 25 of the DSU. In the 'shrimps' case the AB looked to Article X.3 of the GATT for support for its due process findings. This requires the uniform, impartial, and reasonable administration of the relevant national rules affecting trade, and the institution of judicial, arbitral, or other administrative tribunals or procedures enabling the independent and prompt review of administrative action relating to customs matters.

6

The North American Integration Regime and its Implications for the World Trading System

FREDERICK M. ABBOTT*

The past several years have revealed deep flaws in the institutions regulating the world economy. Governments throughout the world now focus their attention on controlling turbulent forces unleashed by the advent of new technologies. Yet throughout the 1997–8 global economic crisis, the processes of regional economic integration in North America and Europe continued, and these processes have lent a considerable measure of security to the regional and global economic landscapes. Though it is easy enough to point to shortcomings of the NAFTA and EU regional integration processes, there is also reason to conclude that these enterprises are on the whole of benefit to the world economic and political system. Evidence is mounting that close market integration coupled with effective legal institutions provides economic, social, and political benefits over more diffuse market integration and the absence of legalization. Though there are certainly risks inherent in the regionalization of the world economy, the success of the NAFTA and EU relative to the world economy as a whole suggests that there is more to be gained than feared from the process.

The NAFTA and EU differ substantially in terms of the level of decision-making authority conferred on regional political institutions and on the degree to which they co-ordinate economic policy *vis-à-vis* third countries. Yet these differences should not obscure certain fundamental shared characteristics. Both systems are anchored by large and globally competitive national economies, both systems are highly legalized, and member countries of both systems share a commitment to democratic political institutions (even if imperfect ones).

* Professor of Law, Chicago–Kent College of Law. This chapter is based on lectures delivered at the Academy of European Law of the European University Institute, Florence, Italy, July 1998. The author is indebted to the directors of the Institute for the opportunity to discuss this subject with an exceptional group of students.

The NAFTA entered into force on 1 January 1994 after a protracted political struggle in the United States. The first five years of the NAFTA's operation have witnessed substantial growth in trilateral trade between Canada, Mexico, and the United States (the 'Parties'). There has been modest growth in cross-border investment and services trade. The Peso Crisis of 1994–5 led to substantial economic hardship and social dislocation in Mexico. Though the NAFTA may have played a role in precipitating the Peso Crisis by encouraging the inflow of foreign capital into the Mexican market, on balance the NAFTA appears to have played a net positive role in stabilizing Mexico's macro-economic situation and in laying the foundation for long-term economic growth. On the legal side, the NAFTA has led to modest gains in attention to the conditions of workers and the environment. The NAFTA was not designed with the intention to manage social welfare conditions. To the extent that the NAFTA has failed to address those conditions, this failure was built in to its institutions. Yet the NAFTA's structure which maintains the centres of political, social, and cultural power in the hands of national government authorities may reflect a reasonable alternative to the EU system. The NAFTA's balance of the advantages of regional economic integration with a more distributed system of political decision-making power may be attractive to states which do not envision the regional creation of a quasi-federal polity.

The legal relationship between the NAFTA and the WTO is ambiguous. Whether NAFTA or WTO rules prevail in the event of inconsistency is uncertain, and the extent to which NAFTA panels may or must consider applicable WTO rules is unclear. The ambiguity in NAFTA–WTO legal relations may reflect an underlying uncertainty in the policy arena. Trade negotiators understand that there are benefits and costs to regional integration, just as there are benefits and costs to multilateral integration. There are policy reasons to prefer each form of integration in specific contexts, and there are political and social interest group pressures for establishing various hierarchies of norms. Though it seems unlikely that NAFTA policy makers deliberately chose to leave the relationship between the NAFTA and WTO Agreement ambiguous, the underlying pressures to do so may account for the lack of a clearly defined relationship. While there may be sound policy reasons for clarifying the relationship between these two agreements, trade policy makers remain subject to conflicting pressures, and the ambiguity may persist for some time.

I THE NAFTA MUTATION OF THE EC MODEL REVISITED

The NAFTA is a significantly different model of regional economic integration than the European Union.[1] The EU is loosely based on the concept of a federal

[1] See generally, by Frederick M. Abbott, *Law and Policy of Regional Integration: The NAFTA and Western Hemispheric Integration in the World Trade Organization System* (1995) [hereinafter

polity with an allocation of power between Union organs—the Council, Commission, Parliament and Court of Justice—on one side, and Member State governments on the other side.[2] The NAFTA is in the nature of a confederation among independent sovereigns, each maintaining autonomous political decision-making authority within constraints defined by agreement.[3] The political decision-making apparatus of the NAFTA is closely circumscribed to roughly include within the boundaries of its central authority (the Free Trade Commisssion) the powers traditionally conferred upon trade ministers by their governments. The European Court of Justice has referred to the EC Treaty as a constitutional charter, and the Court has viewed its role as the guardian of that constitution.[4] The NAFTA does not purport to serve as a constitution in the sense of altering the distribution of powers among its Parties.

The EC Treaty provides for the adoption of directives, regulations, and decisions by the Union political organs. These enactments are customarily referred to as 'secondary legislation' reflecting their status underneath the 'primary legislation' of the EC Treaty. The relationship between primary and secondary Union legislation is similar to the traditional relationship between the constitution and parliamentary enactments of a national federal government. The EC Treaty and secondary legislation may have direct effect in the EU Member States, meaning that this legislation may be relied on by individuals in the courts of the Member States in appropriate circumstances.

The NAFTA political institutions are not empowered to enact secondary legislation except in very limited circumstances prescribed by the agreement (such as in adopting rules of procedure for NAFTA dispute settlement panels). There is no general legislative power allocated to the NAFTA political institutions. The NAFTA is in theory capable of direct effect within the national courts of its Parties. The United States has by legislation deprived the NAFTA of potential direct effect in US courts.[5]

Law and Policy]; 'Integration Without Institutions: The NAFTA Mutation of the EC Model and the Future of the GATT Regime', 40 *Am. J. Comp. L.* 917 (1992) [hereinafter 'Integration Without Institutions']; and 'Foundation-Building for Western Hemispheric Integration', 17 *Northwestern J.Int'l L. & Bus.* (1997) 900 [hereinafter 'Foundation-Building'].

[2] Each Member State government allocates internal political power according to its own constitutional structure.

[3] On the constitutive differences between the EU and NAFTA from the standpoint of US constitutional law, see Frederick M. Abbott, 'The Maastricht Judgment, the Democracy Principle, and US Participation in Western Hemispheric Integration', 37 [1994] *Germ. YB Int'l L.* (1995), 137.

[4] See generally, J. H. H. Weiler, *The Transformation of Europe*, 100 *Yale L.J.* (1991), 2403, and for a review of EC governance preceding the Single European Act and subsequent reforms, Stefan A. Riesenfeld, 'Legal Systems of Regional Economic Integration', 22 Am. J. Comp. L. (1974), 415.

[5] Regarding the non-self-executing character of the NAFTA in the United States, see Frederick M. Abbott, 'Regional Integration Mechanisms in the Law of the United States: Starting Over', 1 *Indiana J. Glob. Leg. Stud.* (1993), 155.

The economic undertakings of the Parties were negotiated in detail. The results of these negotiations were expressed in the NAFTA text. The Parties have so far carried out the economic undertakings of the NAFTA substantially in accordance with its terms.[6] Though a few matters are disputed, in the context of the overall undertaking, these disputes are modest.[7]

The NAFTA prescribes mechanisms for the resolution of disputes between its Parties, and in limited circumstances for the resolution of disputes between the nationals of its Parties and Party governments. The general dispute settlement mechanism of the NAFTA is an arbitral procedure that refers determinations to Party governments for political resolution.[8] This is consistent with the NAFTA's limited design in respect to intrusion on Party autonomy. The NAFTA's anti-dumping and countervailing duty dispute settlement apparatus directly binds Party governments.[9] Party nationals are entitled to pursue third party arbitration of investment-related claims at ICSID or under UNCITRAL rules.[10] Each of these dispute settlement mechanisms is operational.

The European Union is a customs union. The EC Treaty prescribes the elimination of tariffs and other restrictive regulations of commerce on trade between its Member States, and prescribes the establishment of common tariffs applicable to goods originating outside EU territory. The EC Treaty

---

[6] The implementation of the NAFTA's economic terms is discussed below at 179.

[7] This author has recently completed a review of the implementation history of the NAFTA, including analysis of disputes among the Parties. Frederick M. Abbott, *The NAFTA as Architecture for Political Decision* (May 1997) and *The NAFTA and Legalization of International Relations: A Case Study* (Aug. 1998), each prepared for a Project on Legalization and World Politics. The second of these papers will be published in an edited volume of collected works from this project.

[8] The first two NAFTA Chapter 20 panel decisions are discussed below at 184–9.

[9] The NAFTA includes a separate dispute settlement mechanism in respect to anti-dumping and countervailing duty (AD/CVD)-related complaints (Chapter 19, NAFTA). The NAFTA contains no rules regarding the substance of the AD/CVD laws of the Parties, requiring only that each Party act in domestic AD/CVD actions in compliance with its own laws. In the AD/CVD dispute settlement system, arbitral panels constituted on a case-by-case basis make decisions as to whether a country Party has complied with its own AD/CVD laws in a particular action. The decisions of AD/CVD panels are directly binding on the country Parties. There are approximately 30 completed or active Chapter 19 panels reviewing AD/CVD decisions of Canadian, Mexican and US administrative authorities. NAFTA Secretariat, www.nafta-sec-alena.org, 13 August 1998.

[10] The NAFTA also permits investors of Parties to pursue third party arbitration against a host government in the International Centre for the Settlement of Investment Disputes (ICSID) or under UNCITRAL rules. NAFTA, arts. 1115 *et seq.* See *Law and Policy*, at 102. The NAFTA obligates the Parties to make adequate provision for the enforcement of resulting arbitral awards. Several proceedings based on NAFTA investment rules have been initiated in the ICSID by US nationals against the government of Mexico, and claims both by US nationals against the government of Canada and by Canadian nationals against the government of the United States have been initiated or threatened.

prescribes that goods originating outside its territory are in free circulation within its territory following the payment of the applicable common tariff upon entry into any Member State. The EC Treaty prescribes a common commercial policy which binds its Member States to follow a co-ordinated trade policy programme. The EC Treaty prescribes the free movement of services, capital, and persons between its Member States.

The NAFTA is a free trade area. The NAFTA prescribes the elimination of tariffs and other restrictive regulations of commerce between its Parties, but does not prescribe common tariffs applicable to goods originating outside NAFTA territory. Except in so far as goods originating outside the NAFTA are transformed within a Party (or Parties) so as to assume a regional character, such third country goods are subject to the payment of tariffs upon entry into each NAFTA Party.[11] The NAFTA prescribes the free movement of services and capital, and limited free movement of business persons, between its members. Except in so far as the Parties are limited in their relations with third countries by the terms of the NAFTA, the agreement does not mandate that the Parties pursue a common commercial policy.

II THE NAFTA IN THE WTO SYSTEM

A. Customs Unions and Free Trade Areas within the WTO System

The General Agreement on Tariffs and Trade of 1947 was part of the Bretton Woods complex of international economic institutions established to reconstitute the international economy following the Second World War. The GATT 1947 embodied several foundational principles of international trade relations. The most important of these was the unconditional most favoured nation (MFN) principle embodied in Article I. The MFN rule obligated each GATT member to extend any tariff (or related) concession granted to one GATT member to all other GATT members.

The MFN rule should have the effect of accelerating the process of trade barrier elimination since it requires a wide dispersion of concessions among GATT members.[12] However, there was a core political motive for adoption of an unconditional MFN rule. In the pre-war environment, trade concessions were widely used as an instrument of diplomacy. Political alliances were

---

[11] The Parties may each elect to limit applicable tariffs to the single highest tariff payable in any NAFTA Party (so as to avoid double tariffing).

[12] A counter-argument can be made that trade barrier reductions will be faster under bilateral or minilateral negotiating strategies since governments may be more willing to grant concessions to a limited number of countries for particularized reasons. This counter-argument in part provides the theoretical basis for the customs union/free trade area exception to the MFN principle.

created and maintained through economic preferences. Since diplomatic decisions were often made for reasons apart from improving world prosperity, an economic system in which trade concessions were used as political instruments would be unlikely to generate a global welfare-optimizing result. The MFN principle is intended to de-politicize the trading system so as to reduce the chances of breakdown into a system of diplomacy-based alliances. The net effect should be to distribute the benefits of trade widely. The MFN principle was the key 'multilateralism' provision in the GATT 1947.

When the GATT 1947 was drafted, it was recognized that some form of accommodation would be necessary for customs unions and free trade areas. The concept of a European economic union was already under consideration, and the political and economic advantages of creating a pan-European market were apparent. The GATT incorporated in Article XXIV a mechanism for relieving the members of customs unions and free trade areas from the obligation to extend the preferential treatment granted within the CU or FTA to non-members.[13] The central criterion used by Article XXIV to determine whether a CU or FTA should be allowed to maintain its preferential character is whether its members have agreed to eliminate substantially all tariffs and other restrictive regulations of commerce on trade between its members.[14] This criterion was intended as a mechanism for limiting the number of CU/FTAs since it precluded GATT members from using Article XXIV as a cover for eliminating tariffs on a limited number of goods. The 'substantially all' criterion demanded a seriousness of purpose.

The Article XXIV mechanism for evaluating CU/FTAs under the GATT is much criticized. The main ground of critique is that it does not subject CU/FTAs to meaningful review even in respect to its own defined criteria since the outcome of the review process is controlled by members of the CU/FTA.[15] Customary practice of the GATT was that decisions on matters such as Article XXIV review were made by consensus, and the members of the CU/FTA under review had the right to block a decision that might have required them to effect a change to their implementation plan. Just as agricultural trade barriers have been a weak point in GATT/WTO liberalization efforts on the whole, so agriculture has been a weak spot in the regional integration process. A number of important regional groups have made liberalization commitments in the agriculture area which might be problematic

---

[13] For details on Article XXIV, see *Law and Policy*, ch. 3.

[14] The additional main criteria are that the members of a CU do not 'on the whole' establish external tariffs higher than those in place in each member prior to the formation of the CU, and that the members of an FTA do not individually raise their external tariffs.

[15] See, e.g. Frieder Roessler, 'The Relationship Between Regional Integration Agreements and the Multilateral Trade Order', in Kym Andersen and Richard Blackhurst (eds.), *Regional Integration and the Global Trading System* (1993), 311 at 323.

under a rigorous application of the requirement that such groups eliminate substantially all tariffs and other restrictive measures of commerce.

The WTO Agreement adds an Understanding that clarifies elements of the GATT 1994 Article XXIV review,[16] but none that affects the right of members to control the outcome of the mandatory review process.[17] The Understanding makes clear that a non-member of a CU/FTA may bring a dispute settlement action in respect to the application of Article XXIV, and this clarification may lead to increased attention to the CU/FTA phenomenon from the WTO dispute settlement organs.[18]

The Uruguay Round brought trade in services within the purview of the WTO, and the General Agreement on Trade in Services (GATS) establishes an additional mechanism for review of regional services arrangements (RSAs). GATS Article V permits members of RSAs to eliminate barriers on trade in services as among themselves without extending these concessions to non-members, provided that such RSAs involve substantial 'sectoral' coverage, involve the elimination of substantially all discrimination in covered sectors, and do not raise barriers to non-members within covered sectors.[19] The inclusion of a provision requiring that the benefits of an RSA be extended to businesses with commercial presence within the RSA significantly ameliorates the potential discriminatory impact of these arrangements on non-Party national service providers.[20]

The NAFTA clearly meets the criteria prescribed by the WTO Agreement for a free trade area (under GATT Article XXIV) and a regional services arrangement (under GATS Article V). By any reasonable measure, the NAFTA eliminates substantially all tariffs and other restrictive regulations of commerce on trade between Canada, Mexico, and the United States, and eliminates substantially all barriers on trade in services in a substantial number of sectors.[21]

The number of CU/FTAs among WTO members is proliferating rapidly, and this trend has raised serious concern among WTO members and in the WTO Secretariat.[22] It is widely acknowledged, however, that if the subject of

---

[16] Understanding on the Interpretation of Article XXIV of the General Agreement on Tariffs and Trade 1994.

[17] These amendments include a presumption that a reasonable time for implementing the reduction of tariff and related barriers is 10 years (para. 3), and a mechanism for calculation of 'on the whole' tariff rates of customs unions (para. 2).

[18] Understanding on Article XXIV, para. 12.

[19] GATS, Art. V:1. For details on GATS Art. V, see *Law and Policy*, ch. 3.

[20] GATS, Art. V:4.

[21] The commitments of the Parties in the areas of goods and services are reviewed for their GATT Article XXIV and GATS Article V compatibility in *Law and Policy*, chs 4 and 5.

[22] See Renato Ruggiero (WTO Director General), *Regional Initiatives, Global Impact: Cooperation and the Multilateral System*, 7 Nov. 1997, speech to the 3rd Conference of the Transatlantic Business Dialogue, Rome (www.wto.org, visited 5 July 1998).

this proliferation is to be concretely addressed, then reform of the existing review mechanisms is required. The existing review mechanisms are not designed or applied to significantly inhibit regionalization of the world trading system. A working group has been established to consider this situation. This group has yet to reach any conclusions. Since many WTO Members are party to one or more regional integration arrangements, perhaps it is not surprising that WTO Members as a body have not aggressively pursued additional methods to exercise control over these arrangements.

Customs unions and free trade areas such as the EU and NAFTA are derogations from a purely multilateral trading system. They are systems of preference, and they are political alliances. The founders of the GATT 1947 were concerned with preventing the international trading system from breaking down into a system of preferential political and economic alliances. The proliferation of regional integration arrangements appears to carry with it a heightened risk that the multilateral trading system will break down into a world economic system characterized by a series of regional alliances with inter-linkages of varying types.

B. CU/FTAs as WTO Members

The NAFTA does not possess international legal personality, and is not a member of the WTO. As a general matter, CU/FTAs are regulated by the WTO through the participation of their nation-state members.[23] Members of CU/FTAs are obligated to assure that these arrangements are implemented in a manner which is WTO-consistent. The Understanding on Article XXIV provides that CU/FTA members are responsible for measures of regional bodies taken within their territory,[24] thereby appearing to apportion responsibility for operation of CU/FTAs on a territorial basis.[25]

The European Community has international legal personality and is a member of the WTO. The Member States of the EC are also members of the WTO. If the EC votes in the WTO, it does so on behalf of all its Member States which are members of the WTO.[26] If a Member State votes individually, then each Member State votes, and there is no separate vote for the EC. This mixed situation of the EC in the WTO creates a complex internal gov-

---

[23] WTO membership is not limited to nation-states, but may include autonomous customs territories. WTO Agreement, Art. XII.

[24] Understanding on Article XXIV, at paras. 13 and 14.

[25] Alternative bases for attributing responsibility to CU/FTA members, such as joint liability for measures taken pursuant to mandatory provisions of a CU/FTA agreement, are a conceptual possibility.

[26] Stefan Riesenfeld has pointed out that difficulties will arise if the EC admits new Member States which are not also members of the WTO. So far this has not happened. See Stefan A. Riesenfeld, 'The Changing Face of Globalism', in F. M. Abbott and D. J. Gerber (eds.), *Public Policy and Global Technological Integration* (1997), 67.

ernance situation for the EC, and a complex legal situation for WTO members outside the EC which seek to determine responsibility for EC and Member State compliance with the WTO Agreement.[27]

C. The Juridical Interface of the NAFTA and WTO

1. Policy and Norms

The juridical relationship between the NAFTA and WTO Agreements is of considerable interest from the standpoints of policy and technical analysis of legal norms. As a matter of policy, a decision by NAFTA negotiators whether to accord legal priority to the NAFTA or WTO would appear to involve a choice whether to accord a greater degree of attention and concern to more narrow regional economic and political interests, or to broader multilateral interests. In light of the importance that trade policy makers have ascribed to the potential for conflict between the regional and multilateral integration models, NAFTA negotiators might have been expected to make a clear choice in this hierarchy of interests. Evidence from the text of the NAFTA and from the early NAFTA dispute settlement panel reports suggests that no such overarching policy determination was made or that, if it was made, the determination was implemented in an uncertain manner.

The fact that the NAFTA negotiations took place in the midst of the GATT Uruguay Round negotiations may at least in part be responsible for the unsettled state of affairs. Yet each set of international trade negotiations is a process that rarely occurs in isolation from other such processes. The uncertainty surrounding the relationship between the NAFTA and WTO Agreement may reflect the dynamic political tensions faced by the NAFTA negotiators, tensions which continue to influence the formation and implementation of policy in the NAFTA Parties.[28] On one side, the NAFTA was and is portrayed by its proponents as a means of accelerating integration on the North American continent in a way which is consistent with the political and social interests of a variety of disparate groups, including the business community, labour unions, and environmentalists. The NAFTA is politically justified by its attention to interests which are more difficult to address at the WTO multilateral level. If the results of NAFTA negotiations are placed beneath WTO Agreement norms, then in theory this attention to regionally-specific interests might be jeopardized by the superiority of more generalized WTO norms. There are, therefore, political and social motivations for advocating priority for the NAFTA.

---

[27] The European Court of Justice has acknowledged some of the difficulties inherent in 'mixed' EU/Member State treaties in its advisory opinion on EC-Member State adherence to the WTO Agreement. See *Re The Uruguay Round Treaties (Opinion 1/94)*, Court of Justice of the European Communities, [1995] 1 CMLR 205, 15 Nov. 1994.

[28] See generally, 'Foundation-Building', n. 1 above.

On the other side, NAFTA negotiators were and remain well aware of concerns among GATT/WTO Members about efforts by particular countries and regions to gain advantages by extending regional preferences.[29] NAFTA negotiators would be hesitant to make a clear statement of regional legal preference that might galvanize opposition to the agreement, or that might jeopardize future multilateral negotiations. NAFTA negotiators may well have maintained a preference for multilateralism among themselves, yet nevertheless have been reluctant to clearly express such preference in the NAFTA because this might be found objectionable by interest groups within the region whose support was required to assure successful conclusion of the agreement.

Though the NAFTA/WTO hierarchy of norms is uncertain, and while such uncertainty is bound to lead to or exacerbate future NAFTA disputes,[30] the political and social forces which impelled the initial state of ambiguity have not dissipated. While interests in political stability and economic efficiency might be enhanced through the clarification of this matter by the NAFTA Parties through the adoption of a clarifying amendment or an intergovernmental understanding, the Parties may be in no more favourable position to agree on such a clarification in the year 2000 than they were in 1993.[31]

2. NAFTA Norms on Priority

The legal relationship between the NAFTA and the WTO Agreement is determined by examining the text of the treaties, the context in which the treaties

[29] The Canada–United States Free Trade Agreement (CUSFTA) which entered into force in 1989 was reviewed by a GATT Article XXIV Working Party. The Working Party did not make any recommendations in respect to the CUSFTA, but rather limited itself to preparing a summary of members' observations. A concern expressed by a number of members of the Working Party was that the CUSFTA was given legal priority over the GATT in trade relations between Canada and the United States. No Article XXIV working party prior to the CUSFTA review had made any recommendation—affirmative or negative—with respect to a CUSFTA. Subsequent to the CUSFTA review, a working party recommended approval without condition of the free trade area between the Czech and Slovak Republics. See *Law and Policy*, at 41–2.

[30] Interestingly enough, the first two cases brought before NAFTA Chapter 20 dispute settlement panels have involved questions of defining the NAFTA–WTO legal relationship. The first—the Canadian Agricultural Products case (Canada/US)—is largely devoted to resolving a NAFTA–WTO relational issue. The second case—Broom Corn Brooms (Mexico/US)—saw a NAFTA–WTO relational issue extensively argued, but the panel found it unnecessary to resolve the issue in its disposition of the case. See discussion *infra*.

[31] In a 1995 book, this author identified some aspects of this legal relationship, and suggested that it might be some time before definitive pronouncements could be made, saying: 'Because of the number of contextual factors involved in defining this relationship, it may be some years before an authoritative definition of the relationship emerges, whether through action taken by the NAFTA Parties to expressly establish the relationship, or through an accumulation of dispute settlement panel opinions that may establish a common law of interpretation.' (*Law and Policy*, at 107.)

were made, and the rules of international law that govern the relationship between treaties concerning the same or similar subject matter.[32] Both the NAFTA and WTO Agreements are written agreements between states governed by international law, and therefore are 'treaties' within the definition prescribed by the Vienna Convention on the Law of Treaties (VCLT).[33]

The VCLT provides that when states are parties to treaties governing the same subject matter, the latter-in-time treaty takes precedence over the earlier-in-time.[34] The NAFTA entered into force on 1 January 1994 and the WTO Agreement entered into force on 1 January 1995. The NAFTA Parties are each original Members of the WTO. Though this temporal sequence might suggest that the WTO Agreement prevails over the NAFTA, there are a number of factors involving the express text of the NAFTA and the context in which the two agreements were made that raise doubts about this general proposition.

The NAFTA text incorporates a general principle regarding its relationship to other international agreements. It also incorporates a number of specific provisions concerning its relationship to other international agreements. The NAFTA provides:

Article 103: Relation to Other Agreements
1. The Parties affirm their existing rights and obligations with respect to each other under the *General Agreement on Tariffs and Trade* and other agreements to which such Parties are party.
2. In the event of any inconsistency between this Agreement and such other agreements, this Agreement shall prevail to the extent of the inconsistency, except as otherwise provided by this Agreement.

Article 104, NAFTA, provides an exception from the general rule of Article 103(2). Obligations in certain environment and conservation agreements (such as the Basel Convention on Transboundary Movement of Hazardous Waste) as listed in Article 104, NAFTA, expressly prevail over NAFTA rules in the event of inconsistency.

Article 301(1), NAFTA, for example, is a specific NAFTA rule that defines a relationship with the GATT/WTO Agreement. It states:

Article 301: National Treatment
1. Each Party shall accord national treatment to the goods of another Party in accordance with Article III of the *General Agreement on Tariffs and Trade* (GATT),

---

[32] On the relationship among treaty norms, see generally, S. A. Riesenfeld and F. M. Abbott (eds.), *Parliamentary Participation in the Making and Operation of Treaties: A Comparative Study* (1992).

[33] Although the United States has not ratified the VCLT, it accepts that the VCLT substantially reflects customary international law applicable to treaty relations. Canada and Mexico are parties to the VCLT.

[34] VCLT, Art. 30(3). The parties to successive treaties may elect to vary this general rule by agreement.

including its interpretative notes, and to this end Article III of the GATT and its interpretative notes, or any equivalent provision of a successor agreement to which all Parties are party, are incorporated into and made part of this Agreement.

There are various other provisions of the NAFTA which are directed to defining relations with the GATT.[35]

The express text of Article 103(1), NAFTA, affirms existing obligations among NAFTA Parties under the GATT and provides that the NAFTA prevails over the GATT to the extent of any inconsistencies. Article 103(2) does not expressly provide that the NAFTA prevails over any later-in-time agreements. By way of contrast, for example, Article 301(1), NAFTA, expressly refers to a 'successor agreement' to the GATT.[36] If NAFTA negotiators had intended that the NAFTA would in general take priority over the agreements resulting from the Uruguay Round negotiations (i.e. the WTO Agreement and related agreements), they might have referred to such 'successor agreement(s)' in Article 103, NAFTA.

Consider, however, that reference to 'successor agreement(s)' to the GATT may have a broader meaning than reference to the GATT standing alone. The GATT 1994 is incorporated as a Multilateral Trade Agreement binding on all WTO Members in the WTO Agreement. The GATT 1994 is identical to the GATT 1947 which was an agreement existing among the NAFTA Parties when the NAFTA was concluded. The WTO Agreement specifically incorporates the *acquis* of interpretations and understandings with respect to the GATT 1947 into its legal framework, and signals an intention that there be a continuity between the GATT 1947 and GATT 1994.[37] The GATT 1994, as incorporated into the WTO Agreement, is effectively an agreement to which the NAFTA Parties were party when they entered into the NAFTA. This provides a basis for concluding that the NAFTA continues to prevail over the GATT 1994 within the meaning of NAFTA Article 103.

However, this conclusion may be undercut by specific language in the WTO Agreement which states that the GATT 1947 and GATT 1994 are 'legally distinct'.[38] If the GATT 1994 is a new agreement only considered to have entered into force on 1 January 1995 (as part of the WTO Agreement), then it would not fall under the express priority rule of NAFTA Article 103 with respect to existing agreements. Yet the reason why the WTO Agreement creates a legal distinction between the GATT 1947 and GATT 1994 was not to create a break in continuity between the rights and obligations of the par-

---

[35] Article 710, NAFTA, sets forth a rule displacing Article 301, NAFTA, and its incorporation of Article III of the GATT (as just stated above), in regard to NAFTA sanitary and phytosanitary measures. NAFTA sanitary and phytosanitary rules are not governed by Article III (or XX(b)) of the GATT, notwithstanding the terms of Article 301(1) of the NAFTA.

[36] The NAFTA refers to GATT successor agreement(s) in a number of provisions, including in the dispute settlement chapter, which is examined below.

[37] WTO Agreement, Art. XVI:1.   [38] Ibid, Art. II:4.

ties to the two agreements. The legal distinction was provided for with the specific intention of facilitating the institutional transition between the GATT and the WTO by allowing some members of the old GATT to delay their entry into the WTO by remaining members of the former institution, at least for a transition period.[39] Outside of facilitating this transition, the negotiators clearly signalled an intention not to break continuity between the GATT 1947 and GATT 1994.

Whether the 'General Agreement on Tariffs and Trade' referred to in the NAFTA Article 103 rule of priority is limited to the GATT 1947, or whether it encompasses also the GATT 1994, is not susceptible to a categorical answer. If the NAFTA Article 103 reference to the GATT is understood to encompass the GATT 1994, the resulting priority rule is inelegant because the WTO Agreement incorporates significantly more than the GATT 1994, including the new area agreements of the GATS and TRIPS, and a number of supplemental agreements in areas such as technical standards and agriculture. The NAFTA might take priority over the GATT 1994 and a limited number of supplemental agreements, and yet not take priority over other WTO Agreements.[40] The full panoply of WTO Agreements might constitute the 'successor agreement(s)' to the GATT referred to elsewhere in the NAFTA.

The use of the term 'successor agreement(s)' to the GATT in contexts outside the Article 103 rules of priority does not neatly resolve the uncertainty. Consider Article 301(1) of the NAFTA as illustration. In that article the Parties incorporate GATT Article III and its interpretative notes. This express incorporation encompasses the comparable provision of a GATT 'successor agreement'. Yet if the negotiators of the NAFTA thought that the results of the Uruguay Round would take priority over the NAFTA by way of Article 103, the reference to a GATT successor agreement in Article 301(1) would be superfluous. The new GATT or WTO article would by operation of international law take priority over the old NAFTA and/or GATT rule. We might conclude that the reference to 'successor agreement' was included in NAFTA

---

[39] When the Uruguay Round was concluded, it was not clear that all former GATT Contracting Parties would choose to join the new WTO. At least for a transition period, it was contemplated that some states might remain parties to the GATT 1947, and that relations between them, and relations between them and Members of the new WTO would need to be defined. It was foreseen that for an interim period two legally distinct agreements might be needed. See *First Report of the Committee on International Trade Law*, International Law Association, 66th Conf. (Buenos Aires, Aug. 1994) (E. U. Petersmann and F. M. Abbott, Rapporteurs). As it happens, they were not. All GATT Contracting Parties became original Members of the WTO.

[40] The subject matter of these new area agreements is generally outside the scope of the GATT 1947 and does not appear to fall within the GATT continuum. There may be a grey area surrounding certain of the WTO agreements that supplement the GATT 1994, since these supplemental agreements in some cases embody GATT 1947 practices and in others largely embody Tokyo Round Agreement rules.

Article 301(1) because its drafters assumed that the NAFTA would otherwise take priority over the GATT resulting from the Uruguay Round. Article 301(1) of the NAFTA may have been drafted to add clarity to a particular part of the NAFTA, but it does not resolve ambiguity surrounding the meaning of Article 103, NAFTA.

The first two cases decided under the NAFTA general dispute settlement procedure, considered below, reflect the uncertainty surrounding the issue of NAFTA/ GATT/WTO priority.

3. NAFTA Rules on Forum

Determining as a matter of international law which obligation should prevail in relations between states is different from determining what authority should decide a dispute between these states. It is possible for a dispute settlement authority to be limited in regards to which rules it may apply in a dispute by the terms of its charter. Ultimately, states are bound in their relations by the superior norms to which they have agreed, even if they have not conferred on a particular dispute settlement body the authority to make a determination concerning their rights and obligations. The question whether NAFTA or WTO rules will take priority in a particular case involving Canada, Mexico, and the United States is distinct from the question which dispute settlement authority will decide the case.

The NAFTA Chapter 20 dispute settlement rules generally permit a complaining Party to elect either NAFTA or GATT/WTO dispute settlement in cases arising under both agreements.[41] An exception is made in respect to claims involving environmental, SPS, and technical standards matters, as to which the responding Party may demand that the matter be settled by a NAFTA panel.[42] NAFTA Chapter 20 provides that once a dispute settlement procedure is initiated in either the NAFTA or GATT forum, and subject to the right of a responding Party to demand NAFTA dispute settlement on environment-related claims, 'the forum selected shall be used to the exclusion of the other'.[43] The default terms of reference for a NAFTA panel are:

To examine, in the light of the relevant provisions of the Agreement, the matter referred to the Commission (as set out in the request for a Commission meeting) and to make findings, determinations and recommendations as provided in Article 2016(2).

The report of a panel is adopted by a majority of panelists. Panels are not empowered to issue orders to the Parties. The determinations of the panels are instead referred to the Parties for implementation. Article 2018 of the NAFTA provides:

---

[41] Art. 2005(1), NAFTA, refers to cases arising under the GATT or 'any successor agreement'.

[42] Ibid, Art. 2005(3) and (4).　　　　　　　　　　　　　[43] Ibid, Art. 2005(6).

1. On receipt of the final report of the panel, the disputing Parties shall agree on the resolution of the dispute, which normally shall conform with the determinations and recommendations of the panel, and shall notify their Sections of the Secretariat of any agreed resolution of any dispute.

2. Wherever possible, the resolution shall be non-implementation or removal of a measure not conforming with the Agreement or causing nullification or impairment . . . or, failing such a resolution, compensation.

Failure by the Party in default to implement an adequate solution entitles the aggrieved Party to withdraw concessions.

Just as there is ambiguity surrounding the question whether NAFTA or WTO rules prevail in the event of inconsistency, so there is ambiguity surrounding the question whether NAFTA panels may apply the law of the WTO in cases before them. On one hand, since the NAFTA expressly contemplates that claims arising under both agreements may be brought under NAFTA Chapter 20, it can be argued that the NAFTA implicitly allows the panelists to consider the law of the WTO. The NAFTA accepts that cases involving the Parties may involve overlapping rules and overlapping jurisdiction. If NAFTA panels are precluded from examining both sets of rules, then it cannot completely adjudicate a claim, and the Parties might be required to pursue a second proceeding in the WTO before a case is resolved. Since the NAFTA demands that the first selected forum be used to the exclusion of the other, it is clear that such dispute settlement procedures should—at the least—take place in sequence.

On the other hand, Article 2004, NAFTA, expressly provides that the Chapter 20 procedures shall apply with respect to interpretation or application of 'this Agreement'. Similarly, the NAFTA default terms of reference for panels refer to determinations under 'this Agreement'. On the basis of this language which identifies a specific legal instrument, it might be argued that only NAFTA rules may be applied in a proceeding, at least as to matters in which the Parties do not agree on alternative terms of reference incorporating WTO rules.[44]

If the Parties accept that a case arises under both the NAFTA and WTO, and yet a NAFTA panel may not consider and apply WTO rules, a Party found in default which considers that WTO issues were not adequately addressed may argue that it should not resolve the claim (by withdrawing

---

[44] Such difficulties might be avoided if the Parties are able to agree on terms of reference which authorize a NAFTA panel to consider both agreements, though this might indeed lead to difficulties in the WTO if a NAFTA Party suspended concessions based solely on a NAFTA panel determination. Difficult questions also are raised when considering whether the WTO Dispute Settlement Body (DSB) may consider NAFTA rules in the context of claims also arising under the WTO Agreement. The WTO Dispute Settlement Understanding (DSU) does not make reference to agreements outside the WTO Agreement, and a WTO panel may be presented with a claim in which conflicting NAFTA and WTO rules might yield different results. This is considered below.

offending measures, etc.) until its WTO claim is considered at the WTO. Though the NAFTA provisions on implementation may authorize the NAFTA complainant to withdraw concessions based on the NAFTA panel determination, a conflicting WTO result could authorize an off-setting suspension of concessions.

4. *NAFTA Chapter 20 Panel Decisions*

(a) Canadian Agricultural Tariffs (Canada/US)[45]

The first NAFTA claim decided under the Chapter 20 procedure involved an alleged conflict between WTO and NAFTA obligations. Prior to entry into force of the NAFTA, Canada maintained certain agricultural quotas. The NAFTA authorized Canada to maintain those quotas (by reference to an earlier provision in the Canada–United States Free Trade Agreeement (CUSFTA)). The WTO Agreement on Agriculture required Canada to eliminate its agricultural quotas, which Canada (as other WTO Members) was entitled to accomplish by tariffication.[46] Tariffs would replace quotas. However, the NAFTA provides that its Parties may not raise tariffs (including on agricultural products), and when Canada imposed new tariffs on agricultural products from the United States, the United States objected and filed a NAFTA complaint.

Canada argued that it was required by the WTO Agreement to tarifficate its quotas, and that in any case it was allowed to tarifficate its quotas under the NAFTA because it expressly 'retained' certain rights to restrain agricultural imports negotiated under the GATT. The United States argued that the WTO Agreement did not obligate tariffication of quotas, it only authorized tariffication. Canada might have eliminated its quotas without imposing tariffs that violated the NAFTA, and without violating the WTO Agreement. The United States further argued that the rights that Canada retained under the GATT were limited to those that had been exercised when the NAFTA entered into force, and that Canada could not thereafter adopt new measures that were inconsistent with the NAFTA.[47] The NAFTA panel had to decide whether Canada's retention of rights under the GATT included the authority to take new action under an old GATT rule.

The panel observed that the NAFTA uses a variety of terms and formulations to address relations between the GATT and WTO, as well as with the CUSFTA. The panel said:

---

[45] Final Report of the Panel in the Matter of Tariffs Applied by Canada to Certain US-Origin Agricultural Products, 1997 BDIEL AD Lexis 24, at 123 [hereinafter Canada Panel Report].

[46] The Agreement on Agriculture requires WTO Members to reduce tarrificated quotas over time. Regarding the WTO Agriculture Agreement, see generally, David Orden and Donna Roberts (eds.), *Understanding Technical Barriers to Agricultural Trade* (1997).

[47] The United States also argued that the rights Canada retained only extended to the imposition of quotas, so that Canada might not in any case impose new 'tariff-rate quotas'.

The interpretation of these agreements is complicated by a number of factors. The NAFTA incorporates obligations from other agreements including both the [CUS]FTA and the GATT. The terminology used in the drafting of the various provisions, both within and across these agreements, is not marked by uniformity or consistency. As discussed more fully below, words like 'existing', 'retain' or 'successor agreements', appear in some contexts yet do not appear in others where their presence may have been thought apposite. As a result, the Panel has been faced not only with the task of determining meaning from the presence of certain words, but also with the more difficult task of divining meaning from the absence of particular words.[48]

The panel ultimately determined that the term 'retain' as used in the CUS-FTA, and incorporated by reference in the NAFTA, does not import a temporal limitation on the exercise of rights by Canada. A right that is 'retained' may be exercised in the future. Canada's retained rights under the GATT (and agreements negotiated under the GATT) were not limited to those that had been expressly exercised prior to the NAFTA, but could include rights exercised in the future. Because Canada retained rights to impose agricultural restrictions under the GATT, Canada could tarifficate its agricultural quotas in spite of the NAFTA's prohibition of new tariffs.[49]

The panel notes at several points that the NAFTA uses the term 'successor agreement' to the GATT when it intends to make clear that Uruguay Round results are to be included in relation to the NAFTA, but the panel also observes that the NAFTA's terminology is sufficiently inconsistent that general guidelines for interpretation are difficult to extract.[50] There is no

[48] Canada Panel Report, at para. 123.

[49] Canada was not, however, determined to be obligated to tarifficate by the WTO Agreement.

[50] The panel expressly refers to Article 104 of the CUSFTA, which is the predecessor to Article 103 of the NAFTA. Article 104, CUSFTA, provides:

Affirmation and Precedence

1. The Parties affirm their existing rights and obligations with respect to each other, as they exist at the time of entry into force of this Agreement, under bilateral and multilateral agreements to which both are party.

2. In the event of any inconsistency between the provisions of this Agreement and such other agreements, the provisions of this Agreement shall prevail to the extent of the inconsistency, except as otherwise provided in this Agreement.

The panel observes:

'Existing' was used in [CUS]FTA Article 104, which constitutes a general affirmation of rights and obligations under bilateral and multilateral agreements to which both states are parties. The use of the term 'existing' would have made it clear [in regard to the provision invoked by Canada in this case] that the 'rights and obligations' referred to were only those in existence at the time the agreement entered into force. (Canada Panel Report, para. 136.)

This statement by the panel is not particularly revealing in respect to Article 103, NAFTA, because of differences in the construction of the two provisions. Article 104, CUSFTA includes an additional phrase in paragraph 1. It specifically refers to other agreements 'as they exist at the time of entry into force of this Agreement', which precludes a forward-looking interpretation of the relational provision of the CUSFTA. One may indeed ask whether the elimination

sweeping conclusion to be drawn from the Canadian Agricultural Tariffs panel report in regard to whether the NAFTA generally takes precedence over the GATT 1994. The panel effectively confirms that this matter will require further sorting out in the context of specific cases.

(b) *Broom Corn Brooms* (Mexico/US)

The second case to come before a NAFTA Chapter 20 dispute settlement panel directly raised the question whether NAFTA panels are authorized to adjudicate claims arising under both the NAFTA and WTO/GATT. In the *Broom Corn Brooms* case,[51] Mexico objected to the manner in which the United States had imposed safeguard measures against imports of Mexican brooms. Mexico argued that the United States action failed to apply the appropriate injury test under the GATT Article XIX safeguards provision, which provision contains language equivalent to the language of the NAFTA Chapter 8 safeguards text. Since Article 802(1) of the NAFTA provides that 'Each Party retains its rights and obligations under Article XIX of the GATT or any safeguard agreement pursuant thereto', Mexico considered that it was entitled to rely on GATT language and dispute settlement precedent under which the US safeguard action was allegedly taken upon an overly-narrow definition of injury to domestic industry.

The panel did not decide whether it was authorized to adjudicate GATT legal claims. It found that the United States had failed to comply with certain procedural rules that are common to the NAFTA and GATT, and that Mexico's claim could be addressed at the present stage by application of the NAFTA alone.[52] However, the panel summarized the legal arguments of the United States and Mexico on this issue in a concise manner.

27. The United States argued that the Panel did not have jurisdiction to adjudicate legal claims based on the obligations of GATT Article XIX and the WTO Agreement on Safeguards. The United States took the position that both the Panel's terms of reference and the general provisions of Chapter Twenty under which the Panel was created limited the Panel's competence to legal claims based on NAFTA obligations. The United States thus argued that the Panel could not consider GATT obligations unless they had somehow been adopted by incorporation into the NAFTA agreement. In the view of the United States, the provisions of NAFTA Article 802, the NAFTA provision reserving to member governments the right to employ global safeguards authorized by GATT Article XIX and the WTO Agreement on Safeguards,

---

of such language in NAFTA Article 103 indicates an intention to remove this temporal limitation, and thus to refer in Article 103(2) to the GATT as it existed at the time of entry into force of the NAFTA, and as it exists in the future.

[51] *In the Matter of the US Safeguard Action taken on Broom Corn Brooms from Mexico* (USA-97-2008-01) before the panel established under Chapter Twenty of the North American Free Trade Agreement, Final Panel Report, 30 Jan. 1998, www.nafta-sec-alena.org.

[52] Ibid, at para. 50.

did not incorporate the legal obligations of those GATT/WTO provisions into the NAFTA agreement[53] . . . The United States took the position that . . . it was the intention of the parties that claims based upon the GATT/WTO safeguards provisions themselves would have to be pursued through the GATT/WTO dispute settlement mechanism.

28. Mexico noted that NAFTA Article 2005(1) generally gives parties the right to initiate dispute settlement either in GATT or in NAFTA whenever a dispute involves a matter 'arising under both this Agreement and the *General Agreement on Tariffs and Trade*.' In Mexico's view[54] . . . the present dispute does 'arise' under both NAFTA and GATT/WTO within the meaning of Article 2005(1), and therefore can be brought in either a NAFTA or a GATT/WTO forum. Furthermore, since NAFTA Article 2005(6) provides that once a NAFTA or GATT forum is selected that forum 'shall be used to the exclusion of the other,' a NAFTA forum selected under Article 2005(1) necessarily has jurisdiction to dispose of all overlapping GATT issues involved in that dispute.

The text of the NAFTA, including the dispute settlement chapter, allows for reasoned argument on each side of the issue. The United States relies on portions of NAFTA Chapter 20 referring to 'this Agreement' and its standard terms of reference, as well as differences in how references to the GATT are styled in the NAFTA text. The United States accepts that its position would demand that Mexico pursue claims in both the NAFTA and WTO to vindicate rights (or assert defences) that differ under the two agreements. The Mexican government relies on the fact that the NAFTA Parties have authorized claims arising under both agreements to be brought in the NAFTA (or WTO) as evidence that the Parties must have intended that the panels charged with deciding cases could apply both sets of rules, particularly in light of language that makes the selected forum the exclusive one.[55]

It would be difficult on the basis of the NAFTA text to conclude whether the Parties intended WTO/GATT rules to be considered by NAFTA panels only in those cases in which the NAFTA appeared to directly incorporate WTO/GATT rules. On a policy level, the US position demands careful forum shopping on the part of a prospective claimant. It would lead to delays

---

[53] The panel also said: 'The United States contrasted the language of NAFTA Article 802 ("Each party retains its rights and obligations under Article XIX of GATT . . .") with the direct language of incorporation employed in NAFTA Articles 301(1) and 309(1) ("Article [III and XI] of the GATT and its interpretative notes . . . are incorporated into and made part of this Agreement.")' (ibid, at para. 27).

[54] The panel also noted that Mexico included in 'its contentions with regard to the ITC's definition of "domestic industry" [that this] raised an issue of US compliance with the additional conditions stated in NAFTA Article 802 and the definition of "domestic industry" in Article 805 that pertains to those conditions, as well as US compliance with the process requirements stated in Article 803 and Annex 803.3' (ibid, at para. 28).

[55] Article 2005(6), NAFTA, does not expressly address whether a second claim may be pursued in the alternate forum after the first claim has been adjudicated. The United States appears to accept that this must be the case.

in the resolution of disputes as NAFTA Parties assert rights to pursue back-to-back claims. It would appear to encourage political friction as Parties refuse to reach adjudicated settlement of disputes pending lengthy procedures in two fora.

There is no reason to believe that NAFTA panelists are any less qualified than WTO panelists to determine the right of Parties under the WTO Agreement. If, however, WTO dispute settlement is precluded once the NAFTA panel procedure is initiated, this may result in reduced access by NAFTA Parties to more comprehensive evaluation of claims as may be provided by the more extensive WTO Dispute Settlement Understanding (DSU) (in particular, Appellate Body review). Allowing NAFTA panels to adjudicate GATT/WTO legal claims would perforce raise the possibility of a unique NAFTA jurisprudence on WTO law.

Legal specialists are used to dealing with different court interpretations of the same rules, and this prospect does not appear to raise immediate concerns. However, assuming that over the long term a body of regional WTO law that differed from authoritative WTO DSU law developed and that this appeared to be causing difficulties, ways to address this problem could be devised. The development of a procedure by which NAFTA or other regional panel decisions could be subject to WTO Appellate Body review might ultimately emerge, though this is not to discount potential political obstacles to this result.

At a more modest level, there seems no reason based on the text of the NAFTA or as a matter of policy why Parties to a NAFTA dispute should not be allowed to decide on terms of reference in particular cases authorizing panels to determine GATT/WTO legal issues. The WTO DSU itself accepts that WTO Members may agree to resolve claims through arbitration, albeit 'within the WTO' and subject to WTO rules on surveillance and suspension of concessions with respect to awards.[56] The WTO Agreement contemplates that a body of arbitral jurisprudence outside the formal Appellate Body/DSB system may develop.

Two fundamental issues involving the juridical interface between the NAFTA and WTO have been examined. The first is which agreement—the NAFTA or WTO—takes priority as among the NAFTA Parties. There remains no categorical answer to this question. The NAFTA text was drafted prior to conclusion of the GATT Uruguay Round. Negotiators sought to address the prospects of a future agreement in different ways, and perhaps without adopting an overarching view on the matter. As a consequence, unless and until the NAFTA Parties decide to clarify this question by agreeing to a definitive interpretation, the matter will be resolved through the accumulation of a body of decision by government officials and dispute settlement panels.

---

[56] WTO DSU, Art. 25, referencing also Arts. 21 and 22 with respect to awards.

The second issue is whether NAFTA dispute settlement panels may adjudicate WTO Agreement-based claims. Again, the NAFTA text does not provide a clear answer. There are good policy reasons to allow panels to consider WTO rules, but it may be necessary for the Parties to agree to such consideration in prescribing their terms of reference. If NAFTA panels cannot consider WTO claims, there is likely to be delay and political controversy in the resolution of disputes.

5. WTO Norms and Forum

(a) WTO Norms and Their Relationship to Outside Norms

The WTO Agreement does not directly address the issue of its relationship with other international agreements as does the NAFTA, although it does address the interrelationship of its own component agreements, and the status of its predecessor agreements. The WTO Agreement provides that it is binding on all WTO Members,[57] and it provides that each Member 'shall ensure the conformity of its laws, regulations and administrative procedures with its obligations as provided in the annexed Agreements'. The absence of a clearly defined relationship between the WTO Agreement and other international agreements has been a source of concern and controversy, particularly in relation to environmental agreements and measures, and the WTO Committee on Trade and Environment has had this issue under consideration for a number of years.[58] GATT dispute settlement panels, and more recently the WTO Appellate Body, have rendered several decisions in which the issue of the relationship between the WTO Agreement and other international agreements is considered.

Until very recently, GATT/WTO panels have shown considerable hesitancy in considering legal rules from outside the GATT/WTO, although the possibility has not been excluded.[59] In adjudication of claims under the

---

[57] WTO Agreement, Article II:2.

[58] See Abbott reports to the *Yearbook on International Environmental Law*, below at 196–7.

[59] In the *Tuna II* GATT panel decision, the panel accepted that GATT members might be subject to rules of international agreements outside the GATT, which agreements might provide the basis for GATT Article XX exception from compliance with otherwise applicable GATT rules. However, the panel did not find such agreements to be pertinent to the case under consideration. *United States—Restrictions on Imports of Tuna* (*Tuna II*), Report of the Panel, 33 *I.L.M.* (1994), 842. In the January 1994 GATT *Banana* decision, the panel rejected a claim by the European Community that certain action could be justified because the Lomé Agreement constituted a free trade agreement which provided an Article XXIV waiver. In doing so, the panel construed the terms of the Lomé Agreement. However, this determination was limited to whether an agreement constituted a measure justifying an exception from otherwise applicable GATT rules, and so might be viewed more in the context of a determination of GATT law than a determination of Lomé Agreement law. General Agreement on Tariffs and Trade: Dispute Settlement Panel Report on the European Economic Community— Import Regime for Bananas, 18 January 1994, (Not Adopted), 34 *I.L.M.* (1995), 177.

TRIPS Agreement, the WTO DSB will necessarily consider legal claims out-side the narrow confines of the WTO Agreement since the TRIPS Agreement incorporates by reference terms, *inter alia,* from the Paris and Berne Conventions.[60] However, because terms of these agreements are incorporated by reference in the TRIPS Agreement, such consideration may not necessar-ily provide a foundation for adjudicating rights under non-incorporated agreements, for example, regional agreements.

A potentially far reaching development in GATT/WTO jurisprudence is evidenced in the recent *Shrimp-Turtles* decision of the WTO Appellate Body. In the *Shrimp-Turtles* case the WTO Appellate Body extensively consulted agreements and context outside the WTO Agreement as an aid in interpreta-tion of key provisions of the GATT 1994.[61] Although the *Shrimp-Turtles* decision does not directly involve the application of treaty norms outside the WTO Agreement to resolve a WTO dispute, the Appellate Body's extensive consultation of non-WTO sources of law in aid of interpretation suggests a willingness on the part of the Appellate Body to put an end to the view of the GATT/WTO as a self-contained legal regime.

If the Appellate Body is prepared to construe GATT 1994 norms in the context of multilateral environmental agreements, then it may also be pre-pared to construe the WTO rights and obligations of WTO Members in the context of their regional treaty commitments. For example, assume that NAFTA Parties agreed to require compliance with certain health and safety-related labour standards in the production of goods. One NAFTA Party then prohibited the import of goods produced in another NAFTA Party in breach of this obligation. If the NAFTA Party whose imports were blocked sought relief under the WTO DSU because of an alleged breach of GATT Article XI (prohibition of quotas), the Appellate Body might consider whether the express agreement by the NAFTA Parties to enforce labour standards by trade measures might—as between those specific Parties—provide a justification under GATT Article XX(b) for the protection of human health, even if it would not otherwise justify a multilateral exception to Article XI applicable to other WTO Members.

---

[60] Frederick M. Abbott, 'WTO Dispute Settlement and the Agreement on Trade-Related Aspects of Intellectual Property Rights', in E.-U. Petersmann (ed.), *International Trade Law and the GATT/WTO Dispute Settlement System* (1997), 415.

[61] *United States—Import Prohibition of Certain Shrimp and Shrimp Products,* AB-1998-4, WT/DS58/AB/R, 12 October 1998 (98–3899). For example, the Appellate Body referred to a number of environment-related treaties, such as the Convention on Biological Diversity, for aid in interpreting the meaning of arbitrary discrimination in the adoption of measures relat-ing to the conservation of exhaustible natural resources under GATT Article XX(g), at para. 173. The Appellate Body also considered the Rio Declaration on Environment and Development, referred to in a WTO Ministerial Decision on trade and environment, to illus-trate international support for a multilateral approach to adoption of environmental measures within the WTO.

The prospective problem that arises regarding application of non-WTO norms among parties to specialized agreements is that the WTO would develop separate bodies of jurisprudence applicable to limited numbers of its Members. Conceptually, this may not appear a significant problem to the lawyer trained to deal with court decisions limited in application among the parties to specific disputes. However, the 'single undertaking' characteristic of the Uruguay Round result was a major achievement for the new WTO that eliminated the balkanized legal system that prevailed following the Tokyo Round. WTO Members (and the Appellate Body) may be reluctant to introduce a system of jurisprudence that might appear to create different tiers of obligation.[62] This reluctance might be overcome by careful attention to compartmentalizing specialized rules, but it is important to call attention to the issues involved.

There appears to be a trend in WTO jurisprudence toward willingness to apply agreements outside the WTO Agreement to disputes among Members, and this willingness might extend to the application of regional integration agreements. There are prospective problems raised by the development of specialized jurisprudence within the WTO legal system which deserve careful study.

(b) WTO Forum

There is no provision of the WTO DSU that specifically contemplates the adjudication of legal claims outside the WTO agreements. Just as the NAFTA default terms of reference refer to consideration of the NAFTA, the default WTO DSU terms of reference for panels refer to examination of WTO agreements.[63] Though there is little precedent under which a WTO panel might adjudicate a NAFTA claim as between the NAFTA Parties, the WTO text does not appear to preclude such adjudication. There are policy arguments which might favour such action. As with respect to the NAFTA, there is a basic issue of adjudicatory and political economy. If the NAFTA Parties have claims arising under both the NAFTA and WTO Agreements, there may be no point in requiring two adjudications. WTO panelists and the Appellate Body would certainly be competent to review NAFTA rules. A more expeditious resolution of a dispute seems likely to mitigate political conflict. In those cases in which the NAFTA Parties to a WTO dispute agree on terms of reference which authorize the WTO DSB to consider NAFTA rules, there would appear to be constructive reasons to allow this.

---

[62] Concern has been expressed by some judges of the International Court of Justice regarding the jurisprudentially divisive potential of the Chambers procedure in which disputing parties effectively select the panel of judges. See dissenting opinion of Judge Shahabuddeen in *Case Concerning the Land, Sea and Maritime Frontier Dispute (El Sal. v. Hond.)*, ICJ, 1990, Order Regarding Application for Permission to Intervene, 1990 I.C.J. 3.

[63] WTO DSU, Art. 7:1.

6. European Court of Justice

The legal relationship between CU/FTAs and the GATT/WTO has been explored at some length by the European Court of Justice. The ECJ has consistently given priority to the EC Treaty over the GATT and WTO Agreement. The ECJ has made two fundamental determinations regarding the relationship between the EC Treaty and the GATT/WTO Agreement. The first was that the GATT 1947 is not directly effective in the law of the Member States since the 'spirit, the general scheme and the terms' of the Agreement do not import such effect.[64] The Council of the European Communities, in a recital to its decision authorizing the ratification of the WTO Agreement, expressed its support for carrying this view over to the new WTO Agreement.[65] The legal effect of the Council's declaration is not yet known. The ECJ's view on the direct effect of the GATT 1947 is qualified to some extent by a decision that direct application is possible if the Council has acted to incorporate a GATT obligation into EU law.[66]

The second fundamental determination made by the ECJ was that the GATT 1947 does not bind the EC in its relations with its Member States.[67] In *Germany v Council*, Germany invoked the GATT 1947 to challenge the lawfulness of the EC banana regulations. It argued that the EC's adherence to the GATT precluded the Council from adopting and applying regulations which were GATT-illegal, and that Germany had the right to rely on these GATT obligations in a dispute with the Council. The Court of Justice said that Germany was bound by Community legislation—even if it had cast its vote against that legislation—and that the Council had the inherent power to act in a GATT-inconsistent manner if it chose to do so.[68]

7. Observations

Should NAFTA rules as a general policy matter have priority over WTO rules in the event of inconsistency? There are good arguments on both sides.

---

[64] *International Fruit Company N.V. v Produktschap voor Groenten en Fruit (No. 3)*, Case 21–24/72, Court of Justice of the European Communities, 12 Dec. 1972.

[65] Council Decision of 22 December 1994 concerning the conclusion on behalf of the European Community, as regards matters within its competence, of the agreements reached in the Uruguay Round multilateral negotiations (1986–1994), 94/800/EC, 1994 OJ L 336, 23 Dec. 1994.

[66] *Fédération de l'industrie de l'huilerie de la CEE (Fediol) v Commission*, 1989 E.C.R. 1781, 2 C.M.L.R. 489 (1991).

[67] *Germany v Council (Bananas—Common organization of the market—Import regime)*, Case C-280/93, Judgment of the Court, 5 Oct. 1994.

[68] For a critical perspective on the Court's decision, see Ernst-Ulrich Petersmann, 'Proposals for a New Constitution of the European Union', 32 *C.M.L. Rev.* 1123 (1995) and 'Darf die EG das Völkerrecht ignorieren?', *EuZW* 1997, 325–31.

Priority of WTO rules would appear to encourage multilateralism. Priority of NAFTA rules might result in more rapid progress in addressing social issues within the context of regional integration, and the resulting rules might provide a constructive model for the multilateral system.

The present approach which is largely based on application of a 'last in time' rule has manifest drawbacks. The NAFTA and WTO Agreements are each likely to be subject to continuing amendment, and this could lead to a rather confused situation about which rule governs in particular circumstances. Some clarification of general principles among the NAFTA Parties would help to avoid misunderstanding and mitigate future disputes. However, in light of the various political and social pressures affecting the Parties, the present *ad hoc* approach may be the rule for some time.

III THE NAFTA AND THE POLITICAL ECONOMY OF REGIONALISM

A. NAFTA Economic Effects

1. Intra-NAFTA Economic Effects

The economic terms of the NAFTA have been implemented substantially in accordance with its terms.[69] As a consequence, tariff and non-tariff barriers to trade in goods and services among the NAFTA countries have fallen, and cross-border flows of capital and investment have been facilitated.

Economic analysis of the NAFTA's effect is complicated by the Peso Crisis of 1994–5, which dramatically affected the terms of trade between the NAFTA Parties. Regardless of the NAFTA's effect in reducing trade barriers, the sharp drop in the value of the peso would have resulted in a short-term increase in Mexican exports to the US and Canada, and a short-term decline

---

[69] This author has reviewed the implementation history of the NAFTA from a legal standpoint in two papers, Frederick M. Abbott, *The NAFTA as Architecture for Political Decision* (May 1997) and *The NAFTA and Legalization of International Relations: A Case Study* (Aug. 1998), each prepared for a Project on Legalization and World Politics. The second of these papers will be published in an edited volume of collected works resulting from the project. See generally US Executive Branch, *Study on the Operation and Effect of the North American Free Trade Agreement (NAFTA)*, prepared and transmitted to Congress as required by section 512 of the NAFTA Implementation Act (1997), www.ustr.gov [hereinafter US Executive Branch Study]. In the first three years of NAFTA operation, Mexican applied tariffs on US goods declined from an average of 10 per cent to 2.9 per cent. During the same time period, Mexican applied tariffs on goods of non-NAFTA origin increased to an average 12.5 per cent (ibid, at ii and 7). US applied tariffs on Mexican origin goods declined from 2.07 per cent to 0.65 per cent in the comparable time frame, while US applied tariffs on Canadian origin goods declined from 0.37 per cent to 0.22 per cent (ibid, at ii, 7–8).

in Mexican imports from the United States and Canada.[70] Nevertheless, in light of large gains in Mexico's exports dominated in dollars, and the robust pattern of trade among Canada, Mexico, and the United States (which included substantial gains in US exports to Mexico), it seems reasonable to attribute a positive effect of the NAFTA on increasing cross-border economic activity among its Parties.[71]

A US Executive Branch Study emphasized the positive influences of the NAFTA in Mexico's relatively rapid recovery (in aggregate terms) from the effects of the Peso Crisis.[72] After the 1982 financial crisis, it took five years for Mexican economic output to reach pre-crisis levels. Following the late-1994 Peso Crisis (in which output dropped more quickly), Mexican economic output reached pre-crisis levels in two years. Mexico's return to international capital markets was far more rapid following the 1994 crisis than following the 1982 crisis.

On the whole, it appears reasonable to conclude that the NAFTA had a net positive economic welfare effect in its three Parties during its first years of operation.[73] The Mexican economy has substantially recovered from the Peso Crisis, and its economic outlook today is reasonably promising.[74]

2. Effects on Third Country Trade

The classical model of regional integration economics generally posits that the global welfare effects of such arrangements may be determined by examining whether they are net trade-creating or trade-diverting.[75] If there is an increase of trade among members that exceeds the level of trade lost with non-

---

[70] The US Executive Branch Study confirms that it is difficult to isolate the effects of the NAFTA on regional trade or investment flows during the first three years of its operation because the Peso Crisis overwhelms NAFTA-specified changes. The US economy was exceptionally strong during the measurement period, and this alone might account for changes in import-export trends (ibid, e.g., at 12–14).

[71] In the period from 1994 through 1996 covered by the US Executive Branch Study, there was a substantial increase in two-way trade between the United States and Mexico. There was also a substantial increase in the share of US imports in the Mexican market, and the share of Mexican imports in the US market. Economic movements in the NAFTA services markets were not significant during the same three year measurement period (ibid, at 8–11, 29–44). Since the entry into force of the NAFTA, there has been a modest increase in the level of US foreign direct investment (FDI) in Mexico (ibid, at 22–24).

[72] Ibid, at iii–iv.

[73] If we were to attribute at least partial responsibility for the 1994 Peso Crisis to the NAFTA—because the NAFTA may have encouraged over-investment of short-term capital in the Mexican market—the economic picture is more mixed.

[74] A useful source of current data on the Mexican economy is *NAFTA Works* published on a monthly basis by the government of Mexico, SECOFI office.

[75] The classical approach was developed in Jacob Viner, *The Customs Union Issue* (1950). For discussion, including critique on grounds that trade creation/trade diversion analysis does not adequately capture welfare effects attributable, *inter alia*, to accelerated growth within CU/FTA, see WTO Secretariat, *Regionalism and the World Trading System* (1995).

members,[76] then there is a net positive global economic welfare effect. If the level of lost trade with non-members exceeds the increase in trade among RIA members, then there is a net negative global welfare effect. The trade statistics compiled by the United States for its three-year study do not permit a complete evaluation of the NAFTA's net effect on trade creation and trade diversion. The Study indicates that diversion of trade occurred during the first three years following NAFTA's entry into force.[77] It states, for example, that Mexico's market share gains in the US apparel sector displaced imports from China, Hong Kong, Taiwan, and Korea, the US import market share of which fell by 9 percentage points in the relevant period.[78] The fact that the NAFTA has diverted trade is consistent with the expectations of NAFTA policy planners.[79]

The NAFTA has also created a significant amount of trade among its Parties as, for example, Mexico has supplanted Japan as the United States' second leading trade partner (behind Canada). Moreover, the results of the GATT Uruguay Round were implemented after entry into force of the NAFTA. Since the substantial trade barrier reductions following the Uruguay Round should in any case have resulted in substantial increases in levels of world-wide trade,[80] it is unlikely that trade with NAFTA non-members has been diverted in aggregate terms, even if the market share of some non-members has declined in relation to NAFTA Parties.

The principal positive effect of the NAFTA appears to be its stabilizing effect on the Mexican economy. Without doubt, the Peso Crisis hurt the Mexican economy and has resulted in significant social hardship. Nevertheless, Mexico has largely been spared from the effects of the 1997–8 global economic crisis which has had an enormously destabilizing effect on many developing economies, and which has resulted in substantially lower economic growth throughout Latin America. Mexico's economy and capital markets performed well during the 1997–8 period, and the Mexican government has publicly attributed this to its NAFTA commitment.

[76] Trade will be lost with non-members as tariffs are reduced among members, and as these tariff reductions are not extended to non-members.

[77] US imports recorded an overall market share gain of 6.2 percentage points in Mexico's market for imported goods. Mexican imports recorded an overall market share gain (in 22 broad sectors) of 2.3 percentage points in the US market for imported goods. The US share of Mexico's textile import market gained 17.2 percentage points, and the US share of the Mexican transport equipment import market gained 19.2 percentage points. Mexico's share of the US apparel market gained 5.2 percentage points (ibid, e.g. at iv–vi, 35–6).

[78] Ibid, at vi and 39.

[79] Trade economists were aware of the potential for trade diversion arising from creation of the NAFTA. See C. A. Primo Braga, Raed Safadi and Alexander Yeats, *Implications of NAFTA for East Asian Exports,* draft by members of International Economics Department, The World Bank (1994).

[80] For predictive comparison of NAFTA and Uruguay Round trade creation/trade diversion effects, see C. A. Primo Braga, Raed Safadi and Alexander Yeats, n. 79 above.

B. NAFTA Social Effects

The NAFTA's social ambitions are modest.[81] The NAFTA and its
Supplemental Agreements on the Environment and Labor created two institutions: the North American Commission for Environmental Co-operation
(CEC) and the North American Commission for Labor Co-operation
(CLC).[82] The CEC and CLC are each designed to promote social interests
without affecting the legislative prerogatives of the NAFTA Parties and without a substantial intrusion on the administration of laws in its Parties.

The North American Agreement on Environmental Co-operation
(NAAEC) establishes a procedure by which interested persons may request
the preparation of a 'factual record' by the CEC Secretariat. The factual record
will report on whether a NAFTA Party is effectively enforcing its environmental law. The CEC Secretariat has prepared and published its first factual
record in a case involving construction of a port facility in Cozumel,
Mexico.[83] In addition to the factual record procedure, the NAAEC establishes
a procedure under which a Party may seek a determination by an arbitral
panel that another Party has persistently failed to enforce its environmental
law. This procedure has not yet been invoked. The CEC has put together a
programme to map the North American environment, as well as a number of
other research programmes. The CEC provides a forum for periodic meetings
of North American environment ministers, and it organizes environment-
related fora.[84]

Though the tangible results of the CEC's activities are limited, the NAAEC
has on balance had a positive effect. Environmental interest groups in the
Parties have co-ordinated activities in respect to petitioning the CEC in factual record and report matters. If the various research projects are successfully
completed, there will certainly be benefits in planning for future environmental programmes. The NAFTA's environmental record has been criticized

---

[81] Regarding NAFTA and the environment, see by this author, Frederick M. Abbott, 'From
Theory to Practice: The Second Phase of the NAFTA Environmental Regime', in Rüdiger
Wolfrum (ed.), *Enforcing Environmental Standards: Economic Mechanisms as Viable Means?*
(1996), 451; 'The NAFTA Environmental Dispute Settlement System as Prototype for
Regional Integration Arrangements', 4 [1993] *Y.B. Int'l Envtl. L.* 3; 'Regional Integration and
the Environment: The Evolution of Legal Regimes', 68 *Chi-Kent L. Rev.* (1992), 173; and a
series of reports in the *Yearbook of International Environmental Law*, 'International Trade
Rules, World Market Conditions and Environmental Effects', 8 [1997] *Y.B. Int'l Envtl. L.*; 7
[1996] *Y.B. Int'l Envtl. L.*; 6 [1995] *Y.B. Int'l Envtl. L.* 349; 5 [1994] *Y.B. Int'l Envtl. L.* 283;
4 [1993] *Y.B. Int'l Envtl. L.* 281; 3 [1992] *Y.B. Int'l Envtl. L.* 341; 2 [1991] *Y.B. Int'l Envtl.
L.* 227.

[82] See, e.g., Remarks of Lance Compa, 'International Trade and Social Welfare: The New
Agenda', 17 *Comp. Lab. L.J.* (1996), 338.

[83] This factual record is available at the CEC website, www.cec.org.

[84] See, e.g., Commission for Environmental Co-operation, 1996 Annual Report.

by a CEC-appointed group of experts because of a lack of co-ordination both within and among the various NAFTA bureaucracies, and because government funding for environmental programmes has been limited.[85] However, while the NAFTA could certainly do more in the area of environmental protection, the institutional structure created by the NAFTA would seem to be better than the absence of such structure. The WTO has made limited progress on environmental matters, so that the NAFTA appears so far to present advantages over the multilateral trade system structure for addressing environmental concerns.

A similar picture emerges in respect to the North American Agreement on Labor Co-operation (NAALC). The CLC Secretariat does not have the power to prepare factual records as does the CEC Secretariat. However, the NAALC obligates each Party to establish a National Administrative Office (NAO) to hear complaints concerning labour law enforcement in the Parties, and each Party has established an NAO. The NAALC also provides an inter-Party complaint procedure involving allegations of persistent failure to enforce labour laws.

The NAO complaint procedure has been more robust than might have been expected. Labour unions of Canada, Mexico, and the United States have initiated a number of complaints that have resulted in negotiations among Labour Ministers of the Parties, and in several cases have produced concrete results in terms of remedial action by employers or government administrative reform.[86] As the NAAEC led to increased interaction among environmental interest groups, so the NAALC has fostered substantial co-operation among labour unions of the Parties. The accomplishments of the NAALC should not be exaggerated. Nevertheless, a base of inter-Party and inter-Union labour co-operation has been established, and this is a substantial advance over action on labour matters at the WTO.

The NAFTA does not make a compelling case for action on social welfare matters by regional integration arrangements. Yet the NAFTA did not set out with a social welfare charter; it set out with an economic charter. The NAFTA has moved in advance of the WTO on environment and labour matters, and it would be hard to make a case that the NAFTA has harmed the multilateral trading system in the process.

---

[85] NAAEC CEC, *NAFTA's Institutions: The Environmental Potential and Performance of the NAFTA Free Trade Commission and Related Bodies* (1997).

[86] These developments are reported at the CLC website, www.naalc.org, with links to NAOs. Particularly useful is the Canadian NAO website, http://labour.hrdc-drhc.gc.ca/doc/nafta/eng.

C. The NAFTA as a Political Phenomenon

The NAFTA was initially portrayed as the first step in a regional trading arrangement stretching from Anchorage (Alaska) to Tierra del Fuego (Argentina). This strategic vision was embodied both in short-term negotiations for accession to the NAFTA by Chile, and in longer-term negotiations for a Free Trade Area of the Americas. Shortly after the NAFTA entered into force, momentum in the western hemisphere for pursuing this vision stalled. The US Congress was sharply divided by the NAFTA debate, and a Democratic President could not induce his own party members to continue along the path of regional integration. The countries of the Mercosur (Argentina, Brazil, Paraguay, and Uruguay, with Bolivia and Chile associated), have pursued their own regionalization programme. Mercosur countries continue negotiations with Andean Pact and other Latin American countries.

The NAFTA was in part negotiated to counterbalance the growing economic and political influence of the EU.[87] The formation of the NAFTA in turn raised EU concerns over US dominance in the western hemisphere economy. The EU has since pursued negotiations with Mercosur and with Mexico on closer economic relations. The countries of Asia expressed concern over the potential trade diverting impact of the NAFTA. Enterprises of some of these countries have responded to the NAFTA by increasing their investments in North America. Asian countries have also pursued regional integration arrangements, including APEC.[88] These arrangements remain in formative stages, and the 1997–8 economic crisis has set back their progress.

The NAFTA appears to have increased Mexico's strategic economic importance to the EU. From a US standpoint, the NAFTA continues to provide a political and economic counterweight to the ever-expanding EU.

IV THE NAFTA AND THE WTO SYSTEM

Inherent in regional integration are risks to the WTO system. The EU has become such an important political and economic force that this exercise in regionalism may have diminished the importance of maintaining an open

---

[87] See Frederick M. Abbott, 'NAFTA and the Future of United States—European Community Trade Relations: The Consequences of Asymmetry in an Emerging Era of Regionalism', 16 *Hastings Int'l and Comp. L. Rev.* (1993), 489 and 'The North American Free Trade Agreement and Its Implications for the European Union', 4 *Transnat'l L. & Contemp. Prob.* (1994), 119.

[88] Regarding APEC and its relationship to the WTO, see Jonathan T. Fried, 'APEC as the Asia-Pacific Model for Regional Economic Cooperation', in F. M. Abbott (ed.), *China in the World Trading System* (1998), 183.

multilateral trading system from a European standpoint. Similarly, the NAFTA has brought added economic security to the North American region, and it can be argued that this too potentially undermines the role of the WTO and multilateralism.

Yet the threats remain largely in the domain of theory. The EU has enjoyed political stability and sustained economic growth, despite the very costly reunification of Germany and a major world monetary crisis. It was predictable that Mexico would suffer social and political dislocation as its economy was privatized and liberalized, and this prediction has borne fruit. However, in comparison with other countries at comparable levels of economic development and political transition, Mexico is doing fairly well. The North American economy has been strong in the face of economic crisis. The political and economic strength and resiliency of the EU and NAFTA have provided an extremely important anchor for the global economy over the past several years.

There is no proof that regionalization of the EU and North American economies has been responsible for their success. Strong American, British, French, and German economies may alone have provided the necessary engines for economic growth in North America and Europe. However, on the historical record, it is difficult to make the case that regional integration has harmed the global economy, or that there is any near-to-medium-term threat present. The NAFTA is so far a healthy complementary institution to the WTO.

7

Epilogue: Towards a Common Law of International Trade

J. H. H. WEILER*

PROLOGUE

There is, or at least until recently was, a widely shared view that even in the realm of economic law—the law of the market—the EU and the GATT represented very different approaches. At the core of the substantive law of the GATT (1947 and 1994) according to this view, we find the principles of Most Favoured Nation and National Treatment—i.e. an interdiction of discrimination and protectionism in the market place for goods and services. By contrast, at the core of the legal regime governing the European common market-place—Article 30 ECT and related articles—we find an interdiction on obstacles to trade, whether discriminatory or otherwise coupled with a legislative power and a legislative programme of harmonization when elimination of national obstacles is not possible. The consequences of these would-be legal frameworks are profound. The EU ideal type on this view would be a single market with a uniform regulatory regime irrespective of national boundaries. The WTO ideal type envisages multiple markets, each following its own regulatory regime determined by national socio-economic choices, but allowing imported goods to compete without discrimination within those markets; two very different worlds.

The EU and the GATT were considered different in another fundamental sense—the role of law, courts, binding dispute resolution and the like. The

* Manley Hudson Professor of Law and Jean Monnet Chair, Harvard University. The origins of this chapter are in a series of internal lectures given at Harvard and Bruges in the early 1990s followed by a first public lecture at Edinburgh in 1996 and then, more formally, as the 1998 Ledingham Chalmers Annual Lecture in European Law, at the University of Aberdeen which was published in P. Craig and G. de Burca *The Evolution of EU Law* (OUP, 1999). This version is revised in some significant ways. I am very grateful to Miguel Poiares who commented critically and helpfully on some aspects of the thesis presented here, to Grainne de Burca who made numerous helpful comments and suggestions on the first version of this essay and to Sungjoon Cho who provided valuable research assistance.

EU was perceived as the paradigm of a successful import of the rule of law into a transnational regime—with all the trappings of courts, privatization of legal action, and the like. GATT dispute resolution was considered as a paragon of diplomacy masquerading as law.

There is, of course, something of the caricature in the juxtaposition of these two images and in reality the differences between the two may never have been quite as sharp. The EU, for example, adopted from its inception a GATT approach to taxation. And, as all students of the American scholar Robert Hudec will know, the legal regime underlying the so-called diplomatic approach to GATT dispute resolution concealed an impressive compliance pull which, I would suggest, compares well at least to the EC Article 169 record. But a good caricature always tells a truth, and I would submit that both in reality and in perception the notion of two very different regimes had and continues to have much currency.

The advent of the WTO and the much vaunted new dispute settlement understanding have changed many perceptions in this regard. The 'juridification' of the GATT has been a favoured theme in the literature. Whereas the change from pre- to post-WTO may not be quite as radical as some would have us believe, and though even at its strongest the WTO is still a far cry from the full constitutional paraphernalia of the EU, the gap between the two systems in this regard has narrowed and has been widely acknowledged to have narrowed.

What I want to argue in this chapter, a modest claim, is that also in the substantive law area, we witness a convergence trend between the EU and the WTO. It is a convergence that results from developments in both systems.

In the WTO the most notable development in my view is reflected by the *Hormones* case. It represents the most striking attempt under the GATT to reinvoke the original philosophy of Article 11 GATT and make a *Dassonville*-type claim that also in the GATT, obstacles to trade, even if non-discriminatory, may be prohibited unless a 'rational' justification may be invoked. For experienced EU watchers, it is almost amusing to see how the WTO must suddenly grapple with the consequences of a *Dassonville*-style approach with all the difficulties that result from the inevitable encroachment on national sovereignty, policy choices, legitimacy of governance, and accountable decision making.[1]

The focus of this chapter will be, instead, on the European Community, indeed on the heart of the Community, the common market in goods (which over the years has been closely synchronized with the common market in the other factors of production, notably services). I will try and show how (and why), over time, the early radical approach, reflective in large measure of the ideal type described above, has been replaced by a more mature approach far

---

[1] Cf. chapters by Howse and Scott in this volume.

more respectful of national regulatory autonomy. I will further argue that within one generation the doctrinal foundation of the law of the common market has shifted from a sweeping insistence on removal of obstacles to an approach which, at its heart, interdicts discrimination and attacks obstacles only when these bar access to the market place.

My method will be simple enough. I will present snapshots of some of the most significant cases in the area of free movement of goods, cases so well known as to obviate the necessity of any detailed description, and then attempt to transform these discrete snapshots into a cinematographic whole, a narrative over time in which the evolutionary nature of the jurisprudence will receive most attention. I regard this jurisprudence as suggestive of five 'generations'. First, a Foundational Period, stretching from the mid 1960s and culminating in *Dassonville* in the early 1970s. This was followed by a Second Generation in the late 1970s and early 1980s (*Cassis*; *Regenerated Oil*). A Third Generation in the mid to late 1980s (a non-judicial phase of legal evolution consisting, *inter alia,* of the White Paper, the New Approach to Harmonization, and the Single European Act), was, in turn, followed by a Fourth Generation in the early 1990s (*Keck*). The present and near future will constitute the Fifth Generation for the purposes of this essay.

As this story unfolds, the slow convergence between the two systems— WTO and EU—becomes in my view quite transparent.

The metaphor of generations is used not simply to underline change from one period to another but also to underline continuity—the new and different is, in this account, an outgrowth or reaction to that which preceded it. And in describing this change and continuity I will be at pains to suggest some ways in which material constitutionalism can be seen as situated in and conditioned by the structural constitutional evolution of the Community.

The shortcomings of my approach are self-evident: First, it is a story in which only landmarks feature. Much detail, important detail, is thus lost though this might be a virtue too, if the purpose of the essay is to provoke those who are already familiar with the field. The focus on court decisions and jurisprudence is another major limitation. Overall political economy, the dynamics and permutations of regulatory competition and the race to the bottom syndrome, economic analysis of various options adopted by the Court, the true saga of implementing the White Paper are, at best, 'context' against which the jurisprudence takes place. Doctrine also suffers, and not only where my positions or representations of doctrine will be challenged by many—for which no apology is made—but also in eschewing whole areas such as price fixing, intellectual property, and the like for which I *do* make the proverbial apology of time and space.

I THE FOUNDATIONAL PERIOD

On 24 November 1966 the Commission opened 169 legal proceedings against Italy which led eventually to the Decision of the Court in the so-called *Statistical Levy* case.[2]

At issue was a charge levied at an equal rate on imported and exported goods, the purpose of which was to finance the collection of statistical data on Italy's foreign trade. By coupling the levy on imports and exports the charge was, arguably, neither discriminatory nor protectionist. Even if a marginal discrimination did exist (after all, on the Italian market, domestic products competing with imports would not have had to pay that levy) it was, for the most part, infinitesimal: ten lire on every 100 kilogrammes or every metric ton of goods or on every animal or vehicle. If ever *de minimis* had a meaning this would seem to be the place to apply it. In addition, and this was argued by the Italian government, the charge could be regarded as financing a service for which the beneficiaries, importers and exporters, could be made to pay. Moreover, the service which it financed was wholly beneficial to the overall design of creating a common market. Knowledge is power in the market-place too. And the knowledge gained by the trade statistics would enhance transparency and, thus, further the project of transnational market construction.

Why then bring the case at all? The real motivation of the Commission is difficult to reconstruct. It seems as if they considered that the Italian charge contradicted some recently passed Regulations—maybe it was their power which was at issue. But the thrust of the case was that the Italian charges violated the prohibition of Articles 9, 12, 13, and 16 EEC on customs duties and charges having equivalent effect. Perhaps the Commission sensed that this was a good case in which to invite the Court to pronounce for the first time on the definition of a Charge having an effect equivalent to a customs duty. That was important as transitional periods came to an end. Though official customs duties had been abolished, a plethora of other 'charges' remained in place. Perhaps it was just fortuitous.

But maybe Commission ambition went even further—thereby providing the reason to select *Statistical Levy* as a convenient starting point for this disquisition on the evolution of the law (primarily judge-made) governing the free movement of goods in the Community legal order. For this important, principled and, somewhat unexpected, prosecution resulted not only in the still extant definition of charges having an effect equivalent to customs duties but also in a conceptual and rhetorical construct—a true canon—which was, in time, to become the bedrock principle of the Court's understanding of intra-community free movement of goods (and other factors of production) in its most celebrated jurisprudence from *Dassonville* through *Cassis* and

[2] Case 24/68 *Commission v Italy* [1969] ECR 193.

beyond. Indeed, the huge flap attendant on the Court's more recent *Keck's* jurisprudence is precisely because the time-honoured canon consecrated in *Statistical Levy* and cases like it was violated.

At the centre of the *Statistical Levy* case was a dispute which seemed then (and, for very different and hugely important reasons, seems to many today) to cut to the heart of international trade regimes liberalizing transnational movement of goods, service, investment, and the like, whether within the framework of the WTO/GATT or other Free Trade Areas.

Did the legal commitment to free trade (and we must, here, make a supreme effort to reconstruct and re-imagine the legal culture and political sensibilities of the mid 1960s) entail a regime which was directed at the elimination of discrimination and protectionism, but no more (in which case Italy would stand on relatively strong grounds in defending the statistical levy), or did it go further and was directed at prohibiting any unjustified obstacle to trade—whether or not it was discriminatory or protectionist (in which case the Commission would be perched to win its case)? Camouflaged with many masks and disguises this question remains the single most potent underlying source of legal and political tension in all free trade regimes, of which the Community is but one.

The Court, rejecting the benefits of the charge as too general to be characterized as a service for which a fee may be imposed and also differentiating the charge in question from a tax, gave its answer to the principal issue in Recital 9:

[A]ny pecuniary charge, however small and whatever its designation and mode of application, which is imposed unilaterally on domestic or foreign goods by reason of the fact that they cross a frontier, and which is not a customs duty in the strict sense, constitutes a charge having equivalent effect within the meaning of Articles 9, 12, 13 and 16 of the Treaty, even if it is not imposed for the benefit of the State, is not discriminatory or protective in effect and if the product on which the charge is imposed is not in competition with any domestic product.

Five years later almost to the day, in *Dassonville*, the Court made its most famous pronouncement ever, defining this time not a charge having an effect equivalent to a customs duty but the similar concept of a measure having an effect equivalent to quantitative restrictions prohibited under Articles 30 and 34.

All trading rules enacted by Member States which are capable of hindering, directly or indirectly, actually or potentially, intra-Community trade are to be considered as measures having an effect equivalent to quantitative restrictions.

Both cases seem to share the same logic of an obstacle rather than discrimination based regime as well as the same sweeping, formulaic, all-encompassing rhetoric. What seemed to be constructed by these twin-like definitions of Charges and Measures having an effect equivalent, respectively, to customs duties and quantitative restrictions was not a mere legal regime of 'fair' trade but a regime which was, in principle, designed to remove all unjustified

obstacles to trade and not merely discriminatory and protectionist measures—a veritable common market-place. This construct and this philosophy
became the driving force of an entire jurisprudence which slowly seemed to
harmonize the same set of rules for the free movement of all other factors of
production and also define the fundamental way in which the Community
was different from other regimes—principally the GATT. The GATT, to an
entire generation of Community lawyers, was driven by the more 'old fash-
ioned' and primitive notion of a commitment to National Treatment, that is,
non discrimination—but no more. The move from *Statistical Levy* to
Dassonville typified (and typifies to many) the very canon of the economic
constitution of Europe: Removing Obstacles, not merely Discrimination and
Protectionism, is the hallmark of the true common or single market-place.

The (apparent) similarity of logic and rhetoric between the two cases may
also suggest, with no proof, that they sprang from the same mindset, that they
were associated with an identical or similar judicial world view of the
Community and its telos as well as from a hermeneutic sensibility which
regarded the interpretation of Articles 9, 12, 13, and 16 which led to *Statistical
Levy* as involving the same 'moves' which would lead to the *Dassonville* formula.
After all, the prohibition in the Treaty on charges having an effect equivalent to
customs duties and of measures having an effect equivalent to quantitative
restrictions seem equally opaque and equally open textured. With eyes clouded
by the 'heroic period' in the Court's jurisprudence at that time, the text seems
to invite a teleological interpretation conditioned by an overarching vision of
the Community as a single market-place in which presumptively goods can
move freely and any obstacle must have an objective justification sanctioned by
Community law and supervised by the Community Court. In this sense
Statistical Levy and *Dassonville* stand to the material constitution as cases like
Van Gend en Loos or *ERTA* stand to the structural constitution.

This canonical view is implicit in many text books—since the issues are
rarely addressed explicitly—and I have observed in years of teaching thou-
sands of students that once *Statistical Levy* is (superficially) internalized
Dassonville seems predictable and even unexceptional. That this view has
become canonical is also evident by the cries of woe by certain writers when
the Court has adopted decisions running against this orthodoxy—cries of
woe as shrill as when the Court hands down decisions which run against the
structural canon (such as refusing horizontal direct effect to directives).

And yet, placed in context—the context (*économie*) of the actual text as well
as political and economic context—the two cases were and are fundamentally
different and the seemingly easy move from the obstacle-oriented construct in
Statistical Levy to the obstacle-oriented construct in *Dassonville* is nothing less
than fateful.

For all its rhetorical sweep, the legal holding in *Statistical Levy* is based on
conventional reasoning which would satisfy the most conservative canons of

legal construction. It also forms part of a conventional and conservative view of a liberal trade regime which differentiates between rules governing Market Access and rules governing Market Regulation and considers that the former should, indeed, be obstacle based and the latter be discrimination based.

By contrast, *Dassonville*—at least the *Dassonville* formula—is another matter: an important departure based on a more complicated set of interpretative considerations.

Hermeneutically, *Statistical Levy* is a conservative case since it takes seriously the notion of equivalency in the text of the Treaty:

Customs duties on imports and exports and charges having equivalent effect shall be prohibited between Member States.

Customs duties usually are, though not necessarily so, protectionist or discriminatory: after all, they can, and often do, cover products for which there may be no identical, similar, substitutable, or competing domestic items. And even so, they are prohibited. Likewise, customs duties can be very small—*de minimis*—and this alone does not save them from the prohibition. So, charges having *equivalent effect* to customs duties also need not be discriminatory or protectionist in order to fall within the prohibition and may be very negligible too. There is no teleology in this interpretation. This hermeneutic fact does not give the interpretation a necessarily higher order of legitimacy; it simply means that the Court did not need to stretch itself to arrive at this result; that *Statistical Levy* was hardly 'heroic' stuff.

Consider another hugely important aspect to *Statistical Levy*. The Court, in Recital 11, necessarily had to differentiate between a pecuniary charge imposed by reason of the fact that a good crosses a frontier—which would thereby be classified as a prohibited customs duty or charge having an effect equivalent to a customs duty—and internal taxes:

[I]t follows from Articles 95 *et seq.* that the concept of a charge having equivalent effect does not include taxation which is imposed in the same way within a State on similar or comparable domestic products, or at least falls, in the absence of such products, within the framework of general internal taxation, or which is intended to compensate for such internal taxation within the limits laid down by the Treaty.

The distinction, not always easy to apply, is important for practical and conceptual reasons.

The practical consequences, at least to litigators, are self-evident. A pecuniary imposition classified as a charge having an effect equivalent to a customs duty would be *per se* prohibited. A pecuniary imposition classified as falling within the general system of taxation would be prohibited only if discriminatory and protectionist—since Article 95 so decreed. This is a far more difficult and challenging (though also lucrative) task for the litigator.

The conceptual significance cannot be overestimated. *Statistical Levy* seems to articulate a distinction, resulting from the economy of the Treaty, in relation to pecuniary burdens on imports: a pecuniary imposition may occur at, and be part of, a market access regime such as a customs duty or a charge having an equivalent effect. In that case it is viewed as an obstacle which, in principle, is *per se* prohibited. By contrast, a pecuniary imposition may be part of an internal regulatory regime—a tax. In this case it will not be prohibited unless discriminatory and protectionist.

For reasons which will shortly emerge it is worth digressing at this point to paint, with the broadest of brush strokes, the equivalent provisions of the GATT. In the area of pecuniary impositions the EC and the GATT have parallel regimes. True, unlike a Free Trade Area or a Common Market, the GATT did not prohibit, outright, customs duties and charges having an effect equivalent to customs duties. But this should not obscure the fact that in its regime of progressive reduction of tariffs, in relation to both customs duties and charges having an equivalent effect, the GATT regime, too, is obstacle based. Any tariff imposed on an import in deviation from the agreed schedule of tariff reductions cannot be excused on the basis that it is non-discriminatory, that there is no competing product or that it is *de minimis*. Thus, the GATT prohibition of new customs duties and equivalent charges is, in principle, a regime of rigorous (no *de minimis*) and strict (discrimination or protectionism need not be proved) liability.

By contrast the GATT regime on taxes, ex Article III, is limited to the principle of national treatment, i.e. to a discrimination based test. We already noted in discussing *Statistical Levy* that this distinction is replicated in the Treaty of Rome when it comes to pecuniary impositions: pecuniary impediments to Market Access—whether customs duties or charges having an effect equivalent—are, like the GATT, strictly and rigorously prohibited. By contrast, market regulation through pecuniary means—taxes—is subject only to the duty of non-discrimination and non-protectionism. Article 95 EC is remarkably similar to the tax provisions in Article III GATT.

What, then, of non-pecuniary measures affecting trade? Let us first examine the GATT with an excerpt from Article XI.

Article XI: *General Elimination of Quantitative Restrictions*

1. No prohibitions or restrictions other than duties, taxes or other charges, whether made effective through quotas, import or export licenses or other measures, shall be instituted or maintained by any contracting party on the importation of any product of the territory of any other contracting party or on the exportation or sale for export of any product destined for the territory of any other contracting party.

The text is peremptory. Unlike Article III GATT, it does not refer to the hallowed 'national treatment' principle. The prohibition is, on its face, of an obstacle based nature rather than a discrimination based nature though it is, of course, subject to the GATT's overall derogation clause and, as we shall see, played a nominal role in international economic law until recently. We will return to Article XI GATT in the Fifth Generation of Community law.

On this reading, in principle (the practice was to be quite different for a long time), not only are quotas as such prohibited but also measures the effect of which is to prevent, like a quota, access to the market are prohibited unless justified under one of the GATT's derogations. To qualify, a measure need not 'catch' a product physically at the border nor need it be discriminatory or protectionist. Any measure which effectively prevents an imported product from being put into the stream of commerce, which, as stated, bars its access to the market, would be caught by the prohibition. Example? A blanket European ban on the marketing of beef containing growth hormones.

So, regulation by the state the effect of which is to bar the access of a product to the market-place is in principle prohibited, unless it can be justified under one of the recognized public policy justifications in, say, Article XX GATT.

By contrast, under the GATT, state regulation which, like a tax, does not bar access of the imported product to the market-place but simply impedes or hinders its marketing through regulation of, say, use or conditions of sale, is dealt with like a tax; such state regulation is not caught by the GATT and is not prohibited unless it violates the principle of National Treatment, i.e. it discriminates in law or in fact. Indeed, it is caught by the same Article III GATT which deals equally with both dimensions of state internal regulation through pecuniary (tax) and non pecuniary measures.

Article III: *National Treatment on Internal Taxation and Regulation*

1. The contracting parties recognize that internal taxes and other internal charges, and laws, regulations and requirements affecting the internal sale, offering for sale, purchase, transportation, distribution or use of products, and internal quantitative regulations requiring the mixture, processing or use of products in specified amounts or proportions, should not be applied to imported or domestic products so as to afford protection to domestic production . . .

Put differently, the principle of national treatment extends not only to regulation through taxes but to regulation through legislative and administrative measures, provided these do not amount to a quantitative restriction in that they completely bar access to the market—in which case they would be prohibited unless justified under Article XX GATT.

I will make two preliminary comments on the GATT regime which seems in principle to differentiate between state regulation barring market access which is prima facie a violation unless coming within a GATT derogation, and other state regulation, whether by tax or all other regulatory measures which is not a violation unless discrimination against imported goods is practised.

First, it is self-evident but worth recalling that whilst the prohibition on discrimination and protectionism imposes an important restriction on the state *vis-à-vis* imported products, it also grants them an important liberty: the liberty of social and economic regulatory choice. Let us put it differently. Whilst you may not use, say, your tax regime in a discriminatory or protectionist manner, you may use it, freely, to further your statal social and economic agenda. You may not, for example, use taxation to afford protection to your local cognac against imported whisky, but you may, in the words of the European Court of Justice in *Hansen & Balle*, create tax distinctions and apply differentiated tax rates so as to:

serve legitimate economic or social purposes, such as the use of certain raw materials by the distilling industry, the continued production of particular spirits of high quality, or the continuance of certain classes of undertakings such as agricultural distilleries.[3]

We know, of course, that sometimes, in 'hard cases', the duty of non-discrimination will impede full regulatory freedom. We know that a lot will turn on the definition of the product market (must all fruit, domestic and imported, be taxed at the same rate, or may we differentiate between, say, soft fruits such as bananas and hard fruits even if it turns out that the hard fruit is mostly local and the soft fruit is imported?) or even more delicately, on the protectionist purpose of the state. But, for the most part, the principle of national treatment which prohibits discrimination and protectionism is intended to create a balance between free trade and very broad national regulatory autonomy.

This balance is part of a broader logic of the GATT regime. The prohibition on measures which block access to the market is not absolute: there is a broad range of recognized public policies which the state may invoke in justification. But total denial to the market-place of an imported product which is lawfully manufactured and marketed in another country creates not simply a suspicion that maybe a competing domestic product is being protected but also, even in the many instances where protectionism is evidently not an issue, is so drastic and inimical to free trade that a state is called upon to justify itself. By contrast, if the imported product is allowed, as is, access to the market-place even if there it is subject on equal footing with its domestic competitors to regulation through taxation or otherwise which might none the less appreciably affect sales, this is not considered as violating the principle of free trade.

The second comment is equally obvious but also worth making. There is a very powerful logic to the manner in which the GATT 'lumps' together tax and other legislative and administrative regulatory instruments. Imagine that the state, for reasons of public health, wants to discourage smoking. It may do so in one of two ways: It may impose very high taxes on cigarettes which, experience has shown, does lead to a reduction in cigarette consumption. Or it may use its non-pecuniary regulatory instruments and, for example, ban

---

[3] Case 148/77 *H. Hansen & O.C. Balle GmbH & Co v Hauptzollamt de Flensburg* [1978] ECR 1787.

smoking in public spaces which may have the same reductive impact. Or in combating alcoholism, it may impose high excise taxes on alcohol which leads to reduction in consumption and may, too, finance rehabilitation projects, or it may bar public drinking to certain licensed establishments, to certain hours of the day, and the like which could have similar effects to the excise tax.

Does it make sense to apply the principle of non-discrimination and thereby give the state near total freedom to regulate through tax (so long as the tax does not favour domestic cigarettes or alcoholic beverages over imported ones) but to apply the principle of obstacles to any non-pecuniary regulation (even if non-discriminatory) and require the state to justify its regulatory choice such as the smoking ban by reference to some authorized list of exceptions each and every time its non pecuniary regulation hinders the marketing of imported products?

When the choices between the two methods of regulation are fungible a distinction between the two methods of statal regulation simply would not make sense: why treat them differently? And sometimes the choices are not fungible: regulation through product-oriented taxes is typically regressive: a high tax on cigarettes has greater impact on the poor than the rich. In that case the trade regime which maintained such a distinction would be providing an incentive for socially regressive state policies.

Be that as it may, the overall architecture of the GATT regime appears as follows:

- an obstacle-oriented prohibition on point of entry and/or Market Access denial, whether instituted through unauthorized pecuniary charges (duties and charges of equivalent effect) or unauthorized quantitative restrictions and measures having equivalent effect;
- a discrimination-oriented prohibition on internal Market Regulation, whether instituted by pecuniary means (taxes) or legislative and administrative measures;
- an overarching Derogation Clause—the General Exceptions of Article XX GATT—which applies to all aspects of the agreement, i.e. equally to the provisions on Market Access and Market Regulation.[4]

---

[4] 'Subject to the requirement that such measures are not applied in a manner which would constitute a means of arbitrary or unjustifiable discrimination between countries where the same conditions prevail, or a disguised restriction on international trade, nothing in this Agreement shall be construed to prevent the adoption or enforcement by any contracting party of measures:

(*a*) necessary to protect public morals; (*b*) necessary to protect human, animal or plant life or health; (*c*) relating to the importations or exportations of gold or silver; (*d*) necessary to secure compliance with laws or regulations which are not inconsistent with the provisions of this Agreement, including those relating to customs enforcement, the enforcement of monopolies operated under paragraph 4 of Article II and Article XVII, the protection of patents, trade marks and copyrights, and the prevention of deceptive practices; (*e*) relating to the products of prison labour; (*f*) imposed for the protection of national treasures of artistic, historic or

It is against this legal context that we can understand the sense in which *Dassonville* does not represent the natural, seamless extension of *Statistical Levy* but represents instead an important departure.

Though seemingly sharing the same logic and a similar rhetoric, *Dassonville* does the very opposite of *Statistical Levy*. Instead of affirming the GATT-oriented distinction between regulation which bars market access and regulation within the market which, however, allows market access to imported products, *Dassonville* conflates the two and then it applies to both the same prohibition on unjustified obstacles whether or not discriminatory and/or protectionist. We should not jump to conclusions that this is our familiar 'heroic' Court privileging telos over text. Textually, the Treaty itself placed the Court in a difficult position.

Whereas in relation to pecuniary charges the Treaty differentiated between Point of Entry regulation (customs duties and charges having an equivalent effect) and internal Market Regulation (taxation) and also, in the footsteps of the GATT, designated a different regime to each, no such explicit differentiation exists in relation to non-pecuniary state measures affecting imports. Conspicuously Article 95 EC, which is so similar to Article III GATT, is restricted to taxation and does *not* cover '. . . laws, regulations and requirements affecting the internal sale, offering for sale, purchase, transportation, distribution or use of products . . .'. In the EC treaty regime of negative integration the latter are left in limbo. The Article 30 conundrum for the Court was, thus, as follows: how does one treat non-pecuniary state regulation which affects trade in imported products. Surely, on any reading, the measures having an equivalent effect to quantitative restrictions ex Article 30 would catch those state instruments which bar access to the market in which case they should be prohibited and subject to justification ex Article 36 whether discriminatory or not. A quota, including a zero quota, is like a customs duty: it is prohibited whether or not there exists identical, similar, substitutable, or competing domestic items.

But do you, following the logic of Article 95 and the GATT, exclude from the reach of Article 30 all those state measures which do not bar access to the market even if they appreciably affect the sales of and hinder the trade in imported products within the market and subject such measures only to the general EC Treaty prohibition on discrimination on grounds of nationality? Or do you include such measures within the definition of measures having an effect equivalent to quantitative restrictions ex Article 30 EC on the benign assumption that if 'innocent' they can also be exculpated by a public policy reason ex Article 36?

---

archaeological value; (*g*) relating to the conservation of exhaustible natural resources if such measures are made effective in conjunction with restrictions on domestic production or consumption; et cetera.'

Hermeneutically, the fact that the Treaty did not draw a distinction between market access and market regulation in the non-pecuniary area could, in and of itself, be regarded as an invitation to conflate the two. Maybe it was even the intention of the Drafters in deliberately deviating from the GATT model in this respect. The theory of intentional deviation from the GATT is weakened because for so long in the history of the GATT the principle of Article XI was whittled away by exceptions, derogations, lack of commitment to enforce, and failure to grasp its true implication. It is doubtful whether in the 1950s one really thought of the GATT prohibition in Article XI as catching, *à la Hormones*, non-discriminatory state regulation which had the effect of excluding imported products from the market. Just as the EC became, somewhat artificially, dominated by the ethos of obstacles to trade, so did the GATT, also artificially, become dominated by the ethos of National Treatment.

So, in constituting and Constituting a meaning for Article 30 it would make equal interpretative sense to have taken the opposite cue from the economy of the Treaty and argue that the model established in the pecuniary field should be applied also in the regulatory field; that it made no sense to created a distinction between regulation and access in relation to pecuniary imposition but not to have such a distinction as regards non-pecuniary state regulation.

What about the actual language of equivalence in Article 30 which was the key to the interpretation in *Statistical Levy?* We have similar hermeneutic ambivalence here. What measures can be said to be truly equivalent to straightforward quantitative restrictions (quotas)? On one reading it is perhaps more of a stretch to claim, as the Court does in *Dassonville* and its progeny, that any internal measure regulating the market-place (such as a prohibition on smoking in public places) by the mere fact that it 'hinders' trade (and it surely does in the sense that if cigarette smoking is to fall, so will the consumption of imported cigarettes) is equivalent to a formal quantitative restriction. Is a ban on smoking in a public place really equivalent to a quota on imported cigarettes? A total ban on smoking would be equivalent—to a zero quota. It would, exactly as a quota does, bar access to the market. But is a regulatory measure which merely hinders even if appreciably, though without the ability to gauge with precision the exact effect on imports, really equivalent to a quota restricting with precision the number of allowable cigarette imports? Is not the essence of the quota—even the non-zero quota—the pre-emptory and sharp bar to access into the market of imported products which do not fall within the quota? On this reading, a measure merely hindering the marketing of a product which had free access to that market is not equivalent to a quantitative restriction. On the other hand it could be argued that just as quotas larger than zero are prohibited, so should other trading rules which have the equivalent effect of merely restricting the quantity of a product which may be sold on the market. I find this last textual argument less persuasive not simply because the non-zero quota is the exception rather than the rule, but also because even non-zero quotas have a sharp, definable edge which bars access of all imports outside the quota to the market. A regulation which appreciably affects sales but does not differentiate between imports and domestic products is really not equivalent in this sense to a quota larger than zero. This is not simply a formal distinction but one with great substance. Even when a state regulation affects the volume of sale, the imported product can compete on the domestic market and if better in quality and price can displace all its domestic competitors. A non-zero quota does not allow such market competition and it is very rare to have a non-zero quota imposed on imports and domestic products alike.

The purpose of this analysis is not to decide whether *Dassonville* was right or wrong but to indicate that the Court had (and retained) hermeneutic leeway in construing Article 30 and that the route it took represented a definite teleological choice.

That leeway means that the Court could have followed the Article 95 EC and the GATT logic in interpreting Article 30 and holding that it was a Treaty provision designed to prohibit any trading rules which effectively denied access to the market to imported products but was not designed to catch regulatory measures which merely hindered marketing of products. Such regulatory measures would be caught by the general Treaty prohibition on discrimination on grounds of nationality. It would avoid the peculiar situation that social outcomes freely obtainable by taxation would be prohibited unless specifically authorized, by regulation.

How, then, can one explain the choice in *Dassonville*? What was its teleology? Could it be said that this very choice defined the difference between a regime committed merely to free trade (GATT) and to the creation of a veritable Common Market? Had the Court constituted and Constituted Article 30 to catch only measures barring access to the market, would the face of the Community as it evolved be fundamentally different? Would it materially be a different constitutional order?

Our answer must, I fear, be nuanced: As a matter of principle—I do not think so. As a matter of fact—quite possibly. As a matter of legal and general culture—decidedly so. As a matter of principle one must, first, remember that a vast area of state market regulation does have the impact of barring access—primarily all regulation which concerns the quality of the product in the health and safety fields. All these regulations would be caught by Article 30 even if the Court had taken the less expansive approach. Now that the GATT is finally beginning to take *its* prohibition on quantitative restrictions seriously, interesting and contentious days lie ahead even within its more restrictive approach. One must also remember that, unlike the GATT, the Treaty did have Article 100 and a project of harmonization. This, in my view, is the critical principled difference between the GATT and the Common Market; not the nature of the negative integration prohibition. Under the GATT if a measure is justified as a legitimate pursuance of a public policy recognized in, say, Article XX, the matter, in principle, ends there even if the justified measure totally excludes an imported product which would have to be modified to meet the justified safety requirements in different markets. Market fragmentation is inbuilt. In the Community, the matter begins there, for when justified measures fragment the market, legislative harmonization is available. So one could have, after all, taken the more restrictive approach to Article 30 and, in principle, still end up with a Common Market very different from the GATT.

So why not? What explains the Court's alternative choice in its *Dassonville* formula which barred both measures and hindered the marketing of imports?

I have already suggested one possibility, a certain Jacobean conception of the common market-place which regards *Statistical Levy* and *Dassonville* as one of a kind and explicitly or implicitly rejects the GATT philosophy of trying to find an uneasy balance between transnational free trade and broad choice of national social and economic options exercised by states enjoying wide regulatory autonomy, which really has as its implicit ideal type a transnational market-place which is identical to a national market-place.

There is another more benign reading. After all, the *Dassonville* formula does not mean that all obstacles resulting from the activities of the regulatory state are actually going to be struck down. Article 30 is subject to the discipline of Article 36. It is not as if regulatory autonomy is truly removed. The state is left with plenty of social choice under the various rubrics of Article 36. It does, however, mean that such measures would be illegal on their face unless scrutinized and found permissible by reference to the authorized exceptions in Article 36. *Dassonville* restricts the autonomy, not the choice. Why, in turn, would the Court, consciously or unconsciously, wish to keep the choice but restrict the autonomy? Recall in the narrative of Exodus the fateful turn on the way to the Promised Land, a turn that ushered several decades of hardship and travel through the desert. It was a detour necessary so as to create a new consciousness purged of all elements of slavery prior to entering the Promised Land. *Dassonville*'s departure from the GATT symmetry may be regarded as a similar fateful turn, necessary, perhaps, to create a new consciousness purged of the habits and instincts of protectionism which sometimes are so deeply embedded in a Continent with a long history of protectionism. A mechanism which would enable the Court to scrutinize even those measures which on their face seem non-discriminatory and non-protectionist but which, in fact, may be found to be so on deeper scrutiny, especially a scrutiny one part of which included the test of proportionality in the sense of least-restrictive-measure. The importance of *Dassonville* thus is pragmatic (avoiding the much more difficult need of proving discrimination before a state has to come in and justify its measures which impact trade) and symbolic: an all-out rallying cry against the ethos of protectionism.

On this reading *Dassonville*, important as it may be—revelation happened after all during the detour in the desert—must be regarded as a transitory device. *Keck* will be seen as a welcome return to normalcy in the Promised Land of the Single Market and a major move, matched on its part by *Hormones*, of re-convergence of the EC and the GATT as regards the basic concepts of transnational free trade legal regimes. To judge, however, from the reactions to *Keck* there are many a Moses in our profession who prefer the desert to the Promised Land.

There is one final important legal consideration to complete the description of the Foundational Period in the evolution of the material constitution of Europe. It is not only Article 36 which complements Article 30; there are also, as mentioned, Articles 100 and 100a. The precise legal circumstances which must prevail for the Community legislator to enact legislation on the basis of Article 100 and 100a, are not fully explored. The very logic of the triangle 30, 36, and 100 (or 100a) produces, however, the following legal result: when a state measure violates on its face the *Dassonville* formula, the Member State is required to justify it by reference to European law criteria—ex Article 36 or as a Mandatory Requirement ex *Cassis de Dijon* often before the European Court of Justice. If the measure cannot be justified it is inapplicable or must be modified appropriately. Critically, when it is justified and can, thus, be upheld, Article 100 or 100a come into play. For unless this were so, a common market could never be achieved if each Member State could keep its own different regime for, say, consumer safety even if each state measure was legally justified. We can call that the problem of the legally fragmented market-place. It can only be resolved by harmonizing the varying legal state measures. Put differently, the Community legislative competence ex Articles 100 or 100a is triggered each time there is a finding of a prima-facie transgression by a state measure of the *Dassonville* formula, even when, necessarily, the state measure in question is justified. This may not be the exclusive ground for using Article 100 or 100a but it is certainly a sufficient ground..

Evaluating the Foundational Period

We can now evaluate certain aspects of the heritage of the Foundational Period as outlined above.

The Court's choice to conflate in the non-pecuniary area Market Access and Market Regulation and subject both to an obstacle-based test is understandable politically and defensible hermeneutically. When establishing a common market you may want to lean on the side of rigour. But one should not hide the anomalies and other consequences of this basic choice.

(i)   We have already pointed out the anomaly which differentiates between regulation through taxes and regulation through norms, a differentiation which might seem to favour state regulation through tax even if, socially, taxing goods is almost invariably regressive.

(ii) Another anomaly which I shall not elaborate here is the divergence between the Court's *Dassonville* obstacle jurisprudence on imports and its discrimination-based jurisprudence ex Article 34 on exports. This anomaly was prompted by two factors: a more relaxed attitude by the Court to restrictions on exports which are rarely motivated by protectionist impulses and a clearer vision—antedating *Keck* by a generation—of the constitutional implications of *Dassonville*.

(iii) A third consequence of the *Dassonville* jurisprudence is that it expands dramatically the number and type of cases in which a Member State is required to justify its social choices in regulating the market-place and its public sphere. Consequently the pressure on the derogation clause—(Article 36) becomes enormous. It comes, thus, as no surprise that the Court had to enshrine another important principle, namely that the derogation has to be construed narrowly. In symbolic terms this meant, of course, an inbuilt conservative bias, or at least presumption, in favour of free trade, creating an ethos that *any* obstacle to free trade is in some ways improper and has to be 'justified'.

(iv) Institutionally, *Dassonville* thrust the Court to the centre of substantive policy dilemmas. The Court, as a Community Institution, had to become the arbiter of delicate social choices, reconciling trade with competing social policies.

(v)   Constitutionally, as mentioned, *Dassonville* represented a massive expansion in the legislative competence of the Community ex Article 100 and 100a.

How does one explain the relative equanimity of reaction to these significant constitutional, institutional, and substantive consequences. There are several, non mutually exclusive, possible explanations.

Consider first the issue of legislative competences. Who paid much attention to legislative competences in an era governed by the Luxembourg Compromise and in an area governed by the unanimous voting requirement of Article 100? It was neither noticed and, if noticed, not considered of great political significance. Explaining the positioning of the Court is more delicate. On the one hand the *Dassonville* move is even more consequential than its constitutional structural counterparts. For all the drama of direct effect and supremacy, these concepts represented a rather exquisite balance between an emerging constitutional law and Community governance: the balance struck by the Court was to allow the political Institutions and the Governments of the Member States considerable freedom in making their policy choices, in negotiating and in striking their eventual bargains. But once a substantive bargain was struck, the structural constitutional new order achieved through doctrines such as direct effect and supremacy meant that bargains could not be abandoned, that they would be upheld and enforced. Free bargaining but no free riders sums up that part of the constitutional interplay. It is not surprising that despite all, direct effect and supremacy were, for the most part, embraced and not rejected by the governments of the Member States. *Dassonville* and its progeny are different since here the Court itself was making substantive and material policy determinations and not simply enforcing the bargains of others. It should be easy to agree that in the relationship between the Court and its interlocutors this is at least a different ball game, though whether it is as different as ice hockey and field hockey, or baseball and cricket, is something that we can wait to be illuminated by those political scientists who think they can answer this question. But on the whole, if we look at the overall climate rather than the case to case weather, the Court's *Dassonville* jurisprudence could be construed as flushing out free riders trying to enjoy the benefits of the expanded export market, but attempting to restrict imports. For the empirical fact remains that, although the Court insisted that a mere obstacle would snap the Article 30 trap, in most cases even apparently innocuous state measures were found to be either discriminatory or, at a minimum, to fail one critical aspect of the proportionality test—in that their declared objectives could be achieved by means less burdensome on imports.

II THE SECOND GENERATION

The Second Generation in this evolutionary narrative is perceived as occurring around the late 1970s and early 1980s. *Cassis* is the central Second Generation case as regards Article 30 and must be understood as a response to two major unresolved problems from the Foundational Period.

We noted already the need to construe the derogations to Article 30 as narrowly as possible. But Article 36 does represent, after all, the important areas where social policy could be allowed to trump the interest in free trade, a foundation of the modern mixed economy and interventionist state. It was, however, written with the sensibilities of the 1950s: consumer protection, for example, is focused mostly on physical safety and not on fairness and transparency; ecological concerns are minimal and would require true textual stretch to be acknowledged.

What happens—and this is the first Second Generation Problem—when public sensibilities change and Member States wish to introduce for legitimate social reasons measures protecting the interests of, say, consumers which are not recognized in Article 36? It is one thing to construe existing derogations narrowly to avoid their abuse as a means for disguised restriction to trade. It is quite another thing to freeze the Community and its Member

States in defining the balance between free trade and other competing values in a time capsule sealed in 1957. The Court could, of course, give a broad meaning to the Public Policy exception. But that would militate not only against, say, the original French version of the Treaty where this provision seemed far narrower, but would compromise the policy of construing derogations narrowly.

We noted, too, the problem of market fragmentation which results from differing standards adopted by Member States, each one of which is in full compliance with Articles 30 and 36, but which cumulatively fragment the market-place. In theory, as we noted too, Article 100 was to provide the answer, but in practice the unanimity requirement rendered that article useless. The record of harmonization as we enter the Second Generation is poor: there are, apparently, always one or two Member States who are able to block harmonization proposals. How then, and this was the second Second Generation problem, could one address market fragmentation given the *blocage* of decision-making ex Article 100.

The third Second Generation problem I shall briefly mention rested in the area of taxation. Strangely, the Treaty did not provide a social policy derogation clause to Article 95—an equivalent to Article XX GATT or Article 36 EEC. If Britain or Ireland were to impose vaccination and quarantine requirements on imported animals susceptible to rabies, the two countries would be able to rely on Article 36 to justify such a measure. By contrast, if, say, in an attempt to preserve natural resources Italy were to tax natural alcohol at a rate lower than synthetic alcohol, which would become a burden which fell disproportionately on imported products, there would be no Treaty provision with which to defend such a policy preference. Did Article 95 mean that any taxation scheme which resulted in a heavier burden on imported products, even if imposed for non-protectionist reasons, was outside the scope of Member State regulatory competences?

Cassis responded to the first two problems. The doctrine of mandatory requirements was an obvious and welcome response to the first problem since, subject to its various doctrinal hoops, it allowed Member States to plead non-economic policies which were not mentioned in Article 36. Fairness of commercial transactions, public health, cultural policy, and other 'ways-of-life' justifications could now be proffered.

The second great doctrine in *Cassis* misleadingly called by some the doctrine of mutual recognition and more accurately described as functional parallelism, was a valiant attempt to respond to the second problem. After all, in principle, the need for harmonization would appear far less pressing if goods complying with the technical standards required in one Member State could be marketed freely in another Member State, provided the standards of the first State were functionally parallel to that of the second. Why would one need to harmonize a common standard at all?

Finally, cases such as *Vinal v Orbat* and *Commission v Italy (Regenerated Oil)* introduced a *de facto* derogation clause to the field of taxation. Whether one reads these cases as permitting origin-neutral taxes instituted with a legitimate social policy to result in tax brackets that otherwise would be considered discriminatory and protectionist, or whether one simply reads them as introducing an unwritten derogation clause which would redeem otherwise discriminatory tax distinctions is irrelevant. The end result of this jurisprudence was to allow Member States to defend tax distinctions within the EC (which does not contain a written derogation clause) even more effectively than one can in the GATT (which has such a written derogation).

Despite the familiarity of these cases and the doctrines they introduced it is worth highlighting some features important for this evolutionary perspective.

(1) There is language in some Court decisions which suggests (and it is a thesis favoured by several notable commentators) that the doctrine of mandatory requirements differs in at least one fundamental respect from the derogation plea under Article 36. According to this thesis Mandatory Requirements are part of what qualifies a measure for the purpose of deciding whether or not it violates Article 30 in the first place. Thus, according to this thesis, if a state is successful in defending a measure under the doctrine of mandatory requirement, Article 30 will be considered not to have been violated at all. One can have sympathy for the Court in not wishing to acknowledge that with mandatory requirements it simply had written into the Treaty a new open-ended derogation clause complementing Article 36. One can have less sympathy for those judicial decisions which try to camouflage this fact by pretending that Mandatory Requirements simply qualify what is or is not a violation of Article 30 as distinct from Article 36 which 'redeems' or justifies a prima-facie violation.

It is respectfully submitted that this is no more than formalist sophistry. The material test of a violation of Article 30 is the need of a Member State to come into Court and defend its actions as justified in accordance with the doctrinal hoops of *Cassis*: legitimate policy, absence of extant harmonization, proportionality, etc. If a Member State is required to justify in this manner, Article 30 has been violated on its face. It is also clear, and the Court as much as says this in *Cassis* and cases like it, that even when a state measure is justified under mandatory requirements, Community harmonization would be indicated in precisely the same way as would be the case if a measure were justified under Article 36. The only meaningful doctrinal difference between Article 36 and mandatory requirements is the puzzling stipulation that the Court itself imposed as one of the conditions for its successful invocation, namely that the state measure in question must be indistinctly applicable. I say puzzling since if a state has a good reason to impose a distinctly applicable measure (such as in our rabies example) why should it be able to rely on justifications listed in Article 36 but not those deriving from *Cassis* and its progeny?

(2) But for this anomaly, the first cumulative effect of the first doctrine in *Cassis* coupled with the Tax Cases represent in my view the emergence of a general principle of justification operating parallel to the general principle of non-discrimination on grounds of nationality according to which it is always possible to plead any social policy—other than protectionism of course—as a justification for violating fundamental economic freedoms, provided it could be shown that the importance of such policy and its specific implementation in the particular case overrides the interest in the free movement of goods and cannot be achieved by measures less burdensome to trade.

(3) As regards the second doctrine in *Cassis* the Court famously preaches the rhetoric of mutual recognition:

There is therefore no valid reason why, provided that they have been lawfully produced and marketed in one of the Member States, [products] should not be introduced into any other Member State

but practices functional parallelism. After all, it allows Germany to insist that a product lawfully marketed in France be labelled differently as a requirement for accessing the German market. Only with a label indicating its (lower) alcoholic content does French Cassis become functionally parallel to the German regulation of fairness of commercial transactions.

It should also be noted that for all the attention *Cassis* received, 'mutual recognition' or functional parallelism is not a radical hermeneutic departure but in fact a very conservative and fully justified application of the principle of proportionality. For a Member State to insist on a specific technical standard even if a different standard is functionally parallel in achieving the desired result, is to have adopted a measure which is not the least restrictive possible.

I cannot overstate the importance of this doctrinal point since, in my view, it foreshadows that which will, inevitably, happen in the WTO. Under the GATT, proportionality, under the appellation of the doctrine of necessity, is well established in broad terms. Thus, if the logic of *Cassis*-style 'mutual recognition' or functional parallelism is rooted in the requirement that a restriction will be 'necessary', it becomes inevitable that a similar doctrine will emerge in the GATT too. How can a state justify excluding an imported product which meets a functionally parallel regulation? Why would it be necessary under Article 20 GATT to do so? This is already acknowledged in the regimes set up by TBT and SPS in the GATT and their equivalents in the NAFTA.

Evaluating the Second Generation

We may now turn to evaluating the Second Generation.

(1) The doctrine of mandatory requirements was a successful doctrine giving an effective answer to the first Second Generation problem. But it had the

effect of even deepening the enmeshment of the Court in the evaluation and sanctioning of Member State social policies in conflict with free movement, and this in ever more delicate areas. It is one thing, and never an easy thing, for the Court to pronounce on, say, matters of health of animals or humans. It is an altogether more difficult and delicate thing to pronounce on the policies behind Sunday trading bans and the like. As the endless material reach of the *Dassonville* formula began to sink in and as the justifications that may be pleaded by Member States became wider and wider, and as it was, ultimately, for the Court to decide whether a specific policy and its application were so important as to override the interest of free movement of goods, the improbability of its adjudicatory role became more and more acute.

(2) This became particularly so in relation to the Proportionality test. As noted, a central feature of the proportionality test is whether a policy objective could be achieved by a less restrictive measure. Supposedly this is a technical, value-free determination which the Court could make on the basis of evidence submitted to it or review when made, as a matter of mixed law and fact, by a Member State court. Is the insulating requirement of Member State A on a washing machine excessive? Can the safety of the user be guaranteed by a more modest insulating requirement applied by Member State B on its washing machines? Call in the experts, weigh the evidence and make a determination— it is quite amusing to note how these hot potatoes are tossed between the national judiciary and the Court; it appears that often Member State courts would much rather the ECJ took those decisions on proportionality. But the reality is far more complex and involves in countless cases the European Court imposing its values on the level of tolerable risk allocation in society.

Take, by way of example, the least probable case of all, *Cassis* itself. The Court found that the objective of the German government, of ensuring that the consumer should not be misled into buying a liqueur believing it to have a higher alcoholic content, was legitimate. But it also found that that objective could be achieved by a measure less restrictive than the German outright ban, namely by requiring the product to carry a label displaying its alcoholic content. What is involved in this banal and intuitively correct decision? It is clear that even if Cassis and other French liqueurs were to carry that label, some consumers would still be misled: some cannot read, others do not read. The communicative effect of labels is notoriously quite limited. What, in effect, the Court decides in *Cassis* is that the German policy of zero-tolerance to any consumer confusion does not override the societal interest in free movement of goods. Instead, the Court imposes its risk assessment reflected in the label requirement which, in effect, decides that this is an area allowing a certain percentage of consumers to be misled (because of the limited communicative effect of a label) and is acceptable.

Who cares? Well, one does care when one moves to the area of automobile safety, of food and beverage additives and the like, in which such risk determination can decide, for example, the number of persons who will die on the roads each year, the number of persons whose health will be put at risk by certain nutritional substances and the like. And certainly the Court itself feels uneasy in having to take these types of decisions. In these respects, then, the success of Mandatory Requirements is also a ticking time bomb.

(3) 'Mutual recognition' or parallel functionalism was, perhaps, an intellectual breakthrough but a colossal market failure. It simply did not, in practice, solve the second Second Generation problem. There are several reasons for this. The most important is infinitely banal: goods which do not meet the technical standards of the importing country may not be marketed. Litigation may, of course, ensue; victory may even be achieved. But from a commercial point of view this is a nonsense. One cannot plan, produce and market product lines hoping that eventually a court decision will vindicate a claim of mutual recognition or functional parallelism.

(4) There are other reasons which explain the practical failure of the doctrine. In many instances there are product lines where there are genuine differences in regulatory regimes, where there is no functional parallelism. In this case harmonization is simply required and cannot be achieved by judicial means. In some cases, the nature of the product requires a single pan European standard.

Cassis in this respect is a lesson on the potential and limits of judicial impact: there is only so much that can be achieved by the courts.

III THE THIRD GENERATION

The Third Generation of free movement which takes place in the late 1980s moves away from the Courts and is characterized by the New Approach to Harmonization (NAH) by the White Paper and the Single Market 1992 project, by the Single European Act, and the very important modifications introduced by Article 100a and by the adoption, in the legislative arena of the ideas explored *inter alia* in *Cassis*.

This is not the place to describe in detail the NAH and it will be sufficient to highlight its key features. They form an important part of the convergence paradigm since in a fundamental sense the NAH is about a greater respect for national regulatory autonomy.

The first feature of the NAH is encapsulated in the regime of the Information Directives.[5] These require Member States to notify the

---

[5] See OJ L 1983/109, 26.04.1983 Council Directive of 28 March 1983 laying down a procedure for the provision of information in the field of technical standards and regulations; OJ L 1988/81, 26.03.1988 Council Directive of 22 March 1988 amending Directive 83/189/EEC laying down a procedure for the provision of information in the field of technical standards and regulations; OJ L 1990/128, 18.05.1990 Commission Decision of 3 May

Community (and other Member States) of any new proposed measures which would constitute an obstacle to free movement of goods. This regime allows the Commission and other Member States to react before the national measures come into force and if necessary 'communauterize' them or challenge them. On its face this looks like part and parcel of the Harmonization discipline of the *Dassonville* genus. But in fact at a deeper level it is a recognition that in the setting of socio-economic values and the mix of regulation and market, it is the Member States and the organic societies they represent which are the long-term repositories of wisdom and legitimacy.

The central feature of the NAH—as reflected initially in the Low Voltage Directive[6] and then in the establishment of bodies like CEN and CENELEC[7]—is adoption at the *legislative* level of the *Cassis* rationale. Two features characterize the new system. First, a minimalist approach to harmonization, meaning that the Community will seek to harmonize only that which is truly necessary to ensure a common market-place in goods allowing otherwise a fare share of regulatory competition. Second, in the setting of Community standards, where possible, the Community will only set overall standards and allow Standard Setting bodies within the Member States to establish their own specifications which would meet the overall Community standards. Here the deference to regulatory autonomy is clear long before Subsidiarity came into vogue. The key to the success of the NAH was the shift in the presumption: goods certified by a national body as complying with specifications established pursuant to a Community standard would be allowed to circulate freely without having to prove on a case by case basis their equivalence—simply, but with profound market implications. This coupled with the shift to majority voting which made it possible to set standards at the Community level meant a veritable sea change in the evolution of the market-place.

1990 amending the lists of standardization institutions set out in the Annex to Council Directive 83/189/EEC JOL 1994/100, 19.04.1994; Directive 94/10/EC of the European Parliament and the Council of 23 March 1994 materially amending for the second time Directive 83/189/EEC laying down a procedure for the provision of information in the field of technical standards and regulations JOL 1996/32, 10.02.1996 Commission Decision of 24 January 1996 amending the list of national standardization bodies in Annex II to Council Directive 83/189/EEC OJ L 1998/40, 13.02.1998 Corrigendum to Directive 94/10/EC of the European Parliament and the Council of 23 March 1994 materially amending for the second time Directive 83/189/EEC laying down a procedure for the provision of information in the field of technical standards and regulations (OJ L 100 of 19 April 1994).

[6] See OJ L 1973/77, 26.03.1973 Council Directive of 19 February 1973 on the harmonization of the laws of Member States relating to electrical equipment designed for use within certain voltage limits.

[7] See OJ L 1998/204, 21.07.1998 Directive 98/34/EC of the European Parliament and of the Council of 22 June 1998 laying down a procedure for the provision of information in the field of technical standards and regulations Annex I–IV.

It is also a reminder to the limits of judicial power. Functional parallelism may have been a brilliant legal construct but it could not have major market impact without the intervention of the legislator.

IV THE FOURTH GENERATION

The early 1990s see a new departure in the famous or infamous 1993 *Keck* decision and its subsequent line of cases. Advocate General Gordon Slynn in *Cinetheque* jolted the prevailing legal culture. The Court issued intermittently the odd case, such as *Oebel,* seemingly at odds with its normal jurisprudence which was a sign of subterranean cracks appearing in the *Dassonville* construct. Walter van Gerven became the prophet standing at this gate, the intellectual hero of a new phase in the writing and rewriting of the economic constitution of Europe. Already in the late 1980s in, say, the Sunday trading cases, he made a powerful plea for change of direction. Sunday trading represents well the 'endgame' of the *Dassonville* rationale, arguably a pathological endgame. Since a ban on Sunday trading, instituted for deep historical, cultural, and social reasons, affects the volume of trade, notably in some sectors such as the DIY industry, and since that volume reduction would also affect imports, the *Dassonville* formula is triggered and a Member State would have to justify such a rule by reference to the criteria of Article 36 and/or mandatory requirements. Let us assume that the Member State would be successful in mounting its justification. For the Advocate General this was no solution. It was the methodology that he attacked, not the result. His plea was that Sunday trading type cases would not be considered as having violated Article 30 at all. When the Court in, say, *Torfaen* holds that:

Article 30 of the Treaty must be interpreted as meaning that the prohibition which it lays down does not apply to national rules prohibiting retailers from opening their premises on Sunday where the restrictive effects on Community trade which may result therefrom do not exceed the effects intrinsic to rules of that kind[8]

it may appear that the Advocate General had already won his battle in that case. But we should not be misled. These conclusory Recitals in the Court's decisions are just another instance of the formalist sophistry mentioned above. In the Sunday trading cases, the Member States were duly put through their hoops, the measure duly had to be justified by reference to legitimate policies and the test of proportionality was duly applied and, indeed, conditioned the results. What the Advocate General had in mind was a veritable reversal of *Dassonville* to exclude Sunday trading type cases from the very catch of Article 30 so that they would not even have to be justified.

[8] Case 145/88 *Torfaen BC v B&Q plc* [1989] ECR 385 (para. 17).

The change comes in *Keck* where the Court famously held:

. . . contrary to what has previously been decided, the application to products from
other Member States of national provisions restricting or prohibiting certain selling
arrangements is not such as to hinder directly or indirectly, actually or potentially,
trade between Member States within the meaning of the Dassonville judgment (case
8/74 [1974] ECR 837), so long as those provisions apply to all relevant traders operating within the national territory and so long as they affect in the same manner, in
law and in fact, the marketing of domestic products and of those from other Member
States.[9]

From the evolutionary perspective I am first interested in the possible
motives, articulated or otherwise, which can explain this change of direction.
The Court itself, uncharacteristically, addresses in Recital 14 of its decision
the question of motive as distinct from legal reasoning:

In view of the increasing tendency of traders to invoke Article 30 of the Treaty as a
means of challenging any rules whose effect is to limit their commercial freedom even
where such rules are not aimed at products from other Member States, the Court considers it necessary to re-examine and clarify its case-law on this matter.[10]

One may read this statement as a simple concern for docket control, a worry
by the Court that it is being swamped by limitless cases. We should, I think,
give more credit to the Court. If the doctrine is justified on its merits, your
alarm at an increase in case load should be directed at the phenomena that
give rise to the increase, not to the doctrine. You do not address a growing
flood of murder cases by changing the definition of murder. Recital 14 must,
thus, be taken as a rethinking of the very merits of the *Dassonville* doctrine
almost twenty years after its inception: a willingness on the part of the Court
openly to acknowledge that its judicial doctrines are rooted in a socio-politi-
cal and economic reality which changes with time and which calls for revision
even of the most hallowed canons.

What, then, are the conditions which had changed since *Dassonville* which
could explain the new approach by the Court? Speculating, of course, the following come to mind.

(1) 1993 is a symbolic date—the first year of the post Single Market 31
December 1992 deadline (in France it was always 1 January 1993). Twenty
years after *Dassonville* things had truly changed. In large measure the commitment to a Single Market was internalized by national administrations, and
the reflexive habits of intra-Community protectionism had not disappeared,
perhaps, but were certainly not presumptive. This was, after all, post-
Maastricht, a Union committed to EMU and all that. There was, too, a
maturing of economic thinking, as evident in the New Approach to
Harmonization which was much more tolerant to regulatory diversity if it did

---

[9] Cases C-267 and 268/91 *Keck & Mithouard* [1993] ECR I-6097 para. 16.   [10] Ibid.

not have major impact on access to the market, and even the virtues of some regulatory competition became apparent. Unlike twenty years earlier, the harmonization programme had, by comparison, become hugely successful and the need for judicial activism as a means of driving the common market agenda had considerably lessened. Conditions existed for a more relaxed, more mature, doctrinal framework.

(2) The Court will have had its own 'self-preservation' agenda. As noted, the Sunday trading type case puts the Court increasingly into 'no-win' conundrums in which it has to engage in balancing public interest concerns of a delicate and extremely intrusive nature. The hot potato saga of who will decide proportionality—national courts or the European Court—is a veritable sign of the Court's unease at the situation it found itself in, an unease that was not apparent in earlier generations of jurisprudence.

(3) In its human rights jurisprudence the Court had held in cases such as *ERT* that Member State measures in derogation of, *inter alia*, the Article 30 prohibition would be subject to judicial scrutiny not simply for, say, proportionality but also for human rights—a very controversial and delicate even if fully justified position. From this perspective *Dassonville* was a disaster. For even if the Court was to give a clean bill of health to Member State measures, it would find itself in a position which it finds particularly inimical: having to stand as a *de facto* appeal instance *vis-à-vis* national courts. For, after all, national courts will happily refer to the ECJ questions on the correct interpretation of, say, Article 30, but they feel perfectly competent to decide themselves if a Member State measure(!) violates fundamental human rights.

(4) The issue of competences is, in my view, one of the most important issues which explain *Keck*. There are two linked dimensions to it. The first is the general Maastricht attention to limiting competences—through the concept of subsidiarity, through the legislative restrictions imposed, say, in the public health or cultural field. But, even more critical is the fact that since the late 1980s and the entry into force of the Single European Act, the entire issue of limits to Community competences took on a new urgency. The force behind this urgency was the shift to majority voting. Hitherto, the delicacy of Community jurisdictional limits was attenuated by the political fact of unanimity. The Governments of the Member States could block any measure that they did not like. Jurisdictional overreach of, say, the Commission could be checked by an outraged Member State at the negotiating table. Since July 1987 this was no longer so. Suddenly constitutional limits, rather than political power, became very important in the competences game. *Dassonville* is also a disaster from this perspective: the broader the catch of Article 30, the broader the legislative competences of the Community. If Sunday trading rules are held to violate Article 30 ex *Dassonville* even if justified by reference to mandatory requirements, they become 'prey' to the Community legislative process ex Article 100a operating by majority vote. If they are excluded from the catch,

they are beyond the reach of the Community legislator, unless some other independent Treaty legislative legal basis could be found. In *Keck*, knowingly or otherwise, the Court made a major contribution to a more limited form of Community governance, very much in the *Geist* of the times.

Be the motives for *Keck* as they may, there is a second central issue concerning this decision: its precise catch. The Court's formulation restricting the new departure to 'certain selling arrangements' is surely inadequate. The Court, after all, was intent on excluding from the catch of Article 30: '[s]uch legislation [which] may . . . restrict the volume of sales, and hence the volume of sales of products from other Member States', but without barring their access and without discriminating against them. Why then restrict the formula to selling arrangements? Why should, say, a ban on the selling of cigarettes in machines or in candy stores frequented by children come under the *Keck* formula and be excluded from Article 30 (even though it will restrict the volume of sales and hence the volume of sales of products from other Member States), while a ban on smoking in public places, which will have precisely the same effect of restricting the volume of sales etc., but since not a 'selling arrangement' not be caught by *Keck* and thus come under the old reach of *Dassonville* and constitute a violation of Article 30 with all the attendant consequences?

The test, surely, should be the following: rules that bar Market Access are caught by Article 30 and must be justified. Market regulation rules—whether selling arrangements or otherwise—that do not bar access, should not be caught unless discriminatory in law or in fact.

If one could rid oneself of the Selling Arrangements formula, *Keck* would come to represent a departure even greater than it appears at first sight. For it would allow us to reformulate a new 'universal field theory' of Free Movement of Goods and reduce it into a couple of simple propositions.

The General Rule of Free Movement: national provisions which do not affect in the same manner, in law and in fact, the marketing of domestic products and of those from other Member States, must be justified by a public interest taking precedence over the free movement of goods.

This first proposition could be seen as based on General Principles of Community law which derive from, but stand independently of, any specific Treaty provision. Note that it catches both pecuniary and non-pecuniary measures and is, in effect, a National Treatment overarching principle for the Community.

The Special Rule of Free Movement (Article 30): national provisions which prevent access to the market of imported goods must also be so justified.

This represents a re-dimensioning of Article 30 and its repositioning not as the fount from which the field derives, but as a special rule designed to catch a specific (and diminishing) category of Member State measures, those which totally exclude a good from the market—even when such exclusion is not discriminatory or overtly protectionist. It is a reading of Article 30 which regards quantitative restrictions as measures which bar access to the market and, thus, insists that measures having an effect equivalent should also be so construed.

The combined effect of the General and Special Rules is to make the combat against discrimination the key premise of the field and to downsize the old law of obstacles to those cases where the obstacles result in effective exclusion of products from the market. Obviously in operationalizing these Rules one would have recourse to the myriad analytical tools developed in the previous generations of free movement, such as proportionality, such as the various notions of what constitutes discrimination, such as onus and burden of proof. But, none the less, the new 'field theory' will have two virtues: first, it signifies a change, a maturation, to a system which is based on the substantial accomplishment of a Single Market rather than on the need to accomplish it, an accomplishment which permits a greater tolerance of national and local regulatory diversity; secondly, it does away with the artificiality of having different doctrinal regimes for pecuniary regulation and legislative and administrative regulation as well as subdivisions within this last category.

V THE FIFTH GENERATION

The Court, judges, as well as Advocates General are still ambivalent about their *Keck* jurisprudence, uneasy about its extension to other areas of free movement such as services, and still working out its permutations. In the literature it is still contested with the usual strategies of such cases: one tries either to claim that it is wrong, or that it is unimportant, or that it does not change much since we were already there. I have staked my position clearly: it is a good decision and in that sense it is 'right' though it does not go far enough by sticking to the selling arrangements formula; it is very important; it does represent a change. Time will tell whether it becomes the new foundation as suggested in my presumptuously titled universal field theory— which, of course, is hardly a theory at all, but a way to cap the culmination of a new constitutional settlement—or whether it is marginalized.

By way of conclusion I want to suggest what in my view will be the critical jurisprudence of the 'next generation'. Here, too, I detect a strong convergence between disparate trade regimes including the GATT and the EC. This convergence is manifest in many areas and I shall mention but a few.

(1) The GATT until recently never took seriously its own Article XI and the prohibition contained therein. For complex reasons which I shall explain elsewhere, it was rare to challenge non-discriminatory quantitative restrictions even where those totally barred access of imported products to a

domestic market. The *Hormones* Panel Decision represents the GATT attempt to take Obstacles seriously. *Keck* represents a 'bending' of the EC towards the National Treatment rationale of the GATT. *Hormones* represents the 'bending' of the GATT towards the Obstacles rationale of the EC.

(2) I have already mentioned my prediction that 'mutual recognition' or, more accurately, functional parallelism, will inevitably find its way into GATT jurisprudence. Likewise one is going to find increasingly attempts at the transnational level to find equivalents to Article 100 and 100a type harmonization as a means of addressing inbuilt fragmentation. TBT, SPS, and various transnational Codes are the visible signs of this.

(3) As the convergence process progresses, the simplistic dream of 'constitutionalizing' the GATT in structural terms and in some ways using the EU as a 'model' for the WTO (and for other transnational regimes) through the advocacy of Article 177 type procedures will become far more nuanced. European constitutionalism is undergoing a certain crisis and reformation conditioned by the tension and gap between its legal imperatives and its social and political reality. The Appellate body decision in *Hormones*, which clawed back some of the more audacious aspects of the Panel, was apparently mindful of the problems of giving binding constitutional force to standards adopted by faceless officials and enforced by adjudicatory bodies whose legitimacy is a matter of some considerable delicacy. This sounds familiar.

(4) Finally, in a convergence story of which much more could and should be told, there is a new set of cases in which the WTO and EC seem to be facing similar and a new type of problem. The harbingers are cases like *Hedley Lomas* in the EU context and *Dolphins* and *Turtles* in the context of the WTO/GATT. Cases such as these are bound to become more prevalent and more difficult. They concern the ability of the importing state to place restrictions based not on the characteristics of the product but in terms of the methods of production in the exporting state. The classical premises of extant jurisprudence are reluctant to acknowledge such concerns as legitimate justification for excluding products. International trade theory is also ambivalent, especially since place of production concerns can extend to factors of production which are part of the comparative advantage of the exporting state. Political economists are ambivalent since these concerns are often no more than a form of cultural imperialism. On the other hand, the very success of open markets and free trade drives home to people that their own consumption habits and practices are inevitably complicit in practices that would be banned in the country of consumption.

One should not leave this story with the impression that the convergence trend is more than just a trend. Even if the WTO moves increasingly to a regime which is willing to challenge non-discriminatory barriers to access, the reality will surely be that in many cases such barriers will be justified and the problem of WTO fragmented markets will remain. The EU harmonization philosophy, even if attenuated by the New Approach still represents a major difference between the two. But I will repeat two predictions which, I believe, will be part of the next stages in the convergence process. It will not be long before a WTO Panel and/or the Appellate Body will pronounce a WTO version of the doctrine of parallel functionalism (or mutual recognition). One can restate the simple reason. Mutual recognition may seem to some the highlight of Community particularism, a result of its very cohesive nature and unsuited to the broader Community. But in fact it is but a banal doctrinal manifestation of the principle of necessity which is also a pillar of GATT jurisprudence. If an imported product meets the safety or other *objectives* of the importing state regulatory regime but does so by adopting a different set of technical standards which are not authorized by the importing state regulation, how could they ever claim that it is *necessary* to exclude that import from the national market? And if they cannot so claim, how could they justify the exclusion under the Justification regime of Article XX GATT? We already find a legislative expression of this in the TBT and SPS Agreements.

We will also see an increase in the pressure on WTO bodies or WTO-approved bodies to adopt international standards which private operators in the Global market-place could adopt as a way to ensure the access of their products to national markets. The WTO may not call this Harmonization but it will be the functional equivalent. Indeed, the most intriguing development in this respect will be the convergence of national regulatory regimes among the large trading blocs (USA, EU, Canada, etc.) as a means of ensuring smooth operation of 'their' corporations and then the internationalization of such harmonized standards.

Further Reading

The legal literature on the European single market is huge but I want to acknowledge, by way of a selective bibliography, my intellectual debt to the works which most influenced me, both in agreement and disagreement, in the evolution of this essay. The Pentateuch of this field is composed, in my view, of the following Masters: L. Gormley, *Prohibiting Restrictions on Trade within the EEC* 2nd edn. (Elsevier Science, 1998), A. Mattera, *Le Marché Unique Européen* (Jupiter, 1988); P. Oliver, *Free Movement of Goods in the European Community* 3rd edn. (Sweet and Maxwell, 1996); H. Micklitz and S. Weatherill (eds.) *European Economic Law* (Dartmouth Publishing Company, 1997) and H. Micklitz, T. Roethe, and S. Weatherill (eds.) *Federalism and Responsibility* (Graham and Trotman, 1994) and a new book destined to reshape the field, M. Poiares Maduro, *We, The Court* (Hart Publishing, 1998). As regards the GATT, *The Analytical Index* by Ernst-Ulrich Petersmann has the same justified stature.

All these authors are bound to take exception to at least some of the theses advanced in my essay, but my debt to them is very big. If there are any ideas of merit their provenance will be found, one way or another, in one or the other of the above books. The same is true of the following articles.

Alter K. and Meunier-Aitsahalia S., 'Judicial Politics in the European Community—European Integration and the Pathbreaking *Cassis de Dijon* Decision' 26 *Comparative Political Studies* 535 (1994).

Daniele L., 'Non-Discriminatory Restriction to the Free Movement of Persons' 22 ELR 191 (1997).

Dehousse R. and Majone G., 'The Dynamics of European Integration: The Role of Supranational Institutions', (Draft on file with the author).

Ehlermann C.-D., 'Harmonization versus Competition Between Rules' 3 *European Review* 333 (1995).

Garrett G., 'International Cooperation and Institutional Choice: the European Community's Internal Market' 46 *International Organization* 533 (1992).

Gormley L., 'Reasoning Renounced? The Remarkable Judgment in Keck & Mithouard', *European Business Law Review* 63 (1994).

Joerges Ch., 'Paradoxes of Deregulatory Strategies at Community Level: The Example of Product Safety Policy', in Majone G. (ed.) *Deregulation or Reregulation—Regulatory Reform in Europe and the United States* (Pinter Publishers, 1990).

Maduro Poiares M., '*Keck*: The End? The Beginning of the End? Or Just the End of the Beginning?' 1 *IJEL* 30 (1994).

Majone G., 'Market Integration and Regulation: Europe After 1992', EUI Working Paper SPS 91/10 (1991).

Mortelmans K., 'Article 30 of the EEC Treaty and Legislation Relating to Market Circumstances: Time to Consider a New Definition', 28 *CMLRev.* 115 (1991).

Nicolaidis K., 'Mutual Recognition of Regulatory Regimes: Some Lessons and Prospects', *Harvard Jean Monnet Working Paper* No. 7/97. <www.law.harvard.edn/Programs/Jean Monnet/papers/7.

Petersmann E.-U., 'Constitutional Principles Governing the EEC's Commercial Policy' in Maresceau M. (ed.) *The European Community's Commercial Policy afer 1992: The Legal Dimension* (Kluwer, 1993).

Regan D., 'The Supreme Court and State Protectionism: Making Sense of the Dormant Commerce Clause' 84 *Michigan L. Rev.* 1091 (1986).

Schapf F. W., 'Negative and Positive Integration in the Political Economy of Welfare States', EUI Jean Monnet Chair Paper 28/95 (1995).

Snyder F., *New Directions in Community Law* (Weidenfeld and Nicolson, 1990).

Waelbroeck M., *Les règlementations nationales di prix de le droit communautaire* (Editions de l'Universitè de Bruxelles, 1975).

Weatherill S., 'After *Keck*: Some Thoughts on How to Clarify the Clarification' 33 *CML Rev.* 885 (1996).

Wills P. J. W., 'The Search for the Rule in Article 30 EEC: Much Ado about Nothing?' *ELR* 475 (1993).

Index